Dear Alice:

Letters Home from American Teachers

Learning to Live in China

Dear Alice

Letters Home from American Teachers
Learning to Live in China

edited by

Phyllis L. Thompson

with letters collected by
Alice Renouf
of the
Colorado China Council

INSTITUTE OF EAST ASIAN STUDIES
UNIVERSITY OF CALIFORNIA • BERKELEY

A publication of the Institute of East Asian Studies, University of California, Berkeley. Although the Institute is responsible for the selection and acceptance of manuscripts, responsibility for the opinions expressed and for the accuracy of statements rests with their authors.

Library of Congress Cataloging-in-Publication Data

Dear Alice : letters home from American teachers learning to live in
China / edited by Phyllis L. Thompson ; with letters collected by
Alice Renouf of the Colorado China Council.
     p.   cm.
     Includes index.
     ISBN 1-55729-060-1 (alk. paper)
     1. China—Description and travel. 2. China—Social life and
customs—1976- 3. Teachers—United States—Correspondence.
I. Thompson, Phyllis L.
DS712.D43 1998
951.05′9—dc21   97-49591
                                                                      CIP

Contents

In Memoriam

John Redman

Who talked me into going
to China in his place,
and then laughed and laughed

Foreword

The idea for this book came about in 1991 when I was corresponding with Professor Phyllis Thompson, who was teaching in China. The Colorado China Council had recently begun sending college graduates halfway around the world to teach English in Chinese universities and was getting letters back from them. These letters were alternately vivid, poignant, filled with angst, informative, and deliciously humorous. As teachers were placed all over urban and semirural China, the program expanded rapidly, and we began to realize how special these letters really were.

The letters' common theme was an intense love-hate relationship with China and the Chinese. China had only been "reopened" to the West in 1979, after forty years of isolation, and Western ways appeared at times almost antithetical to those of the Chinese. Being in China was thus a profound and paradoxical experience, as the teachers struggled to establish their own Western-based identity while trying to understand and blend into a radically different sociocultural and political milieu. They were discovering that, in spite of all they had tried to learn in advance, their preconceptions and ideas about China were about as accurate as their conceptions of Mars.

The first round of Americans who went to China to teach in the 1980s (Tani Barlow and Donald Lowe, Mark Salzman, Bill Holm, Rosemary Mahoney and Naomi Woronov, to name a few[1]) wrote of a China in the early throes of awakening and reaching out beyond its traditional borders. Westerners were treated with intense curiosity, sometimes hostility, and often great warmth and kindness.

They also found a China where deprivations were the norm, not the exception: they often lacked heat and hot water and had to contend with broken windows, mice and rats, poor sanitation, and a bureaucracy so

---

[1] For information on the writings of these early travelers, see the reading list toward the end of this book.

entrenched and dehumanizing that Westerners found it both monstrous and malignant. Getting a simple train ticket could take hours if not days of intense finagling or overwhelming frustration trying to maintain both position and "cool" at the train station window while being roughly jostled by others on the same mission.

Going to a Chinese post office in the 1980s could make grown men cry, and making a phone call—well, it simply couldn't be done. There were almost no computers, TVs, phones, or even washing machines available to teachers. Americans could really test their mettle and "come of age" in China. It was tough "surviving" a year in China, but in hindsight it was usually an exhilarating and life-affirming experience.

In the 1990s, however, China began slowly to offer a different physical and cultural environment for many teachers, at least on the surface: heat and hot water were a little more dependable; phone service appeared; and washers, dryers, and color TVs popped up in teachers' apartments. Even the twin *bête noires*—the post office and travel arrangements—while still frustrating, started to become more user friendly. There were still a lot of "hardship" teaching posts throughout China, but they were not quite as hard as they had been. By 1997, every university had telephone service and was hooked to a fax machine, and most had e-mail. Compared to 1991, when international mail took from three weeks to a month, communications both internal and international had become instantaneous. What a spinning world!

On my annual trip to China in November 1996, I visited teachers in nine cities, in western China and on the east coast. I am no stranger to China, having lived in Taiwan in 1970–71 as a Chinese history graduate student and having visited China regularly since 1979. The fall 1996 trip, however, was a watershed. Instead of complaining (usually justifiably), many teachers felt comfortable in their surroundings, and some even grumbled that the experience was just a little "too easy." Where were all the hardships and deprivations we had warned them about? Not only were many teachers connected with their families via e-mail, but some could even sit in (relatively) comfortable apartments and have excellent pizza delivered right to the door. Was China becoming more like the United States and less like Mars?

Living and working in China have certainly become more comfortable. Beneath the outward signs of modernization, however, China and the Chinese people (especially the 70–80 percent who don't live in the big east coast cities) have not changed much. Five thousand years of Chinese history and culture can hardly be extinguished by a little more than a decade of telephones, TVs, computers, e-mail, and an improved infrastructure. The "real" China is still there, and, as has been true for centuries, more of it happens behind the curtains than appears on stage. It is true that many facets of traditional China have unfortunately been diluted by modernization, but the puzzles and paradoxes of Chinese culture remain. This is one of the greatest seductions of China—it is like a puzzle people work on for a lifetime, hoping to figure it out by peeking behind the curtain.

It is as though the China experience infects people with a mysterious virus. Since 1979—or 1879, for that matter—Westerners have gone to China to meet and become friends with Chinese people and to encounter a non-Western culture. They often hate being there, get angry with the size of the puzzle, and long for the day they can return home. But as soon as they hit their home shores, the virus flares up. They have been exposed to a few behind-the-scenes glimpses of China through the eyes of their students and colleagues, and they have experienced a small part of the Chinese drama firsthand. China is under their skin or in their blood for a lifetime like a virus—sometimes dormant, sometimes raging, but always there below the surface. As these letters attest, the infectious fascination with China is as alive today as it ever was, and will be tomorrow.

Boulder, Colorado   ALICE RENOUF
1997

Acknowledgments

Thanks go primarily to all the letter writers, named and anonymous. Without their courage and generosity, there would be no book. And thanks also to the loved ones who received these letters, thereby opening themselves to considerable confusion and anxiety from a great distance.

Dr. Janet Bennett and her creative staff at the Intercultural Communication Institute in Portland, Oregon, are silent partners in this project in ways too numerous to list—everything from introducing me to the theory of culture shock years ago to coordinating the distribution of my own letters from China. Dr. Bennett's insight and experience are a constant support to any traveler she befriends as, for example, when she instructed me that "chocolates mail perfectly well to the tropics," and then proved it.

This book was produced upstairs from the archetype of Virginia Woolf's "angel in the house"—my mother. First she raised me up to travel and adapt, and then she did all the shopping while I tried to explain to others what good can come of it.

Janet Bennett and Margaret Pusch made comments on the "Culture Shock" chapter that helped make it more precise. Vicki Hannon and Sally Susnowitz took time to consider the whole book and thereby contributed much to its usefulness and accessibility. Joanne Sandstrom believed a collection of letters could be made readable and convinced others to act on that faith. And Cathy Lenfestey made countless artful refinements to the computer files in order to produce the book.

Finally, this book exists because Alice Renouf inspired the letters then kept them for years, saw the use in publishing them, and talked the rest of us into it. She tracked down a huge number of details and kept everything moving, while she herself shifted house twice. Zubin Emsley says what so many feel about dear Alice: "You helped me in a caring, professional, personal, responsible way. Thank you from the top of my heart." Amen.

P.S. from Alice Renouf: I want to thank my family, Jon, Cassidy, and Whitney Rush. When I should have been busy being wife, mom, and housewife, I was writing my teachers instead. My husband's unflagging support made this venture possible.

Preface

"My name is Phyllis Thompson," I said the first day of every class I taught in Changsha, China, "and I travel." I wrote my name and the word "travel" on the board and drew a rough outline of the United States. I then put a dot for every city I had lived in, hopping back and forth from California to Rhode Island to Washington State and so on (my father was in the Navy), and then after high school to other places within and outside the United States—Holland, Ohio, New York, Puerto Rico, Oregon, Mexico . . . It was in this way I discovered that by 1991, when I was forty-five years old, I had lived for a year or more in twenty places. "China," I said, "is number twenty-one."

Not only do I travel, but I think about how to travel well. My mother first taught me basic skills—how to make friends and settle in quickly, how to throw away all but essentials when we moved, and how to sense what was essential for me. She showed me how to keep friendships alive over time and distance and generally imbued me with the belief that it is possible to feel at home and to find true friends every-where.

More advanced lessons in travel followed when I made my first trip abroad and alone. Just after high school I went to Holland as an American Field Service foreign exchange student. There I began to notice the deeper psychology of settling in—how the first thing we see is what's different from where we started and how our early impulse is often to resist the differences. I remember stalking around my Dutch family's beautiful old home muttering, "Their language sounds like a throat disease and they can't even make flat glass!"

After I learned Dutch and came to love my Frisian village, it struck me as odd that I'd been upset by a language and antique glass, but scholarly articles helped me understand that these reactions were signs of culture shock. Many serious travelers imagine that, if they just got better somehow, they might be able to avoid this sort of transition shock, so I have used the opportunity of Alice's letters to reconstruct the story of how sojourners in general fall into it. I join here with others to argue that the shock of transition is inevitable for the well-adjusted traveler and that it is worth the trouble.

In spite of its psychological thread about travel, however, this book is not really about traveling. It is more a collective attempt to answer the simple and impossible question "How did you like China?"

For anyone who has lived there, China is no longer an abstract noun. It is neither a country nor a way of life. It is a photo in the newspaper that stops us because it looks like one of our students. It is the memory of our favorite Chinese dish called up by a whiff of sesame oil. It is the confusion we feel when someone says, "Those Chinese all just do what they're told," and we remember the courage with which friends stuck by us when they were told to avoid foreigners. China was a rich and challenging life for each of us for a year or more. It led many of us to parts of ourselves we had never seen before. How did we like it? Without a lot of details, it's a little hard to explain.

Explaining is even more difficult because the media in both China and the United States often simplify and vilify the other land. Communist or capitalist, oppressed or free, manipulated or exploited—whose side are you on? Anyone who has lived in China—or in the United States or any other country—knows that these are not the real questions of daily life. "What will we have for dinner?" we ask one another wherever our home is. "What do we have to do today? Shall we go for a walk?"

This book is a tapestry of answers to the real questions of daily life in China, woven by me and thirty-six other Americans who found that my mother was right: Even where the look of home and friendship was strikingly different from anything we had experienced before, we could eventually find our place and make true friends. We spread this tapestry before you with the hope that it may help you understand how we liked it and as a long song of thanks to those on both sides of the Pacific who helped us weave it.

Granada Hills, California   PHYLLIS THOMPSON
1997

WARNING
This book is not about China.
It is about Americans encountering China.

If you want to understand the
difference, read on.

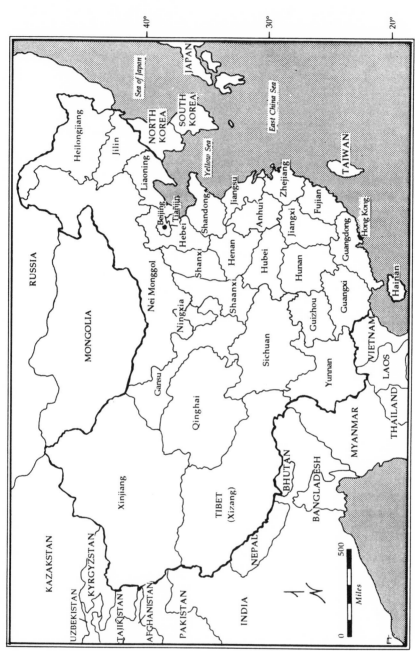

Map 1. The People's Republic of China, showing its provinces and surrounding countries.

CHAPTER ONE

A Looking Glass World

KEVIN LAW-SMITH: Mind-expanding. Frenetic, crazed, hairy, mad, ecstatic ups and downs. Saw parts of myself unseen before.

PJ: There is no denying, no denying that we deal every single moment with the exact opposite of our home culture. Chinese obligation vs. U.S. individualism is only the beginning. They put prices above an item, we put them below. They see time as long, we think time is short. They know how to accept things, we know how to change them.

MICHAEL MAY: China is one truly screwed up country which I have come to love and hate at the same time, maybe even in the same day.

"The very frustration" of journeys to the Third World, says Ivan Illich, "can lead to new awareness: The awareness that even North Americans can receive the gift of hospitality without the slightest ability to pay for it; the awareness that, for some gifts, one cannot even say 'Thank you.'"[1] Indeed, a year or more in China is packed full of both frustration and gifts, especially for North Americans.

In this century, middle-class North Americans have been born into more freedoms and luxury than the average king and queen before 1800.

---

[1] Ivan Illich is an outspoken international activist based in Mexico. He made this comment to a group of young American volunteers on their way to work for a summer in rural Mexico in 1968, and he was trying to convince them not to go. Whether the letter writers in this collection could have profited from the same speech is something you must judge for yourself. "To Hell with Good Intentions," *Combining Service and Learning*, ed. J. C. Kendall and Associates, 1:314–320 (Raleigh, N.C.: National Society for Internships and Experiential Education).

Traveling from the United States to any other culture is likely to involve obvious loss of comfort and subtle gains of perspective that can be utterly confusing—especially when that culture is on the opposite side of everything you can think of.

Stepping from the United States of America into the People's Republic of China is like stepping through Alice's Looking Glass—everything is backwards, but it's not quite clear at first what that means.

The Drama of China

To get a sense of the problem, it might help to take a brief look at the Chinese opera. This is a Chinese tradition that many Americans have a vague sense of, and perhaps a quick image pops up for you—painted faces, stylized costumes, unearthly music. If so, our first important lesson lies before us: Most quick images of China are too shallow. One of the letter writers in this collection puts it this way:

> JEANNE PHILLIPS: I'd mostly seen local troupes working in a park and hadn't thought I much liked Chinese operas—too long, too screechy for my taste. Boy, was I wrong. First I saw the local company do a new comedy with modern humor and set, about medieval corruption of officials (not an accidental theme), and I loved it. Then today, a complete contrast, the top Sichuan company doing a classic fairy tale that I happened to know well, about a white snake/beautiful woman—lots of acrobatic feats, dancing, dramatic acting, fantastic costumes, and not-piercing singing. Loved it too. It turns out that each region has its own style of opera, so seeing many different companies is a rich and varied diet.

Each region of China has its own style of opera and also its own dialect, its own foods, its own weather. Although the distribution of basic housing and electricity, of rice and cooking oil is coordinated by the Chinese central government in Beijing, ancient local differences pervade everyday life throughout China, a country as large and diverse as the United States and older by three thousand years.

Every foreign teacher, therefore, must adapt to a different regional "style" of China. And each year, each term, each month—sometimes each day—China can show a different face. Like its opera, China often seems to shift dramatically, fantastically, and inexplicably. At an opera festival, such dramatic changes can be exciting, but is anyone really prepared for constant quick-change in daily life?

One other basic lesson can be learned from attending an opera on the other side of the Looking Glass: Foreigners easily misunderstand the nature of the show. Another of our letter writers describes this well:

> MARLA JENKS: We arrived a few minutes late, but this was no big deal. People came and went freely throughout the performance. They also tended to talk quite loudly with one another, smoke, rustle food wrappers, play with their cigarette lighters, etc.
>
> The auditorium itself was very nice by Chinese standards. Across the stage was a heavy green velvet curtain that looked like the stagehands had stepped all over it before stringing it up. The ceiling was quite high, and several fans hung down to provide a little circulation in the otherwise stuffy room. Throughout the performance we could hear dogs barking, people shouting, and motorcycles driving by outside. It wasn't exactly a peaceful experience, and you had to work hard to block out the outside noise.
>
> What I found most amazing was the cameraman. He stood down front with a huge TV camera and filmed the performance from all angles. Then he climbed on the stage and got his close-up shots. The next step was to film the audience. Suddenly a huge spotlight blinded all the spectators, and the cameraman moved up and down the aisles. We sort of ducked down in our seats hoping the cameraman wouldn't see us, but it did no good. As soon as the camera people realized there were foreigners in the audience, they set their spotlights right in front of us and started filming away.

At the opera and in the classroom, foreign teachers might *think* they have come to learn something about China and to teach English. But they soon find the spotlight is really on them.

Without realizing it, each teacher in this volume stepped into a grand drama being played out by foreigners all over the Chinese republic. Sitting on sunny balconies or in cold apartments, they jotted down a few of their own scenes and sent them home. Taken as a whole, these letters show why a year or two in Zhongguo, "the Middle Kingdom," is truly like grand opera—full of paradox and passion, confusion and despair, deep meaning and deep love.

Let us see what tempted these players onto the stage.

The Cast of Characters

What draws anyone to teach in China? Most commonly, in the case of the authors here, it was an ad like the one on the following page.

The Colorado China Council is one of many nonprofit organizations that place people in China. For example, the U.S.-based China Teachers Consortium includes ten institutions that together find jobs for more than two hundred teachers each year.[2] Evangelical groups still send teachers, as they have since the West set up permanent bases in Asia in the eighteenth century. And teachers, missionaries, and technical experts come from many other countries as well.

Yet all these people fall into one category in China—they are "foreigners." The Chinese word for foreigner is *waiguoren*, meaning, literally, "outlander." In a country that places a high value on fitting into the community, this word carries subtle shades of meaning that most foreign teachers come to sense only slowly. One of our contributors explains:

RACHEL COLEMAN: [I live in] the Panda House, as the foreigners'

---

[2] China Educational Exchange, Oberlin College, Princeton University, Stanford University, the University of Puget Sound, Wellesley College, Western Washington University, Whitman College, WorldTeach, and Yale University.

TEACHING IN CHINA

You're wondering if you should go to China and, if you do, how you will grow and change and what benefits you will derive. Some observations: A year in China will give you the opportunity to teach some bright and dedicated students. You will form friendships with colleagues and students so profound and long-lasting that you will wonder how you ever lived without these people. It will give you the chance to travel to one of the most amazingly beautiful and geographically and culturally diverse places in the world, not as a tourist, but as an insider— someone who is living and working in the country. It will give you insight into the oldest, most populated, culturally rich and complex society on earth. You will observe and participate in the fastest-growing economy of any nation in the last 1,000 years. You will witness extraordinary pollution, poverty, bureaucratic suffocation, and crowding of terrifying proportions, but you will learn to love the country so much that at times you may hate it with a passion, but you will always want to go back.

The Colorado China Council, a non-political, non-religious, and not-for-profit organization, was established in 1977 as an educational out-reach program to enrich people's understanding of China. It is a member of the China Teachers Consortium, founded by the Yale-China Association, 1990. Our primary objective is to send Americans to teach at Chinese universities, institutes, and secondary schools. The council has placed over 180 teachers throughout China. Alice Renouf, the director and chief administrator since 1977, holds graduate degrees in modern Chinese studies.

compound is lovingly known—although it's hard to say "lovingly." The Chinese definitely view us "foreigners" with a lot of disdain, and the Panda is considered something of a well-kept pet . . . a bit slow & stupid & precious. So it is often hard to know whether the titles the Chinese give us are straightforward or backhanded. And knowing China, they are probably both.

As these letters will eventually make clear, not all meanings of "foreigner" are bad in China. But the Chinese government does see every foreigner—teacher and student, visiting lecturer and organizational consultant—as presenting the same basic set of administrative problems, whether the person comes from Australia or Zaire, Bombay or Yemen, Chicago or down-home Kentucky. All foreigners need help getting tickets and medicines because they have no family to do it for them; their work units need special allocations of cooking oil and electricity to cover foreigner excesses; and they need unusual amounts of foreign currency. To make coordinating these special services easier, universities usually collect their band of outlanders together in some version of "Panda Land," in houses and high-rises, often set off from the rest of the campus behind gates and walls.

Sometimes as many as fifty *waiguoren* might live in one complex, with foreigners who teach English, French, or Japanese living alongside foreigners who study Chinese language and medicine. (We will see this situation described in more detail by Rachel Coleman in Chengdu and by Marla, Matt, and Brian, who live together in Quanzhou.) More often, from four to twenty foreigners share a house or an apartment building on campus, with the higher-status foreign teachers getting better quarters than lower-status foreign students. A few foreign teachers work entirely alone (represented here by Inger in Shantou), though "alone" is a word used ironically in a country with 1.2 billion people.

Among the letter writers in this collection, the following people live near or with one another on the same campus:

- Brian Campbell, Marla Jenks, and Matt Thibodeau in Quanzhou, Fujian
- Nicole Combs and Max Tuefferd a year later in Quanzhou, Fujian
- Todd Lundgren and Eileen Vickery (married) in Qufu, Shandong
- Greg Collins and Amanda Myers in Changsha, Hunan
- Stephen and Joe Márquez in Xi'an, Shaanxi
- Dalkkon Hurtt and Doug Thompson in Fushun, Liaoning

In addition, most Chinese cities have several institutions of higher learning. A major city might have ten or fifteen different institutes, colleges, academies, and universities, each needing one or more teachers of English. Therefore, it is possible to commute within a city to visit fellow foreigners and also to get together with compatriots in other towns. Among writers here, the following people lived close enough to visit one another:

- Joe Márquez (in Xi'an) and Jim Page (in Yan'an)
- Kevin Law-Smith and Adam Williams (both in Tianjin)

Other people placed by the same agency are not always a foreign teacher's best friends, however. The foreigners' quarters in China host an exceptionally mixed and fluid group called the "expat community"—that is, *expatriates,* or people who are "away from their homeland." Expats often come together to share stories about the "weird" place they all find themselves, to drink and play together, and in the best cases, to support one another through the difficult process of adapting to another country. Such communities form in every land—you can find them among foreign students at any U.S. or Canadian university—and for some, these groups yield the most satisfying friendships forged during time abroad. But there is also a danger here. Some experts feel that intense involvement with expats in any foreign setting can divert sojourners from engaging in the difficult but exciting work of really immersing themselves in the culture around them, from really "learning how to walk upside down and write backwards," as PJ describes it in a letter from Changsha.

Inevitably, however, whether they view the expat network as a support or a diversion, each foreign teacher in China is automatically caught up in it. And as these letters will show, its connections can be extended through time: Teachers from one year pass heartfelt advice (and cherished vegetable peelers) down to those who follow. In this collection, we will meet thirty-six of these expats, all very different except for two things: They all chose to step into the drama of China between 1990 and 1995, and they all sent letters to Alice Renouf of the Colorado China Council.

Name	Years in China	City and Province
Dale T. Asis	1994–95	Xiangtan, Hunan
Bruce Bender	Spring 1994	Dalian, Liaoning
Mary E.R. Bracken	1991–92	Guangzhou, Guangdong
Brian Campbell	1993–94	Quanzhou, Fujian
Rachel Coleman	2 years: 1991–93	Chengdu, Sichuan
Nicole Combs	1994–95	Quanzhou, Fujian
Paige Davies	1992–93	Nanchang, Jiangxi
Zubin Emsley	1994–95	Hangzhou, Zhejiang
G (Greg Collins)	3 years: 1992–95	Changsha, Hunan, & Guangzhou, Guangdong
Todd Hamina	1991–92	Changsha, Hunan
Dalkkon D. Hurtt	1992–93	Fushun, Liaoning
Inger	1993–94	Shantou, Guangdong
PJ	1993–94	Changsha, Hunan
Marla Jenks	1993–94	Quanzhou, Fujian
Teddy Kellam	2 years: 1992–94	Guangzhou, Guangdong
Todd Lundgren & Eileen Vickery	2 years: 1992–93 & 1994–95	Qufu, Shandong
Joe J. Márquez	1993–94	Xi'an, Shaanxi
Michael May	1992–93	Fuzhou, Fujian
Megan	1995–96	Hangzhou, Zhejiang
David Moldavsky	1993–94	Nanchang, Jiangxi
Amanda Myers	1992–93	Changsha, Hunan
Jim Page	1993–94	Yan'an, Shaanxi
Jeanne Phillips	1992–93	Fuzhou, Fujian
Matthew Rees	1992–93	Yan'an, Shaanxi
Patrick	1992–93	Yan'an, Shaanxi
Katie Showalter	1994–95	Fuzhou, Fujian
Kevin Law-Smith	1993–94	Tianjin
Stephen	2 years: 1992–94	Xi'an, Shaanxi
Matt Thibodeau	1993–94	Quanzhou, Fujian
Doug Thompson	2 years: 1992–93 & 1994–95	Fushun, Liaoning, & Changsha, Hunan
Samantha Tisdel	1993–94	Qingdao, Shandong

Name	Years in China	City and Province
Max Tuefferd	1994–95	Quanzhou, Fujian
Justin Van Wart	1994–95	Tianjin
Adam Williams	Fall 1992	Tianjin
Kristen Wood	1992–93	Jinan, Shandong

As you can see, some of these writers prefer to veil their identities with initials and shortened names, and two ask to remain anonymous. We have also masked the names of any people mentioned in these letters who have not given us express permission to use them. A long history of dramatic reversals in relations between the United States and China suggests that we err on the side of caution.

Not quite all these letters came originally to Alice Renouf. Samantha Tisdel's material comes from letters she gave to the Ouray County (Colorado) *Plaindealer*, published as a "Dispatch from China" on April 28, 1994. And not quite all the teachers found their positions in China through the Colorado China Council. But all these writers eventually found their way to Alice and felt a sympathetic and responsive connection during strange times far away. They have risked sharing their letters because they all hope, in the classic sense, to both teach and delight.

They may have gone to China just out of college for the adventure. They may have left a good job that seemed hollow in order to do good works. When she wrote the letters used here, Jeanne Phillips was an emeritus professor of psychology returning to China for a second year of teaching. Zubin Emsley was an aerospace engineer looking for something entirely new. Whatever their motives, they found more than they bargained for—things unexpected, frustrating, and ultimately valuable, "some gifts," as Illich said, for which they "cannot even say 'Thank you.'" By laying these letters side by side, we hope to develop a sense of this mysterious gift.

In addition, this composite portrait might allow us to glimpse the real answer to the question that began this section: What draws someone to live and teach in China? What qualities do these writers share that pull them to pass through the comfortably reflective surface of the Looking Glass and enter the unknown land on the other side? Perhaps we can peer through these stories to the tellers behind them and discover what spirit and skills they might have in common as they arrive—clutching their passports and wrestling their luggage out of planes and trains, stepping down onto uncertain ground.

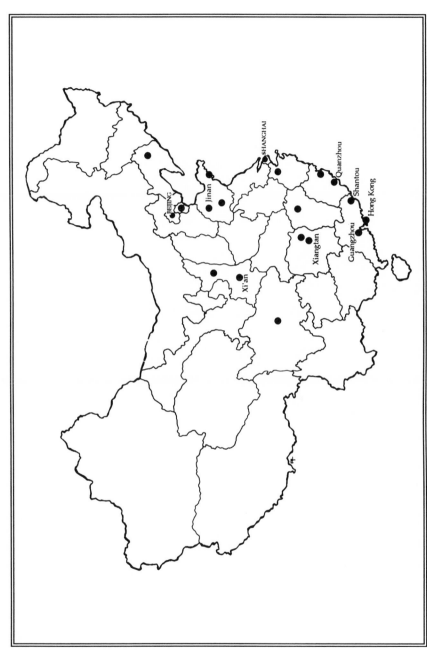

Map 2. The People's Republic of China, showing the cities from which letters in chapter 2 were written.

dan, rou, cai, pao cai (dahn, row, tsai, pow tsai): egg, meat, vegetable, pickles—the food words Inger learns first in her stay.

doufu (dough-foo): the pinyin spelling of *tofu,* a soft soybean cake.

mei you (may yoh): "Don't have any," a phrase that is frustratingly common in China!

renminbi (ren-min-bee, abbreviated **RMB**): the general term for Chinese money, which means literally "people's money."

NOTE: The letters in this book come from China. The language is different there, of course, and some ideas are different too. A new vocabulary develops among these foreign teachers, both because they pick up bits of local language and because they have new things to say. Each chapter therefore begins with a list of new words the writers use and a rough pronunciation guide. These words are collected in a complete vocabulary list at the end of the book.

All the Chinese in these lists is rendered in pinyin, a system developed in mainland China for converting the sounds of Chinese characters into our alphabet. Most pinyin spellings can be pronounced commonsensically in English, but four exceptions show up fairly often:

- *ou* (as in *mei you,* "don't have") is pronounced "oh," so this phrase can be pronounced approximately "may yoh."
- *zh* (as in the city names Guangzhou and Quanzhou) is pronounced "j," so these city names are approximately "Gwahng-joe" and "Chuan-joe."
- *xi* (as in the city name Xi'an) is pronounced "shee," so say "Shee-ahn."
- *qi* (as in *qi gong,* "practice controlling energy flow") is pronounced "chee."

CHAPTER TWO

Arrivals

Hong Kong

Alice,

Hong Kong. The air is heavy, the smells of people and sticky food and car exhaust, tropical plants. I remember this place from my nose, like the scent of an old lover's perfume. I love it. As I walk around these streets I sense a cleanliness I do not recall. Was Hong Kong dirtier thirteen years ago? Wasn't there more debris and refuse thrown in the street, every other person squatting and smoking? Either the face of this colony has changed or I developed a myth years ago that has shaped my expectations.

I'll write again.

G

Jinan, Shandong

Dear Alice,

Hello from China! Well, I've made it—amazingly enough! Safe and sound but without my luggage, which was lost somewhere in San Fran I believe. But not to fear; it's on its way, and should be here by Monday—hopefully everything's still in it! China is most definitely not what I expected. Like you said, no matter what type of preparation and preconceived notions exist, one will never know what they'll find until they get here.

My university is very plush I think—my apartment is incredibly large and well-equipped. I have a large bedroom, a bed with bug netting, a large living room, all kinds of neat old furniture, a TV!, a phone!, a small kitchen, and a bathroom (and washer). Most everything is filthy dirty—especially the floor. Jinan is quite dry, dusty, and smoky, and it's been very hot—until today. It's raining. The rain is such a nice relief. It's easier to breathe and much cooler.

My classes do not begin until September 9 because my students are in military training.[1] I've met a few of the other teachers and students, and tonight we may go to a "Dance." Tomorrow I'm going downtown on a BUS to exchange $ and buy some things. I've braved the market and the department store in town with another teacher who is from Pittsburgh, PA! She's already become a good friend.

There will be a total of fourteen foreign teachers here—mostly couples (from Australia, Japan, and the U.S.). The woman who lives upstairs from me is an older woman from Australia. She's been here since last (spring) semester and appears to have adapted quite well. September 5 has been arranged as an outing to climb the most holy mountain in Shandong (maybe in China?). I can't remember the name but I know it's "Confucius' Mountain." I've called home to Mom and Dad and also to Ben. It took some time getting through to Ben (three days), but he's already making arrangements for a passport, and Mrs. Lu (one of the foreign expert's directors), after seeing me bawling, said, "Don't worry. Have him come and visit!" Everyone's very nice here. More soon.

Love,

Kristen Wood

As Kristen's letter suggests, one thing that can help with arrivals is the presence of other foreigners. Some, like the teacher from Pittsburgh, are good companions in adventure; some are guides who have been in China before, occasionally even from the same placement agency.

---

[1] Most incoming college students in China receive military drill and tactics training. Chinese students usually enter the university in a "class," which stays together throughout the entire course of study.

In the next letters we hear from three groups who arrive in China together—first, from Joe Márquez arriving for a year in middle China with Stephen, back for his second year, then from two other groups landing in the coastal city of Quanzhou in two different years, as they encounter some unexpected neighbors.

Xi'an, Shaanxi

Alice,

I'm here! But getting here was quite eventful.

I have to admit I wanted to go home until we arrived in Xi'an. I hated it. I think culture shock hit me when I stepped on the plane. That whole time I probably looked like a psychological wet dream (laugh, I meant this to be funny).

The airplane was ugly. The fabric all looked like it was put together by Timothy Leary on one of his trips. It seemed like the whole time we were flying, the plane was constantly ascending. I thought, "We'll reach the moon by sunrise." The food was horrible. You had your choice of chicken feet or dog tongue stew —I'm kidding, but it left much to be desired.

After take-off, someone's alarm went off. They didn't realize this until 45 minutes had passed. We saw three movies—only one had subtitles.

I met Stephen in customs in Shanghai. We made it from Shanghai to Beijing with our bags. We got in around 11 P.M. and Stephen talked someone into letting us stay at a guest house at one of the universities. We were able to get a shower and a few hours of sleep. In the morning we grabbed breakfast there (rice porridge, Chinese bread, spicy cukes, and some *doufu*). After breakfast we went to the train station.

Our train didn't leave until 11 P.M. We were in the station for about thirteen hours. We took turns watching our stuff. On one of my free times I took a walk around the station. There must have been close to a thousand people inside and outside the station, sleeping on the ground waiting for trains. I was amazed. I wanted to videotape this to show people back home but was afraid that it was too rude, even if I held the camera at my side. After seeing what I saw I feel I cannot complain, because the Chinese have it far worse than I will, and this is their country.

Our train finally arrived so we "queued" Chinese style—in other words a mass of people trying to fit through one turnstile. I got a little pissed off but kept my cool. We finally made it *onto* the train (soft sleeper)[2] and settled in. We had so much stuff we had to sleep with our duffel bags on the cots. (This is the making of a great adventure and travel book.)

I ate in the dining car the next day, which I probably shouldn't have. I'm fine now, though.

We finally arrived in Xi'an—extremely exhausted and de-hydrated. I thought I was going to pass out. Xi'an was a bit more run-down than I expected but I like it. It was great to see the city wall and the bell tower. I have read so much about the city that it was numbing to see them. I was actually here—in Xi'an—I asked for this? It reminds me of Boston because of all the sites and history. But Boston has blue sky; Xi'an has Gray Drab covering the city.

Oh yeah, I almost forgot. Make sure you tell all the teachers from now on to take a Swiss Army knife, vitamins, something to eat, and eating utensils with them. I did not know how long it would be before I reached Xi'an, but at least I had my Swiss and my vitamins. The vitamins were helpful because I was unable to eat properly and felt kind of down and dragging. I didn't have any raisins or dried fruit, which would have been helpful to boost my energy. Stephen and I had to eat with pocketknives at the Beijing station because they were *mei you* on the chopsticks. Thank god for my Swiss.

I'm fine, Alice. And I can laugh at my adventure getting here. It was fun. It wasn't fun doing it, but if you think about it, it is

---

[2] The highest class on Chinese trains—a semiprivate room with four beds, mattresses, sheets, and other amenities.

funny. Maybe when the Poodles[3] get together we'll swap stories to see who had the toughest time reaching school. If I win I'll probably get a beer out of it.

I just finished dinner and realized that there are no other people my age. I'm bummed about that but I'm sure I'll be all right. And I think the whole "getting here" experience helped. It was tough and I was a bit depressed, but it helped make my initial adjustment to Xi'an better. I'm not saying I won't go through culture shock, but I now think it will be easier.

Please thank J—— for teaching me Chinese. I have had a couple of difficult times because of a lack of vocabulary, but I also talk to whoever I meet. Some people in Shaanxi speak with their teeth clenched and it is difficult to understand them but fun trying to communicate.

Alice, take care. I'll keep in touch.

Sincerely,

Joe Márquez

Quanzhou, Fujian

Dear Alice,

Well, we made it. We're here, in our rooms, which are quite acceptable, but as Brian says we're about to get "hosed" out of them, because they want to shuffle us around. This is an ongoing source of tension, because we're quite happy where we are, except for the dead rat—but Brian can tell you about that.

We got to Xiamen without a hitch; the ferry was great, except when we got off there was no one to meet us and we had to take a cab, and we can't get reimbursed because we didn't get a receipt!

---

[3] At orientation in Colorado, one presenter told an incoming group of teachers that foreigners were not always hired to teach language so much as to entertain students with examples of American culture in action. He called this the "Dancing Poodle Show."

Please fax us our group's addresses and phone #s, and fax #s A.S.A.P. Thanks.

Love,

Matt Thibodeau

Quanzhou, Fujian

Dear Alice,

As we rode into Quanzhou from Xiamen, I kept wondering what I had gotten myself into. Everyone here is nice. The "veterans" who have been here for two to five years are really helping us out. As Matt mentioned, I found a dead rat in the bottom of my closet. It was underneath the boards intended to keep them out. We had to pry them up to get rid of it. This is the worst of it so far. I am ready to start teaching. Now I'm a bit bored. Our (mine and Matt's) department head stopped by today and gave us books and schedules. We're Here! I guess that's it for now. We just wanted to say "HI"!

Brian Campbell

Quanzhou, Fujian

Hi Alice!

I guess those guys just about covered everything. Things are going well with only a few minor hitches. Our rooms are fine (except for the rodents), but my closet is inaccessible. They have explained that it's the storage space for blankets and pillows, and the maid with the key is gone for an indefinite period of time. Food is okay, but I think I'm going to need a pizza before too long! Take care,

Marla Jenks

Quanzhou, Fujian
(different year)

Dear Alice,

As we pushed our luggage out (as well as being pushed out ourselves) of the Xiamen Airport, there was P—— waiting with a car to take us back to Quanzhou. I think both of us were pretty nervous that there was not going to be anyone there—so we were pleased!

We have gone into the city a couple of times. It is amazing. I absolutely love it!—all the people, bargaining, food, bicycles, did I mention people?—are massive. It is absolutely wonderful. I feel fortunate that I studied Chinese before coming here, but sometimes that really doesn't matter!

I cannot believe I am in China! I want to absorb all the culture I possibly can this year. We were taken to a traditional music/puppet (marionette-type) show Tuesday night. What a wonderful treat of welcome.

Nicky Combs

Quanzhou, Fujian

Dear Alice,

My impressions in the first week are of being in a Third World country. The conditions are generally poor but livable. I believe they are about thirty or forty years behind us—but gaining rapidly.

One thing I hadn't realized—everyone here (that is, every foreigner except Nicky and me) is a missionary of sorts.

Max Juefferd

Not everyone has the cushion of companions, however, although they may wish for it at the start.

Shantou, Guangdong

Dear Alice,

Here I am, safe and sound in Shantou.

Mr. Lu (FAO)[4] picked me up at the ferry without incident. He was a bit late but I ignored all the pedicab and taxi cab drivers who harangued me, loaded down with my three HEAVY bags. Hoping to get the foreigner to overcharge, I'm sure.

I'm strongly hoping that Mrs. G—— doesn't back out. Her last fax sounded pretty suspicious. I don't see why she would assume the Chinese contracts are so sticky when there have been so many of our foreign teachers over here without problems. Without major problems, anyway.

For personal reasons I'm hoping Mrs. G—— comes. I have been pretty intensely homesick since I am the ONLY Westerner on the medical college campus here in town. I would very much like to have a Western roommate, and her landing would be much softer than mine was since I would be here to cushion it.

I have just received my monthly salary. I got my full month's salary even though I arrived the 9th. Mr. Lu floated me RMB 300 for my first week.

Otherwise, things are going fine. I'm feeling pretty stupid with my Chinese (I can say things in four languages that I can't say yet in Chinese.) I'm getting along fine at the dining hall though: *dan, rou, cai, pao cai!* The post office is O.K., although they overcharged me by almost twice my first visit. I guess you really *can't* trust most Chinese where money is concerned. Not that I couldn't afford it, of course.

Inger

---

[4] "Foreign Affairs Officer" or "Foreign Affairs Office" (the same initials are used for both). This important office and its officers handle negotiations between foreigners and various state agencies. Thus the FAO hands out monthly salaries and (theoretically) helps with things like work visas and train tickets.

Some say it directly, some by implication: Landing in China can be like landing on another planet. But as Dale Asis reports, the "natives" seem generally to welcome the arriving "aliens."

Xiangtan, Hunan

Ms. Alice Renouf,

It has been an extraordinary month for me. You are right, I love and hate something about China every day. It is everything and nothing I expected. It is a mental explosion both inside me and around me. I know less, and more, than when I left. And you are right again, I could never prepare well enough for China. It is like going to Mars.

But it is not a place of cold aliens. My China is full of warm and caring people, the most curious students I have ever met, and the most enduring, deep friends I have found. In America, I was so busy doing things, doing errands, finishing deadlines and finishing lists that I had made the day before. I was always racing with time. But in China, it is different. I find time to look at myself. I find time to develop true friendships. I find pleasure in the simplest things, like a hot shower!

Dale Asis

Listen:
Billy Pilgrim has come unstuck in time. . . . [He] is spastic in time, has no control over where he is going next, and the trips aren't necessarily fun. . . . He said that he had been kidnapped by a flying saucer in 1967. The saucer was from the planet Tralfamadore, he said. He was taken to Tralfamadore, where he was displayed naked in a zoo, he said. He was mated with a former Earthling movie star named Montana Wildhack.
Kurt Vonnegut, Jr.
Slaughterhouse-Five

Xi'an, Tralfamadore Sector
Friday 4th or so

Dear Alice,

Sorry about our lack of communication but we just returned from Tralfamadore. We're not sure when we were first kidnapped; it seems we've acquired the ability to exist in multiple dimensions of time and we're debating the question of present reality. Therefore we thank you for your letter which has indicated to us that we are indeed living at some period at the end of 1992.

We're going out on a limb to tell you about Tralfamadore for it is a world known only to the Tralfamadorians, sagging porn stars, Billy and ourselves. Upon returning to this world, we found ourselves located in the middle of China, literally in terms of geography and figuratively in terms of communism, a place where time is elastic and action must be considered, at least to some extent, superficial.

It is difficult to relate events that have happened to us here because we've been duped. Whereas at one time we were being educated, now we are the educators. Of course you cannot separate these two because, as you know, time is the fourth dimension, so what appeared in the past, what is at present, and what will come in the future is and always will be. So it goes.

Upon our arrival in China, albeit separately, we discovered that the Chinese, as did the Tralfamadorians, provided us each with another of our kind so as to ease our transition into this particular dimension of time. Although we get along wonderfully and are grateful to have one another to talk with about difficulties, we both agree that Montana Wildhack would have provided a deeply missed entity, but that's for another dimension.

The FAO, like the AAO (Alien Affairs Officer), is very kind and willing to go out of his way to aid us in times of difficulty. The accommodations provided for us here are exactly the same as those accommodations on Tralfamadore. We live together in an apartment that has a kitchen, a bathroom, a sitting room, one office, and two bedrooms. Thus we are quite comfortable in terms of living conditions. However, here the water and electricity can and do go off periodically without notice. Without water, our personal hygiene sometimes is less than that of the Tralfamadorians. To compensate for the infrequent bathing, we are forced to change our attire on occasion. This is quite abnormal behavior, for it appears that most people here have only two sets of clothing.

We exist, and yet we don't. As sometimes we are on Tralfamadore. And yet we teach, therefore we are—at least today.

Now we have just returned from Tralfamadore. We know not how long our stay was, for the time warp which we must pass through has distorted our sense of time. The residual taste of cheeseburgers still lies heavily on our tongues, as a weeping baby lies in its crib.

We see, hear, feel, taste, and smell that it is time to teach class and thus we must sign off for now, whenever and wherever that may be.

Until next . . .

Mr. Patrick[5]
Mr. Matthew

Guangzhou, Guangdong

Alice,

Things *couldn't* be better! I have a wonderful apt. (w/AC [air conditioner], TV and phone). I was shocked! Things are a lot different here. There's much more freedom and openness. The

---

[5] Chinese names have the surname first, then the personal name—Mao Zedong could politely be called "Mr. Mao." Therefore students sometimes call teachers by their personal names, thinking they are being formal. Since Americans tend to be informal, this suits most of them just fine.

influences from Hong Kong are very evident! The food is the best Chinese I've ever had and dirt cheap. Mr. Tang is very nice as are other heads in the department. My classes don't start 'til end of month because all freshmen are doing three weeks' military practice—wild! Until then, I was told to "enjoy life" and perhaps help with making tapes. Facilities are great!! Definitely made a good choice. Only bad thing is it's hotter than hell—makes Houston look air-conditioned. Met a guy on the plane from Denver-LA who was going to Xi'an to teach at medical school. Small world!

Mary Bracken

"We made it!" these letters say, with vast relief. Smooth or rough, the long trip from a place called Home to The Foreign Land is complete. People here seem to care about us, they give us money and comfortable rooms, and they sponsor trips around town.

But clearly this *is* a foreign place. The freshmen have three weeks of military practice? People have only two sets of clothes? "At one time we were being educated," say Patrick and Matthew, "now we are the educators." Somehow, everything *has* turned upside down. The next few weeks in China (like the first weeks in any new land) are filled with intense learning—almost like the first years of a child's life—trying to piece together how this new world works.

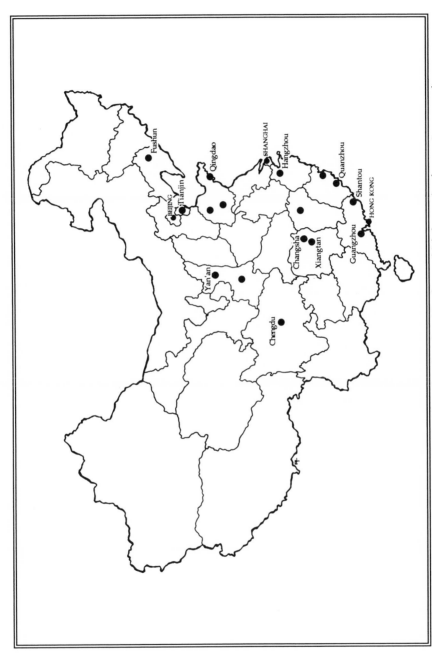

Map 3. The People's Republic of China, showing the cities from which letters in chapter 3 were written.

baozi; baozi cooker (baow-tsuh): *baozi* are steamed rice-flour buns; a *baozi* cooker is the steamer, a straight-sided round container of woven bamboo that is set over water boiling in a wok.

gong fu (gong foo): the pinyin spelling of *kung fu,* any of several forms of Chinese martial art.

guanxi (gwan-shee): the complex web of obligations and favors that pervades Chinese society, explored in this chapter at length by Jeanne Phillips.

jiaozi (jow-tsuh): crescent-shaped wontons (dumplings); can be boiled or fried.

mei xin (may sheen): "No mail."

pijiu (pee-joe): beer. Since Chinese beer is quite tasty, this is often one of the first words a foreigner learns in China.

tai ji (tai gee): often spelled and pronounced *t'ai chi* in the United States; a flowing exercise and "soft" martial art.

waiban (wy-bon): Foreign Affairs Office (or officer); in charge of foreigners.

Xiao T—— (she-aow): *xiao,* meaning "young," and *lao* (laow), meaning "old," are friendly or informal titles in China. Many of the writers here develop friends they call *xiao,* and several call their housekeepers or immediate bosses *lao.*

yuan (yu-en, abbreviated ¥): the primary unit of Chinese currency. At the time of these letters, $1 = 5–8¥.

CHAPTER THREE

Learning to Live in China

If China has taught me anything, it is to respect the high probability of the improbable.

G

What If Everything Mother Taught You Is Wrong?

Yes, indeed: On the other side of the planet, they do things a little differently.

Guangzhou, Guangdong

Hi Everyone!

I've just finished meeting with Xiao T——, one of my postgraduate students. We meet every Friday morning at 7:30. She is thoughtful and fantastic—teaches me more than I could ever teach her. This morning, she found a poinsettia tree on campus and made a vase from a shaft of bamboo—now I have a bit of Christmas cheer perched on the corner of my desk. Although Xiao T—— is an overworked computer science student, she has the vibrancy of a handful of colored ribbons rippling in the wind. I have never met a person with such a delicate reverence for the beauty of life—she is fascinated by the colors of trees, by the words of poets and the sounds and details of her every day. She approaches life with such wonderment and romance and stunning clarity—I anticipate each visit. She always pulls a flower or a book out of her bag—and one time she brought a green bouquet of flowering cabbage for my lunch! Time with Xiao T——, like time with many of my students, is delightful.

And life in China is ripe with intrigue. I look out my east window onto the courtyard of a kindergarten watching the children play. In bold colors they dash wildly, this way and that, sending *gong fu* kicks into the air, waving their arms, or just running in silly circles. Guangzhou, where I live and teach, is much the same: frenzied and bustling, colorful and alive. When I first arrived here, I saw a gray, dilapidated-yet-modern Chinese city. But now, I relish the energy, the activity, the passion in Guangzhou—the Garden City.

How can I describe it? I'll take you on a brief tour. I walk out of the south gate of my university campus (a serene oasis of bamboo trees, ponds, and antiquated brick buildings) onto the street. Suddenly the pace of Guangzhou hits you like a burst of hot exhaust. On the left hover the bicycle repairmen, waiting to net a broken chain or a flat tire from the steady stream of bicycles flowing like a school of fish down the bicycle lane. The street is packed with contrasts: a curious blend of the modern, the archaic, and the bizarre—a Japanese-built taxi vies for space with a motorcycle carrying a family of five and a bicycle hauling thirty live chickens bound and hanging upside down like ornaments on the family Christmas tree. Hawkers along the street sell everything from pig-stomach shish kabob to padded bras to Mao Zedong keychains.

Across the street (after many clever, calculated steps!) a bountiful open-air food market entices. As you draw closer, though, your first instinct is to plug your poor nose, which has suddenly been assaulted by the pungent aroma of slaughtered pig. As you meander among the cement counters, you learn all there is to know about Cantonese cuisine. The vegetables at this time of year are sparkly and fresh—lumpy carrots and cilantro, huge red and yellow onions, flowering greens and curious squash, long thin eggplant and stubby mushrooms. The veggies are similar to those grown in the West, but they always have a *slightly* different shape—indeed, a bit more character than the ones I'm used to! Even vegetable shopping is fascinating here.

Turn the corner, and you meet the fruit-hawkers. This

month, papaya, mandarin oranges, and starfruit are prevalent—and, oh yes—four-foot shafts of sugarcane. Down the next aisle, naked chickens dangle, hanging in rows by their beaks. You can buy a live one and chop it yourself or "settle" for one that has been killed and de-feathered within the hour. Next are the eggs. You choose one and sit it on top of a wooden tray, flip a switch, and a bright light bulb allows you to check for signs of life in the egg. If you see nothing, it's a good egg. Next we move on to the pork and *jiaozi* aisle. On one side they are chopping busily, and on the other side, you can buy the filling and the wrapping for *jiaozi*. There is a special technique to folding the dumplings, and you end up with a lovely crescent moon–shaped creation. The *jiaozi* are boiled or fried, then gobbled eagerly with chopsticks!

If you're up early enough (6–7 A.M.), you'll see the most beautiful human painting. Against the backdrop of the rising sun are young and old Chinese doing morning exercise—badminton, running, and martial arts. It's breathtaking and peaceful at the same time—a human collage of swirling and grace, sinuous, fluid bodies with simultaneous rocklike strength. The Chinese seem to understand their bodies so well, and health is paramount—blended into their traditions. I'm awestruck by this natural wisdom: no goals of strength or thinness or elusive perfection; they simply listen to their bodies, and they have the ability to make their minds quiet enough to hear.

As for the psyche, the philosophy of the people, of this society—I could ruminate for years, torment myself with the quagmires and complexities, the paradoxes, and the elusive simplicities. How can I even communicate my questions? I go out into the street, and there are so many people—yet they manage to "flow by" one another. People seem to be able to tune out the frustrations of China—the overpopulation, the chaos and confusion, the inefficiencies, strange rules, and ineffective regulations. They have the ability to cope, to avoid getting hot under the collar or frothing at the mouth the way we Westerners often do. I watch people in the street calmly avoiding calamities—one after the other—leaving themselves to instinct.

I, however, have two choices: to bumble through my day absentmindedly, tripping over this and that, spilling my tea (on these days, I'm in imminent danger of traipsing into the path of a bicycle or a minibus); or to inch through my day, cautiously measuring each careful plod of my foot, ready to dart from each potential hazard. (Potential hazards in China are a *riot*. One time I slid on a piece of raw pork—just like a banana peel. Another time, I was hit with a plastic container of discarded rice. I've been whacked by a bicycle, and even a motorcycle; and last month, while A——— and I shared a chair, the seat exploded into plastic shards, depositing us on our derrières in the middle of a group of students!)

So you see, my life is surprising and intriguing, rich and bizarre, and always, always humorous. It's China . . . I love it.

Teddy Kellam

Yan'an, Shaanxi

Dear Alice,

Where to begin? My life in Yan'an. All in all, in a nutshell, more or less, or in sum, my existence here is wonderful. I'm really enjoying myself. I'm not saying that my pleasure is in the absence of minor problems. Hey, I'm in a remote area of central China! Perhaps I'd suffer similar setbacks in larger cities, as well. Who knows? The problems really are quite trivial. They range from no copies, books, water (hot or cold), or electricity . . . to severe ass-biting cold weather, toxic coal fumes, and constant dust particles in my lungs. I could continue but it would be pointless. I'm not complaining but commenting on different (and sometimes bizarre) survival techniques. For example, my theory here is, warmth and comfort first, style second. At any rate, it provides my students with numerous laughs. Who's really getting the last laugh, though?

My living arrangements are fine. My building is brand new. But as a result of local (and widespread) corruption many utilities frequently break down. The electrical outlets can sustain only a certain amount of energy. This problem has resulted in my blowing the whole unit of power for the entire building. However, my neighbors know where to go when this happens. After the second time I did this, many of the neighborhood men came downstairs wielding tools. Fortunately, they were for the electrical breakers and not me. After a short time all is restored— until I try to use my radio, TV, refrigerator, boiler, and space heater all at once.

I've got two bedrooms, a living room, a walk-in kitchen, and a bathroom (with a door too small for a dwarf; many a night I have nearly severed my head from my shoulders). There is no carpet, but now I understand why. After twenty-four hours and a hundred students, my apartment contains much of the Gobi.

Speaking of students, many come by for occasional visits (normally they stay as long as any in-law). Because they're used to using the Chinese squat system, I had to show a couple of the first-years the ropes in using a Western toilet. After they left I noticed two perfect shoe prints on my toilet seat. The good part of this story is that most of them had adequate aim.

How about me? I'm doing well. My life is basic and now full of routine. Get up. Drink tea/coffee. Go to school. Go to lunch. Carry water. Read. Rest. Work. Eat dinner. Carry water. Read. Work. Read. Have a *pijiu*. Go to bed. This alternates with wonderfully exciting variation. For example, Thursday night I teach German, Thursday day I oversee first-year English corner [where students meet informally to practice speaking in English], Friday afternoon office hours, and every day (my fault for this imprudent omission) I have a one-hour *Chinese* lesson.

Thanks for your letters and sorry for my lack of response. I'll try to improve but probably won't.

All is well. Keep in touch.

Love,

Jim Page

Every country's ways and means are a bit different, and the main project of early weeks anywhere is to learn as fast as you can and try to keep things in perspective.

DALE ASIS: My hometown, Xiangtan, doesn't have a lot of tourist spots. We do have a park with a small pond with paddle boats. We also have a small sandy "beach" by the Xiang River, packed with picnickers every weekend. It is quite scenic, but I have to share it with at least a thousand other people.

The foreign teachers at a nearby university are all grinning with envy at my college's royal treatment of me. I even get a car to use when I go visit them on weekends. But my stay is also filled with frustrations. The water is erratic, the broken window in my classroom is never fixed, and sometimes they change the schedule without telling me. Am I complaining? No. I'm enjoying the ups and downs, the happiness and frustrations that come with my stay in China.

SAMANTHA TISDEL: [The entrance to the library is through] a side door . . . small, inconspicuous, and guarded at all times by an "uncle"—an old man whose only job is to sit at his little table and monitor all comings and goings.

Every important building on campus has its own uncle—the teaching buildings, dormitories, and, annoyingly, the "foreign teachers building" where I and my cohorts are kept. We have two uncles, dubbed "Happy" and "Grumpy," who take turns on twelve-hour shifts to provide us with neverending protection. Chinese friends must sign in and out when coming to visit. All visitors must be out, and inmates in, by the 10:30 lock-up at night, or else.

We have not been provided with keys to our own front door and so must arouse the doorkeeper if we come home late. Woe to the stupido who comes home late if Grumpy is on duty! Grumpy (otherwise known as Sleepy) doesn't like to have his beauty rest disturbed. He likes to let you pound on the door, shivering in the cold, for what feels like hours before dragging his sweet behind out of bed to let you in. And once you're in, he'll let you know in a volley of incomprehensible Chinese just what he thinks of the decadent hours kept by certain pesky foreign devils. That's okay; you can explain to him in a volley of incomprehensible English that he'll need a whole lot more than his precious beauty rest if he wants to pass for a human being. The language barrier . . . ain't it great?

ADAM WILLIAMS: I'm a little disappointed that I'm the only foreign *teacher* living in the foreign *students'* building. My room is far inferior: no kitchen area, and a ceiling that collapses a little bit more every day. It has also made friendships with other teachers close to impossible. I'm overlooked when it comes to invitations from the school. It's very inconvenient to go and visit them in their building, and when I do I'm often accused of being a student—"You must sign in."

However, I have made some wonderful friends with undergraduate and graduate students here from Carlton University. These students only stay until December 7, so I'm kind of unhappy about that.

I tried to go visit Kevin Law-Smith but he wasn't around. I'll try again later. His school is 'way across town. It's unbelievable how enormous Tianjin is. I'm living in a seaport where it takes anywhere from one and a half to two hours to get to the ocean— depending on where you live in "nonindustrial" Tianjin (although I don't think there is a nonindustrial part to this city). It's so nice to have our campus as a haven.

MARLA JENKS: Absolutely *everyone* employed by the university lives on campus. There are no private houses. People are all in dorm-style buildings—teachers, administrators, food service workers, *everyone*.

Shantou, Guangdong

Dear Alice,

Things have much improved now that I'm over the first two weeks' crash landing. Of course the students are wonderful! I've met the other foreign teachers at Shantou U. outside of town, and I'm beginning to really feel at home in my apartment.

I don't mind so much now that Mrs. G—— isn't coming. Not only has the loneliness subsided, I now am so busy that I'm grateful to have been "stuck in town by myself," because the time alone is really nice. It's turning into a really nice adventure.

The Shantou U. campus is about thirty minutes out of town by the school buses, which run about six to eight times a day, back and forth. They have nine foreign teachers there who are all very nice. I see them fairly often, as I teach out there three days a week and sometimes I meet them for their regular Saturday morning shopping jaunt in town. This weekend, to celebrate having been here over a month, I am planning a fried chicken dinner out at the U. with all of the foreign teachers who can make it and possibly a couple of our Chinese friends. My new, good friend Grace, a Chinese who is an English major, will go out Friday night to arrange for three chickens to be killed and plucked and buy them for me on Saturday A.M. I found some white flour at a supermarket in town. Mashed potatoes, steamed vegetables, fresh fruit and (if Mrs. J—— will make it) gravy will round out the feast, to be washed down by some Tsingdao beer for the drinkers and Tang for the abstainers.

Shantou is an SEZ,[1] and is in Guangdong province, so perhaps things are more readily available here. Almost everything you need is available. Of course you must adjust to a completely new system of monetary value; it doesn't work to simply convert prices to U.S. equivalents. Everything made in China is, naturally,

---

[1] Special Economic Zone. There are many of these in China, cities where the dominant socialist system is loosened to allow experiments with free-market capitalism. SEZs mentioned often in these letters are Shantou, Xiamen, and Shenzhen.

reasonably priced. Imports are quite pricey, but if you must have milk for your strong American bones, you must pay. Thus you must budget. Enough to make a bit over one gallon of powdered milk costs the equivalent of sending fifteen letters home (provided the post office doesn't return any to you).

I don't mind being a bit overcharged. I look upon it as a fee for your ignorance. The more you know, the less of this fee you pay. Besides, our salaries ARE higher than those of most Chinese, and we can afford to pay a little bit extra. I save most of my shopping for when I'm with Grace. She is quite a good business-woman and is fun to watch in action—her expressions of doubt, suspicion, and disbelief are great. I know not to take the over-charging as a racial thing because in Shantou, where the natives speak the difficult Chaoshan dialect, anyone who can't speak Chaoshan is overcharged. My brown hair and height only mean that I don't have to open my mouth to get the treatment.

Mr. Lu has been very good about getting what I need. He just brought me my bike—a sparkling new green Phoenix—a couple days ago. So yesterday Grace and I went shopping and I rode her on the back. No mishaps, but of course a lot of stares. I also might get Star TV, which has some English programs (e.g., *Doogie Howser*, MTV Asia) but no news. Mr. Lu said he will pay for the cable people to put it in, even though I told him I didn't want it. Believe me, MTV Asia is a very disorienting show to watch while you're here. All the evening videos are Western, and if any Chinese see this program, it's no wonder they think American women are loose and trampy. Of course, it's nice to hear some home music after the syrupy stuff they're fond of here.

I've taught my freshman classes two Beatles songs ("Hello" and "Eight Days a Week") and "I've Loved and Lost Again" by Patsy Cline. I didn't know how the old country music was going over, so I told one class I wanted their opinion on a singer named Johnny Cash. I said I'd play it for them. They said, "Yeah, we like." And then they kept trying to tell me something about "CATS, King of Cats." Until finally I think I figured out that

they already know him, except as the "King of Cats." Johnny =
Jun = "supreme ruler"?—I'm having a good time.

Inger

TODD HAMINA: I'm 28 years old and I've seen the best fireworks
of my life. It's all downhill from here.

PJ: The school took us to a fireworks show down at the lake.
Two hours of fireworks, two complete one-hour shows, each very
different. Five yuan to a dollar, Alice—this was an eight-million-
yuan show. A fireworks expert friend of mine recognized several
of the items as state-of-the art. The "choreography" was one of its
magnificent features.

They opened with a ground show that spurted light and
color—raining pouring skyrocketing up. And smoke built and all
the colors glowed and reflected in the smoke and then they shifted
colors—red-white-green became all-green became green-blue became all-blue became blue-red became all-red. Then all-yellow and
the air show started, and they used only a golden yellow shining,
falling kind that dripped down like willow trees, placed all around
the sky. Magnificent, sensitive explosions.

The best of this part was a big popper that goes 'way up and
does a little sort of chrysanthemum but not much to speak of,
then slowly, all over in a slow rain, come out these glowing red
apples drifting down—fifty bright red lanterns slowly sifting down
from the sky into the water like music.

The second half was louder, more works, but with long,
ungainly pauses between sets. The triumph here was the very end.
We'd had our necks craned far back for nearly two hours and
were pretty spacy. They have these chrysanthemum fireworks
going off, those big ones, all colors, right? Lots and lots of 'em
going up and going off, coming right at you through the air.

Now, your average chrysanthemum is no small firework, you
know? Behind this lot comes the Big Mama of All Chrysanthe-
mums, Big Blue. This mother went off behind and encompassed
a span of at least three normal ones, spreading across the black

sky. It *loomed* back there while the others drifted down, huge. Huge, and the world stopped making sense.

You should have seen it.

ZUBIN EMSLEY: In a few minutes, I'll jump on my bike (very carefully because of its flimsy, rusty condition) to be swept by the torrent of bicycles down to the market to see life while I eat lunch. The post office is on the way.

I suppose this is China in the way you spoke of China. It's beautiful. It's ugly. It's wholesome and pleasant and disgustingly dirty. The air drifting through my torn screen door is laden with horns and bells and black dust that coats everything in disappointingly short order.

I'm very pleased to be here. I love being thoroughly in this place. I've rattled around the city, usually in the company of my students. I sometimes yearn to go alone.

KEVIN LAW-SMITH: It's quite something living with eight million people. It's like every day is a holiday, and everyone is out on the streets. Crossing the road was my first test.

MARLA JENKS: Well, I've made it through another week! I left Denver three weeks ago today, and it seems like much longer! No, things really are okay. I'm in a pretty good mood tonight, and I think it's attributable to the fact that a new foreigner from London just moved into the room next door to me. She's about 23/24ish and seems really nice. She graduated from college last year, and after a year of waitressing she thought she'd try something new and different—so here she is in China. I think that's why I'm in a good mood.

She's currently going through the shock of finding out about the immediately apparent horrors of living in China. We told her about the rats and advised her to keep all food tightly sealed and in the refrigerator. She reacted as most people do. Then, when I was trying to help her pry her closet open (it's also locked), a gigantic spider emerged from the crack. She screamed and leaped back, and that's when I realized that I'm starting to develop an acceptance of this place. While I wasn't excited to see the spider, I was nowhere near as horrified as she was. I saw it more as a routine nuisance than the shock that it was when I discovered my first arachnid. I don't think I'm fully integrated into this weird place, by any means. But I think I'm going to make it.

Fushun, Liaoning

Dear Alice,

It has been a while since I last spoke to you, but I have been rather busy as of late. So I am setting aside a little time now in which to write you.

Good news: (1) The pollution, although noticeable, is hardly what was expected. Dal and I have played basketball quite a few times with no breathing problems at all. They say the winters are sometimes bad, but the city has improved greatly over the last couple of years.

(2) The students are very nice and our fellow teachers have accepted us with little or no animosity. Sometimes you sense that some are a bit frustrated because they are aware you make a great deal more than they do. But that soon dissipates once you thoroughly describe the living expenses in the United States.

(3) Not only is the school aware that we may want to travel, they encourage it. They help us in buying tickets and such.

(4) Our Chinese is improving. Dal just got his TV working and we watch, always trying to comprehend the shows. But I'm afraid we have little success at the moment. Perhaps in a couple more months.

(5) Fushun and Shenyang *are* developed interior cities. I can buy practically everything I could have in the States with little or no problem. Anything, just name it and either city will have it.

Bad news: (1) The school desperately needs a third foreign teacher. We each are carrying sixteen hours, and other English teachers (Chinese people) are also extremely busy. The going gets a little tense, especially when you ask for assistance.

(2) My feeling at the moment is that I am being closed in, without any relief. The school wants me to do certain tasks, and meanwhile I am to perform other things during my so-called free time. On top of that, during my spare time, not one, but usually two or three things are asked of me at the same time. I can't accept them all, and yet I am expected to never decline anyone. I am finding myself giving excuses in order to decline.

(3) Fushun isn't very polluted, but it is dirty and not very pretty. Picturesque isn't the word to describe Fushun, or Shenyang for that matter.

(4) People in general are nosy and meddlesome. I have lost some freedom and independence. Not entirely bad, just slightly irritating.

Other than those, I am getting along *very* well. Living in China is by no means a difficult task physically; it is the customs and mind-set that come in conflict.

I am busy as I said, so another letter may not come for some while, but worry not.

Sincerely,

Doug Thompson

Fushun, Liaoning

Dear Alice,

[As Doug said,] the pollution in Fushun is bad but bearable. We live two kilometers away from the world's biggest coal mine. We have counted thirty smokestacks within a mile's radius, all of which stand amidst the numerous petroleum refineries. Yes, we are in an industrial city.

Of course, the people here are very kind. The school has gone out of its way to make us comfortable. Doug and I each have our own room and a personal cook. The food is delicious. We have become quite adept at using chopsticks.

Dal Hurtt

There's a certain amount of loneliness
involved in leaving home and traveling
to the other side of the planet.

I take an abstract comfort
in the fact I'm not in love.
You can feel the way
not being in love feels
anywhere.
>   Todd Hamina
>   (from his collection of poems *By the Xiang Jiang River*)

Utilities

Learning to live in a place far away from home can be, as Todd Hamina's poem suggests, a wistful experience. But it can be full of excitement and wonder as well. There is much to do and much to learn, and constant pressure to do things differently.

Differences rise up on every hand—different vegetables, different numbers of people on the road, different music and fireworks. But as Marla Jenks and others note, the physical differences are not troubling for long. After a short while, local arachnids and pollution levels become part of the acceptable world. What remains disturbing is what Doug Thompson calls the "customs and mind-set" beneath the surface. Constant hints of these subtler differences drift and rustle in the back of the mind, like leaves before a rising storm.

PAIGE DAVIES: We have H_2O from the tap from 6:30 A.M. to 8:30 A.M., from 11:30 A.M. to 1:30 P.M. and from 5:00 P.M. to 8:45ish P.M. *Hot* water from the tap is unheard of. The shower water is in a reserve and takes 20–40 minutes to warm up, depending on the month and how cold the apartment is.

JOE MÁRQUEZ: I have AC and hot water twice a day. I have a TV and plenty of lights. I have my own two-burner stove and a large refrigerator. The bathroom has a raised tub with a hand-held nozzle. The hot is cold and the cold—hot. Last night I turned the water on, but I turned it too much. So much so that the head pointed upward; the whole room was wet. There is a main drain by the toilet with a rock in it. Stephen says it is there to keep out the rats. Alice, I think I need a bigger rock (ha!)

MARLA JENKS: We lost the power once this week, and we usually have to go without running water for about twelve hours every day. There's no telling when the water will stop, and you're often left standing in the bathtub with a soapy head. What's really foul is when the toilet won't flush.

There are several reasons for the shortage. For one, it's the end of the summer and the reservoir is very low. We've been hoping and hoping for rain, but it just won't come. Even a typhoon would be welcome at this point. Additionally, there are more people here than the water supply can support. The campus added 2,000 more students this year and just built another huge dormitory which opened this week. Also, our building is built on a slight rise, so our water pressure is doubly bad. The first floor (where the maids are) gets enough so we have enough to drink. The second floor (where I am) can sometimes get enough of a trickle for washing hands. The third floor is often bone dry.

On Thursday night I was relaxing on the toilet when we suddenly lost water and power. Y—— sat outside and shined a flashlight under the door so I could finish my business. But then we were doubly distressed because our favorite cheesy British game show *Crystal Maze* comes on on Thursdays. We look forward to the event all week. We all gathered in the hall to lament our fate, when suddenly the lights came back on. Everyone scurried back to their TVs, relieved that the crisis had passed.

ZUBIN EMSLEY: [A note written at the top of a page that is filled front and back] You may recall how precious paper is here. I have access to this computer, but there's no instruction book, no paper, and no one available to fix busted things on it.

JEANNE PHILLIPS: Back at the hotel, the electricity went off, bringing loud groans from the workers on the all-night shift of the high-rise being built next door. Indeed, I looked up from my fourteenth-floor window with dread at the crane and men on the bamboo scaffolding, thrown into pitch blackness when their big spotlights went suddenly off. But happily no one fell or dropped a crane load onto anyone else. The hotel lights quickly came back on, presumably with their own generator, while the neighborhood remained dark for some hours. My room was so hot that my balcony door and drapes were open all the time, and I knew when the cement mixers went back on next door. Since there is all-night construction in several spots in my own neighborhood, however, I am quite acclimated to the noises.

MARLA JENKS: Speaking of phones . . . calling home isn't going to be anywhere near as convenient as I had hoped. Matt spent three days trying to find a phone on which he could contact an AT&T operator.

TODD LUNDGREN AND EILEEN VICKERY (first year): Our accommodations remain amazing and, in the crux of a Shandong winter, we are often forced to go in T-shirts inside. Our students have to shed nearly every layer they have to keep from melting. Let us say the central heating is satisfactory—but we wish it were a little less central, that we could turn it down or off. We also have a tape player and this handy manual typewriter on loan for the year from the *waiban*. It is frightening that we live better here than in the United States.

JEANNE PHILLIPS: Well, the monsoons are upon us. . . . At least I thought the rains would bring our two days per week without electricity to an end—if the reason is, as they say, low water in rivers and reservoirs that generate power. Of course, no-power days hit just when it is terribly hot and humid and you are dying to use a fan, but usually the power comes back on by 7 P.M. or so.

Since our water requires a pump to get up to its roof tank, when *the pump* doesn't come on, it is a dark and dirty and hot night indeed! So anyway, just when we thought power was guaranteed for a while, we hear it will be off 24 hours per day for three days (gasps for our freezer treasures)—yet it is still on now. But this letter may end in mid-word and my typewriter blow up from a power surge. . . .

Yes, the power just dropped down, my lamp is giving about 15 watts of light, and the typewriter has retired for the day!

TODD LUNDGREN AND EILEEN VICKERY (second year): Our program has lost a great deal of face because its new building is not completed. Everyone else on campus has coal heat, but as they sold the old building's furnace earlier this term to the chemistry department, we have only our AC unit to heat with.[2] Sometimes it shorts out after a few minutes. They've repaired the breaker box a few times. Hopefully it will stay fixed. But to see the octopus of wires connected to this end of the building for the AC units is frightening. And the wiring's old. None of us use them at night, and Mrs. Li says we shouldn't all use them at the same time during the day. She says she'll draw up a schedule for use. We told her politely not to bother, because we are (mainly) Americans. It's impossible to get us to make such sacrifices.

AMANDA MYERS: My mother would be horrified at my living conditions but as you know, compared to my Chinese neighbors, I live like a queen. My only complaint is the serious lack of hot water, but I do believe we are the only people on this campus to receive hot water AT ALL, so I can't complain. I had bedbugs for a while. When I showed our housekeeper, she screamed and immediately stripped and burned my bed. So, although things are broken more than they are fixed, we are well taken care of.

TODD HAMINA: Living in China is like camping.

---

[2] The Chinese call all adjustments of room temperature "air conditioning," and many units that look like U.S. air conditioners actually heat as well.

Transportation

If utilities are handled differently in China, at least teachers can imagine that the differences arise from natural causes. The differences that build up around transportation are more complex and unclear, hinting again at some "customs and mind-set" not so easy to explain.

MARLA JENKS: I have a rusty, rickety, red bike whose bell rings every time I go over a bump. It also lacks gears, which makes hills a special challenge. I need to be thankful, though, that the tires don't leak and the brakes work. Y—— likened it to a company car.

JEANNE PHILLIPS: At the bottom of our hill, down by the ancient stone bridge across the Min River that separates our huge island from the main part of Fuzhou, there used to be a little green shed, headquarters for a stand of pedicabs (bicycle rickshas) and three-wheelers. Three-wheelers have the pedicab's seat-with-awning for passengers but are powered by a "walking tractor"—a sort of multipurpose gas engine used in water pumps, farm equipment, and everything else, including these vehicles. The driver sits on something like a bike seat on a pole that surmounts the front-end engine.

Now the stand is gone, no three-wheelers at all, and pedicabs are visible only downtown near the big hotels on one of the two main streets, for short shopping trips. Taxis abound, with meters that drivers try not to use. Engines smoke and sound like the old three-wheelers, so one is never sure of arriving, especially at our hilltop location. Taxi drivers are said to clear between five and seven times as much money as university professors or managers of a government enterprise. Despite their numbers, competition has not forced them to scrounge, so they exact five times the meter price to bring me home across the jam-packed bridge and up the hill on a steep, narrow lane.

MARLA JENKS: We waited for the bus just outside the university gates as buses, bikes, minivans, carts, and motorcycles whizzed past us honking their horns and ringing their bells. Luckily R——— can read characters, so she knows which buses are going where.

We found the appropriate vehicle and crammed our way in among the grimy, curious faces and managed to locate a vacant seat without too much vinyl ripped off it.

The interior of the bus was filthy, and through the cracks in the floorboard planks we could watch the road going by beneath us. The ride to town is a noisy, bumpy, dusty experience. The bus stops frequently, as the driver and "crew" attempt to lure any pedestrian walking along the road onto their bus. Everybody passes everyone else simultaneously, while the on-coming cars do the same. Bikes and pedestrians weave unpredictably in and out of the maze, and everyone, no matter what their mode of transport, beeps and honks at everyone else.

Anyway, we got to the center of Quanzhou, and the whole town seemed to be under construction. There was rubble alongside the streets and bamboo scaffolding covering everything. The sun was beating down mercilessly and the air was full of dust and exhaust fumes. After our foray into "civilization" I was left feeling exhausted, slightly rattled, and thankful it wasn't an experience I have to endure daily!

INGER: I have an idea for a skit at the next Orientation. It has to do with all those sweet little ladies out in the park every A.M. doing *tai ji* exercise. This is not only for health reasons; it is also guerrilla training so they can get onto the buses.

I almost had my friend hoist me through the window of today's bus to the university, but he thought it would be unseemly (he's American). It didn't matter; today there were enough seats. But the push and crush onto the bus EVERY TIME always reminds me of elementary school when the teachers used to try to establish fire-drill-order by telling us the story (or myth) of the students who got trampled to death in the stairwell because everyone kept pushing. I've only gotten into the fray a couple of times when I was particularly pissed off and wanted to shove a few people. Mostly I do the block method and simply try to keep people from pushing under my arms to get ahead of me.

On the surface, all these writers seem to be reacting to the odd and rickety qualities of Chinese transportation. But the real source of their frustration may lie deeper: Most Americans are unused to public transportation of any kind except airplanes. Eventually it will be possible for some of these writers to be impressed that ordinary Chinese transport is so cheap and that it goes almost everywhere. At first, however, for people used to traveling 55 mph and more in their personal speed-pods, only the disadvantages of communal movement shine clear.

And in China, even personal transportation is a community affair, as Jeanne Phillips discovered when she tried to get a motor scooter. It was here that she blundered into the *"guanxi* net," a web of rights and obligations so complex, pervasive, and vital in Chinese society that Americans who work in China seldom escape tangling with it.

The *Guanxi* Net

Fuzhou, Fujian
December

Dear Alice,

The friend of a colleague turned out to have several unused motor scooters on hand—old junk but with the usually unobtainable license—so now I am tooting around anywhere within one tank of gas (short, as it burns gas and oil like a truck), putting on brake and accelerator simultaneously so it won't stall (no clutch), and wondering if it will start again when I need to go home. The repairs to get it moving at all were done, of course, by a young teacher's boyfriend who won't accept pay. Also, his logic is that, since it isn't my machine, I must not spend any money on parts and repairs in any case, though he freely says it is a piece of junk. His logic doesn't take in the fact that it is I, not the owner, who will have to push it home—nor that the free loan is such a boon that a little money to fix it is a bargain. Do you manage with that logic a lot better, Alice, because you can speak Chinese?

January

Maneuvering within this area of *guanxi* makes cultural differences suddenly stand out. *Guanxi* is often translated as a sort of *quid pro quo* algebra of favors exchanged, but it is really much more than that, entailing networks of relationships and degrees of closeness. While the free enterprise spirit is changing some of this, much of the time I cannot pay to get something done because the only people I know to ask to do it (or to help me find someone to do it) have a relationship with me that makes them want to help me out of friendship, and to help me to a far greater degree than I can be comfortable with. Thus I can't get the thing done at all.

A young graduate works in our Foreign Affairs Office, and I early on asked her if we could have an arrangement on the side whereby I could pay her for errands outside the usual range of taking-care-of-foreign-teachers. She protested, and proceeded to explain a word that means "connected to someone to the extent of being willing to die for them"—clearly, going to the post office was covered. So I rarely ask her help and have to do the errands myself, which is fine except that the asthma limits exertion and mandates setting priorities.

More striking has been dealing with my borrowed scooter, which ran for one glorious day of going places but not before or since. A young instructor helped me in 1989 when I had a scooter here, so this time she and everyone else assumed she'd help me again. So it is her driver boyfriend who took the borrowed scooter off to repair, who misguidedly protects my finances by not spending money to replace most of the parts, who does the work himself and therefore only when he has free time—which is thus free for me, but long in between.

So finally, a month later, he delivers it in working order (though probably in need of minor adjustments after I use it awhile) and with instructions to take the less steep road up our hill, given my bulk. It has never really started since then. Truly hating to impose on this chap's very scarce free time (he works long hours six days, has the usual home chores to do on Sunday, plus his courting) and hoping to get fast and thorough, guilt-free service, I found a commercial shop through a student who knew a reliable one near by, managed by her cousin. So I took it there with her as guide/translator. Sure, you guessed it—when I went back the next day, the guy wouldn't let me pay for it. He'd done enough so it started that day, but not since.

Meantime, my original helper found out I was going to take it elsewhere and called to say her boyfriend was available to come over that hour. But I'd already left it at the shop. So she was hurt and baffled by my behavior, which implied I didn't trust the boyfriend's work, but—more important—that I didn't trust our relationship enough to accept her help. This was a rebuff. It denied the depth of her caring and friendship, and it cast doubt on her trustworthy character and sincerity. The young woman in the FAO (my die-for-you friend) was aghast at my awful behavior and stupidity about cultural differences. She did reassure me that the woman who helped me is so good-natured and easy-going—and amused by ignorant foreigners, perhaps—that I would be forgiven. But I think some real trust building on my part is now necessary.

Nothing is simple. Often favors are huge nuisances to receivers as well as givers. Things are automatically done through networks, even when other routes would seem more efficient or qualitatively superior, partly because using the networks was for so long the only solution in the face of scarce resources. It became the ingrained approach to every problem. So accomplishing what one needs to do can be extraordinarily complex and difficult, while people knock themselves out being the most generous and helpful friends you can imagine—which is the cause of the obstacles! But these favors are the heart—and fuel—of the society.

Jeanne

Every American teacher in China has stories like these and experiences the feelings that accompany them: Irritation. Exhaustion. Frustration. Feeling "slightly rattled." Although it may look at the start as though physical inconveniences like lack of water and rickety buses cause some of these feelings, Jeanne Phillips's analysis of *guanxi* illustrates that the ultimate problem is usually cultural—differences in what Americans and Chinese value.

In the face of no central heat or push-and-crush "queuing," Americans new to China are asking themselves, "Why do these people put up with this?!" In the face of the *guanxi* system, Americans are saying, "How do you manage with this logic?" What these questions really ask is, "What makes this mess tolerable to you?" The answers to these questions lie at the deepest level of *value* and *meaning*.

What is the *meaning* of a bicycle in America, and what is its *value*? Bicycles generally mean exercise or sport, and perhaps transportation for children. Their value is fairly low on the scale of status and usefulness. Autonomous adults in America travel by car. In many countries including China, however, to own a bicycle is to be wealthy. A bicycle says you are at least middle class, and unusually footloose and free. Most of your neighbors walk or ride the bus. So the meaning and the value of a bicycle can shift, and many small shifts like this can begin to rattle the world.

Central heating, many changes of clothes, mechanical service that you pay for—things the American middle class thought were "normal"—turn out to be rare luxuries in much of China. *No* heat becomes normal, and U.S.-style efficiency is an otherworldly ideal. To expect these makes you . . . well, listen to PJ discuss the conflicts she began to feel.

> PJ: What are the characteristics of the Third World? The biggest category seems to be LACK OF CHOICE. You have few possessions, so you don't have (say) one kind of towel for washing dishes, one for your body, one for your hands, one for drying dishes, one for your face. You use the same one for all operations. They sell only blue notebooks at your store this month—you don't hold out for a green one, or even expect there will be a choice. Everyone who buys this month also has blue notebooks. You live where you were born because you can't afford to travel; you drink the water you have because you can't afford a bottle or a filter. You drink unboiled water because the rice chaff you use for fuel is running low.

ERRATIC SERVICES. Electricity, piped-in water, and a phone are luxuries. You may have systems to deliver them, but the expertise to fix them (i.e., people who can afford to take time out from getting food and shelter in order to be trained) and the time to fix them are spread thin. There is not enough money loose in the culture to create goods of good quality, so things break. There are not enough time = money and money = tools loose in the culture to mend them.

EXPENSIVE "NECESSITIES" ARE LACKING. We take for granted paper, pottery dishes (which break easily), a variety of glasses for different beverages (choice again), your own bathroom, your own room (let's not even mention your own house), privacy, quiet, screens to keep out bugs.

In the Third World you learn how simply, how basically you can live, yea, how basically most of the un-American world does live. And you learn that to live even simply, gathering water, wood, food, and clothing literally from scratch takes up all your time.

Next to this, my need for a typewriter (which I share with three other Americans, and which we all quietly wish we didn't have to share), for my own stereo, for a room with a door I can close, for hot water when I want it (I'm charting times of availability in hopes I'll find a pattern)—these needs are striking and disturbing. Next to these people, I'm greedy and dissatisfied with my lot, and yet my lot is so much better than theirs it doesn't bear talking about. I get tired of the embarrassing contrast.

We are rich here, so they confine us to tourist hotels that cost more. In a good socialist context that's correct. But it strains my budget; I can't travel as much. OK, travel is a luxury. But the inner paradox of being (in American terms) thrifty and flexible and gutsy to be slugging it out here in the Third World, versus (in Chinese terms) living in the lap of luxury amidst poor relations—this paradox is not pleasant.

The Post Office

PJ is not alone. For many American teachers learning what it means to live in China, a split begins to develop. The distance widens between who they used to be and who they are now; the gap grows between the past where things made sense and this strange (if exciting) new present. This split is not comfortable, and it is often salved by letters from home—that far-off place where it is still possible to understand What Things Mean.

> MARLA JENKS: Your letter arrived today and I was so excited I couldn't see straight enough to rip the envelope open! I received it fourteen days after you wrote it. I wonder if that's standard processing time.
>
> I've gotten all your letters unopened and in order. They're fantastic! I live for them, and I've hung the postcards on the walls.

> PAIGE DAVIES: If any prospective teachers want to write and ask me further questions, I'd LOVE to get mail. My friends are being pretty lame about letter writing, so any mail is appreciated.

> MAX TUEFFERD: We are all glad to get the notes that you send us. We are starved for mail (or I am anyway). So every little bit is a morale booster.

But here, too, at the heart of connection with a loving and predictable world, profound differences exist. At first, they can look like just another case of learning new rules.

> INGER: The post office is another of those Chinese institutions where you shrug it off with a wry smile and say, "That's the Chinese postal system." When they send a letter back to you for whatever reason, the stamps are cancelled so you must buy new ones. One of the Shantou U. teachers first had a letter sent back to her because, if you have more than two stamps, you must put them *all* on the back. The next time she tried, it came back

because the stamps had been put too close together. On my first visit to the post office they charged me double what I should have paid, yet they can't have done it to pocket the overcharge because I paid face value for the stamps. They just told me I had to put more on than was necessary. It's like learning poker games with a bunch of people who won't tell you the rules. You just have to find them out as you play and lose a bit of money in the learning.

But soon those obscure, troubling differences begin to rustle in the background, and foreigners have to choose how they will respond.

TODD HAMINA: The Chinese are veritably intoxicated by foreign stamps. They've been known to steal them. Sometimes I think that if I had enough stamps I could take this place over. (Truth is that foreign stamps are actually much more attractive than the local variety, although I must admit the tiered *baozi* cooker stamp does hold a special place in my heart.)

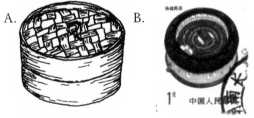

A. *A bamboo* baozi *steamer.* B. *Todd Hamina's "baozi cooker" stamp. The stamp actually shows an unusual and famous circular communal village.*

I say thwart their council and spend even more time picking out beautiful stamps. Don't get stuck in a rut. I'll tell you, if I see another Amelia Earhart wannabe stamp I'll roll over and die. And metered mail is the absolute worst, maybe as bad as no mail at all.

INGER: It turns out my paranoia about my mail being stolen *was* founded. I don't think it's censorship unless they're being *really* clever and careful about it, since the only letters to get through have been the metered ones and, recently, those with the most common stamps on them: American flags and the female aviator. I talked to a friend on the phone (he was quite alarmed by the tone of one of my depressed letters), and he informed me he had sent at least a dozen letters since I came; I had received only four. I'm also missing one confirmed from my sister-in-law, and who knows how many other uncounted ones. They do seem to be taken to enrich someone's postage stamp collection, so I've asked everyone to send metered mail.

At this great distance, even the "predictable" world far away can find ways to go wrong.

INGER: It's fine to give copies of my letters to L——— since I don't have his address. I thought I'd remembered it and I sent my last letter to them at the end of October only to have it stamped "Return to Sender" and "Use the US Postal Directory . . . It's Free!" and boomeranged back to China. It was at the 80220 post office so it was within a mile or so. I guess it's not only the Chinese post office that gives me problems.

As things become increasingly uncertain, despair can grow . . .

INGER: I would love to work on a post office skit at Orientation next summer, only I don't know if I will have any humor left about the situation. It's been two weeks since I've received any mail and every *mei xin* only increases my suspicion of theft. Then my opinion of things Chinese drops another fraction and I feel doubly in exile.

. . . although sometimes there's a happy ending:

INGER: Post office still acting up, but I'm getting my mail and there's a new lady in our post room who is really nice to me.

All through experiences like these, we hear the rustling of value differences again, shifting the rules and the ground under our feet.

Fuzhou, Fujian

Dear Alice,

Some misunderstandings are ascribed to language problems, when really the difficulty is disbelief. I hate going to the post office to mail letters because it entails the usual push-and-shove routine that replaces any idea of a queue and then getting little batches of stamps for each letter which one must paste on from a dirty, almost-empty paste pot with no counter space or else struggle to find a spot to use one's own glue on them.[3] So I brought a postal scale and finally got it recalibrated to grams and went to the PO to get a lot of stamps so I could do all the fixing in the comfort of home and just drop them in the slot.

First, I discover that the POs near me don't have commemorative stamps, only the ordinary ones. But then the woman wouldn't give me the forty stamps of this and that denomination that I asked for. I kept reiterating my needs in Arabic numerals and sign language. Then some students came in and offered to help, but their limited English kept me frustrated with our inability to get my order across.

Finally all became clear: The clerk initially couldn't understand my order because it was inconceivable that one person would buy forty stamps each of several denominations, some as high as 5¥ (about 70 cents). When finally she believed it, I couldn't believe what the students were trying to convey—the PO not only had no 5¥ stamps, but couldn't give me the equivalent in smaller ones because they didn't have enough—e.g., didn't have 80 2¥ plus 40 1¥. The PO had very few stamps early in the day, except for the 0.40 ones for local letters. They limited the number of 2¥ I could buy so they'd have a few left.

I go next week for R&R in Hong Kong and will carry with

---

[3] Chinese postage stamps have no adhesive backing, partly because tropical humidity would make them stick together.

me a few small things (besides letters) I want to mail to the U.S. Why lug them? Anything that doesn't look like an ordinary letter (which means a thick envelope or any parcel) must be inspected by a customs representative at the PO, hence cannot be sealed and fastened up at home. More important, the PO folks have their own strong notions of what constitutes proper packaging, so that my carefully repaired and secured and labeled once-used bubble envelope mailer was refused. I had to go buy some rough white cloth and (with the PO staff's generous and amused assistance) sew up a muslin bag, which was addressed with India ink. For anything that won't take that sort of exposure to damage, one can buy unassembled small wooden boxes at the PO and borrow a hammer or go to the big central PO downtown where you can pay a chap to make wooden and cardboard boxes and pack things for you—a one-man package store operation. I have sometimes gotten my PO to accept my own humble packaging efforts, but it is always iffy. So if your postman one day delivers, with amazed bafflement, a muslin bag, you'll know that one of the tougher clerks was on duty that day.

Jeanne

And the final blow to is to discover that rules that seem strange may have a purpose! Alice has in her collection several plastic bags containing torn and empty envelopes from China. They came with the U.S. postal notice depicted on the following page.

On the other side of the Looking Glass, they tell us, everything is backwards. Slowly, slowly, Americans living in China begin to build up a sense of what this might mean. The old ways they knew are less predictable now, and some of the strange new ways might work. At this point they face directly the real challenge of learning to live in a new culture—living with daily levels of uncertainty and novelty seldom experienced at home.

For some, this challenge is welcomed like a blast of hot air!

United States Post Office
Denver, CO 80266-9701

DEAR POSTAL CUSTOMER:

The enclosed was found loose in the mails or has been
damaged in handling in the Postal Service (whichever is
applicable to the enclosure).

Damage can occur if mail is insecurely enveloped or bulky
contents are enclosed. When this occurs and our machinery is
jammed, it often causes damage to other mail that was properly prepared.

We are constantly striving to improve our processing methods
to assure that an occurrence such as the enclosed can be
eliminated. We appreciate your concern over the handling of
your mail and sincerely regret the inconvenience you have
experienced.

Chengdu, Sichuan

Dear Alice:

Hello, hello! Howdoya like this stationery? Kinda like
writing on tissue paper!

Well, I'm here, I'm alive, and it's goddamn wonderful!

I've been here a week and a half so far. I've met more people
than I can count on both my hands and feet. I have an unbelievable, Gargantuan-sized apartment. I've just found out what my
classes for the semester will be . . . though who the students are
. . . how many . . . what textbooks I'll be teaching from (!)—all
remain vague. (Mind you, we were told classes begin a week
ago—?). Bicycled to the zoo on the outskirts of town my second
day here and almost got lost. Just had my first lesson in Chinese

Hardball—i.e., Bureaucracy—and won! And I'm writing in the dark as we "speak" because the electricity is out and has been for an hour (shocking!)

First of all Chengdu is MANIA! It is not the quaint little burg I had pictured. It is a full-on crazy, jammed-packed, infernal cacophony of honking, clanging chaos—and that's on a slow day! The humidity here is nine million percent. Really—you expect to see fish swimming by in the thick soup they call air here as well as in the, well, sludge they call water. It is still *very* hot—"pot pie weather," I heard a comedian refer to it once. Like when you open the oven door to check on a pot pie but lean over a wee bit too far, and that BLAST you get in the face—yeah, like that! Actually, it's not searing heat, just stagnant and suffocating so you wish for a tub of cold water to soak your constantly dripping body in!

Apparently, it never snows here, is quite tropical (palm trees) in the winter—never drops below 40° F.—So I didn't need to bring the winter jacket—I guess. We'll see.

The apartment: This is *unbelievable!* I'm not very good at dimensions but it is at least 50 feet long by 40 feet wide. It is this palatial mansion—by Chinese standards. It is carpeted—yes! Wall-papered. Has built-in *cedar* wood shelves, cedar stacking cabinets, shelves, dresser, and desks and chairs. The place has a kitchen with a refridge, gas stove, and cabinet. And bathroom with a huge old Victorian-style tub with a hand-held shower nozzle, FLUSH toilet, *hot* running water in the tub and sink ("My Gawd!"). It has a dining area, living room, big bedroom. It has a standing, modulation electric fan, an air conditioner (!), a TV, and a plug-in large standing heater. It has a total of three balconies, one of which has clotheslines strung up—oh, yes—and a European-style washing machine! You know the kind where you have one compartment to wash and to rinse and one compartment to spin down the clothes—God, it's Grand!

The apartment building is set in a courtyard of four four-story buildings with the dining hall at the end, the gatehouse at the mouth, and the apartments on either side (two on each side). In the center of the courtyard is a carp pond and moss rockery that, if the water weren't so scummy, would really be quite beautiful.

The campus itself is quite green with many trees (yes, with white-washed trunks) and lawns (clumps of grass in rows), and beautiful foliage and flowers all growing semiwild. The campus is huge. It houses students and teachers plus everyone who works here and their families—from the university president to the gate guards, street sweepers, and bus drivers (oh, and their chickens . . . which no one admits to owning because they are "illegal" on campus, but they run and peck about *well* taken care of). It has its own middle school and preschool and its own small shops where you can buy anything from porcelain bowls to pens to moon cakes and Sprite!

As for people, I have found the Chinese people here to be warm and affable. The people on the street are nonchalant about seeing foreigners. They turn and look, but I've had no one come up to me, even to practice their English. Little kids and some adults will yell a big "Hah-lo!" from out of shop doorways or atop speeding bicycles, but that's the extent of their "need" to engage a foreigner in any way.

When I first arrived I was met by a man and a woman, both from the department I'm working in. The woman told me a story—how it is said they get so little sun in Chengdu that when the sun does come out, all the dogs start barking at the "stranger"! (Actually, we've had many days of sun, but the sky is always *very* hazy from the air pollution; you never see full sun, or the stars.)

The next day the woman took me around campus, then to Mr. Yang's office in the language center—he's the acting head of my department. We chatted and then he took us over to his apartment for tea. This really touched me. Head of the department, but his apartment was tiny, bare cement floor and walls, half the size of mine—and he's been at the university fifteen years! We talked about his pet birds, a film project he's working on, and other small talk. Then he led us back down the dingy, dark concrete stairwell to the courtyard where he produced a tiny key and unlocked a bike—an old, black, rusted, clunky bike with a small red tassel on the handlebars. He solemnly pointed this out as a way to identify it in a sea of black, rusty bicycles! As we contemplated this beauty, it had another identifying mark—a nice flat tire. So he personally walked it over to the-place-where-you-get-your-bike-fixed, waited while they fixed it, paid for it, turned to me and said, "Well, I will see you tomorrow!"

My hostess and I then bicycled into Chengdu. Holy cow! Bicycling here is like . . . uh . . . riding through an oncoming herd of rabid buffalo stampeding from a raging forest fire! (Only, probably, that is easier . . . and less noisy). It is an absolute phenomenon! There is this "flow" that happens. Nobody signals. Trucks, cars, and motorbikes have the right-of-way—barreling and honking madly down the street. The rest is just the safety in numbers rule plus pure chicken—whoever looks like they are *not* going to stop gets the right of way. My god, it's a study in intuitive flow—something like a school of fish. It all works, but god knows how or why. It's absolute mayhem!

Anyway, that was the first day. On the second, a visiting professor invited us (me and the two other new foreign teachers) to visit the zoo. (Ugg, it is pitiful—half-dead diseased pandas in concrete cell blocks.) Bicycling through the mayhem, we stopped for a drink at a roadside stand and I lost them. I rode fast ahead to catch up, but they weren't there. Maybe they were behind me? So I stopped and waited . . . and waited. After a few minutes had gone by, I realized I was in DEEP Shinola! "Great," I thought. "My second day here and I am going to die somewhere on some god-forsaken street in this city of eight million people I can't talk to because I won't EVER be able to find my way back!!!" I decided to go straight, some gut feeling, and I did that about two miles before my resolve buckled and I was just about to turn around and try to head back when—there they were (!) waiting on the corner, just outside the entrance to the zoo. "Omigod!" Never did an animal prison look so good! What an unbelievably scary deal.

Other people I've met so far have been the other American teachers (there are four of us, including me) plus one Fulbright Professor and his wife. We are all here for a year, though two of the new teachers are very negative, hate the Third World experience, and may leave after one semester. There is also a Brit woman, who is a gas, and a Russian lady, who speaks no Chinese or English so it's a wee bit hard to get to know her.

There have been three British economists staying here for the past week, giving lectures on poverty alleviation. They're all Ph.D.s from the University of London, extremely erudite in their field, plus an absolute riot on a personal level. The university held a reception last night for all the people who attended the lectures—governors, high officials, and big boo hoo's from all over China. One of the Brits came banging on my door, "You must come down—there's loads of food and tons of people. Come and impress them with some of your Chinese." "Chinese?" I thought. "Which of my seventeen decent words will impress them the most?!" But I ran down there with him and I met the deputy-something of the Beijing Office of Economy, the governor of some city in southern Sichuan, and some leader of economic reform from Guangxi province. It was a blast.

After the reception split up, one of the professors said, "Good God, we're here to alleviate poverty and look at all this food. Go round up your starving student friends and get them in here!" It didn't take much coaxing—Americans, Germans, Japanese, Italians studying Chinese at the university all streamed in with pots and pans and emptied the tables like heathens. It was disgusting and hysterical at the same time.

The three Brits then invited me for a drink at the Bamboo Bar, an absolutely seedy dive just up the river that runs alongside campus. This too was hysterical. Any drink we ordered, they didn't have. So finally we asked what they DID have and got a bottle of god-awful syrupy wine. But we drank the whole thing and conversed about world economies, China, what have you—and had an absolute howl over everything late into the night.

So that was last night. Now I've got cold, soggy banquet food in the fridge. The electricity is back on due to a blessed American student having the wherewithall to replace a fried fuse-wire-thing in the ancient fuse box contraption outside the patio door. But now I can't use the air conditioner because it's got some short and that's what blew the fuse.

Ah, China—precious insanity!

So the last bit I'll leave you with is duking it out with the Chinese "system" and somehow coming out on top.

Hardball lesson no. 1 was over class scheduling. The head of the department, Mr. Yang, good-naturedly decided to change my schedule and give me more classes. Ha! And some little feisty bit in me said, "No way! You need me more than I need you. This is just a ploy to overwork the ignorant foreign teacher," which I had heard was pretty much what they do initially when you are still innocent, ignorant, and trying to give a good impression. So I just stuck by my guns. "Well, there's a mistake here," he said, jabbing at the tissue paper my schedule was written on. "You should have Fast Reading class also. Only two hours." Without a blink I said, "Ah, yes, but I like this one better," pointing to the first schedule. He ruffled through lots of papers and official-looking things, pointed out "the mistake"—I just sat calmly like a lump of lead. This went on for two more rounds and then suddenly he said, "OK, this schedule is all right. We will cancel the Fast Reading." And without a twinge of my usual Puritan guilt, I said, "Fine. That seems like the best thing."

Wow! Howdya like that?

Classes start tomorrow (I'm finishing this letter Sunday A.M.), and we will see how it goes. I've met some of my students and they are absolutely beautiful and eager. I love Mr. Yang. He's a wily old coyote, but he's a full-on character, and as long as I keep two steps ahead of him, it will be absolutely a gas!

That's all for now.

Take it easy,

Rachel Coleman

And Now for a Look at Our Weather

The average American lives in a highly "conditioned" environment. Screens keep out bugs, storm windows and shutters keep out the cold. The atmosphere inside buildings and cars is adjusted for every season—made warmer in winter and cooler in summer. Houses tend not to leak, and windows tend to be airtight. As you have probably sensed by now, things are different in China.

These Americans in China are exposed to the elements in ways they have never experienced before unless, as Todd Hamina notes, they go camping. Atmospheric pressure and temperature gain power in their lives, and weather reports are often delivered with passion and pique. Good days are a blessing; bad ones seem to go on forever.

American teachers slowly learn that their students have never experienced the levels of indoor climate control the teachers assumed were normal. The Chinese government distributes resources for heating (such as furnaces and coal, pipes and steam) only *north* of the Yangzi River. South of the Yangzi there is no central heat, except in special hospital wards and some foreigners' housing. (To get a sense of how this geography affects our correspondents, see map 4.)

Thus in the south, public buildings such as restaurants, offices, movie theaters, student dorms, and (yes) classrooms are unheated. Sometimes common rooms or special events are "warmed" by small metal stoves that slowly burn cakes of pressed coal-dust. Rice left on the stove overnight will boil into porridge, but the heat is so low that the stoves can be covered with a board and used as impromptu poker tables. Generally, people keep warm by wearing lots of clothes and staying in bed.

On the other hand, when heat is provided, things can go to the other extreme. As Jeanne Phillips reported, "My hotel room had a thermostat that seemed not to function at all, and the central heating level was oppressive. It was so hot that my balcony door and drapes were open all the time." And you might recall Todd Lundgren and Eileen Vickery wearing T-shirts in mid-winter during the year they had heat in Shandong.

In summer, air conditioning is unknown in China, except in high-class hotels and (when it works) the apartments of foreign teachers.

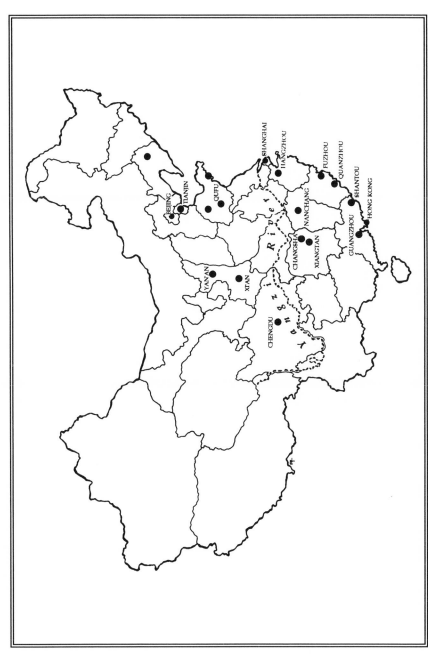

Map 4. Weather Map. The People's Republic of China, showing the position of letter-writers' cities relative to the Yangzi River.

Weather Reports: Fall

September

SOUTH Fuzhou: Evening was approaching, but it felt as if it were high
       noon. The moisture was collecting all over my body.

       Guangzhou: Hotter than hell. Dreary.

       Quanzhou: HOT, sunny & very humid.

       Xiangtan: Sticky and humid every day. After two-hour periods,
       my shirt is soaking wet with sweat.

NORTH Chengdu: Pot Pie Weather . . . like when you open the oven
       door to check on a pot pie but lean over a wee bit too far,
       and that BLAST you get in the face.

       Xi'an: It rained almost the whole month.

October

SOUTH Guangzhou: The sun is shining, the air dry and cool. The heat
       has subsided now and we've had a little rain, so the AC only
       goes on at night because the "Anglo-Saxon-sucking mosquitos"
       are a pain in the —— some nights. They're most persistent!

       Quanzhou: I'm lying on my bed watching the rain fall outside.
       It's a warm, tropical shower. Not heavy, but steady.

NORTH Beijing: Crisp and busy!

       Tianjin: It is still very much like summer here: Bats, mosquitos,
       flowers, and green trees. I'm quite impressed with the lovely
       lotus plants growing in the many lakes and canals.

       Yan'an: It's cold in Yan'an now. Jim has a thermometer in his
       room and it read 45° F inside!

November

SOUTH Guangzhou: A beautiful day, sunny and cool. The nights are
       chilly now, so we bundle up, whether indoors or out, but re-
       gardless, somehow the immortal Chinese mosquitos manage to
       find a plot of uncovered skin to snack upon. I do not like to
       get out of bed in this weather—it would be a great time to
       have a warm boyfriend to cuddle.

Quanzhou: I can't believe your picture of the snow and traffic jam! It seems like a completely different world! I walk around every day in shorts and sandals among the palm trees and hibiscus bushes.

NORTH Beijing: Cold, real cold—the first time I've been in snow in years, and it was nice.

Tianjin: The ice, the snow, it's all begun in sunny China. The snow puts a blanket of color across the dreary cement scenery—the trees leafless, the sky grey-black—Smell of CO_2 in the air. People miserably cold, bundled up in every article of clothing they own. The weather here is growing very cold. And as I'm sure you know, Chinese buildings are not known for heat efficiency; hot noodles keep everyone warm.

Qufu: It's been gray for weeks, and I'm ready for some sunshine and a big Siberian blow.

MARLA JENKS: It's colder than a well-digger's ass around here! I'm sitting here in bed shivering. Lately there's been a watery sun in the sky, but a cold wind blows day and night and is very uncomfortable. We all have come down with colds too, which is annoying. I would think, since I'm on the same latitude as Cuba and the tip of Baja California, that the weather would be more tropical year 'round. I sure hope it warms up. I've become spoiled and can't deal with the cold. I should quit griping, though, because I'm sure it's much colder where you are. I don't know how I ever survived in upstate New York—actually, I do. We had central heating, which makes a huge difference. Well, guess I'll go to bed. It's much warmer under the covers.

Weather Reports: Winter

December

SOUTH   Nanchang: When I'm not teaching I'm usually in my apartment which is comfortable though, now that winter has come, *really* cold. I have a dinky little heater which doesn't do much good since the cold pours through the windows, which do not always shut and sometimes have cracks and holes.

Quanzhou: Christmas was a bright, sunny, beautiful day.

Guangzhou: It's Christmas Eve and it's sunny and warm.

NORTH   Chengdu: The *China Daily* was recording Chengdu temperatures in the late teens.

Qufu: Qufu has been gray and cold and we haven't seen the sun for three weeks.

It's snowed the last two mornings (a first for us in Qufu!) and has turned to drizzle in the afternoon. Gray, gray, gray!

January

SOUTH   Changsha: CHANGSHA'S WEATHER SUCKS! Had to say that, couldn't suppress it any longer. How can a city on the same latitude as Southern Texas have snow? Rain I can understand, but snow? And when it rains, it's an all-day thing. Rather cold, with temperatures dipping below freezing. Cold humidity.

It is cold in Changsha and rainy; my timely departure coincided with reports of the season's first snow.

Nanchang: January was nearly unbearable, even with a space heater in one room where I kept the doors shut at all times. But I survived.

Xiangtan: It is cold here in Xiangtan. I am wearing at least five layers of clothing. I think my students are wearing all their clothes on a cold day.

NORTH   No reports. Everyone went traveling, for example to Kunming: Sunshine, air with a hint of altitude.

G: I like a little cold, and when I walk from class I like to feel the rain on my head. But every time—or at least, almost—someone rushes up to me, awkwardly walking or riding a bike while holding an umbrella over my head. I can't help laughing, not at this person's kindness (usually a student, friend, colleague), but at their obvious discomfiture. They never seem to mind, and if the person is of my station or higher (according to Chinese custom), I await the polite scolding for not having an umbrella. If I sneeze, he or she will inquire if I need drugs. "Yes," I tell them, "but I don't think you can help me."

Weather Reports: Spring

February

SOUTH Changsha: It's warm today, 60° F, and sunny. God, talk about something to uplift the soul! It's been warm all week, though cloudy.

Fuzhou: After a week of cold, rain, power off two days a week, today is sunny and HOT, beautiful, birds singing, camellias out.

Hangzhou: Cold like January (35° at night, and 10 degrees higher in the afternoon.

Quanzhou: The fierce winter still has not come. Today it was balmy and sunny, as it has been since I've been back. I wore shorts today even. It was even warmer in Hong Kong a couple weeks ago.

Shantou: We're now on the tenth day of rain, and it's getting unnerving to wake up every morning to the same sound of rainfall.

NORTH Chengdu: Cold and damp.

March

SOUTH Fuzhou: Our "warm" spring was not going too well for a few weeks. But the last few days the rain stopped and it feels like summer! My students had a good laugh the other day when I showed up for class in shorts.

Guangzhou: Aiyah—the rain season is upon us. (By the way, it's freezing tonight—I've been able to see my breath in my room for two days.)—Cold and wet—I feel like a frog.

Quanzhou: It's now spring—the weather is warm and rainy, but really nice.

NORTH Xi'an: The weather is finally breaking. It'll be hot soon. I'm actually looking forward to it.

April

SOUTH Changsha: The sun has broken through today and finally hatched that low egg of gray clouds. In the rain I walk right past the trees which in the warm light insist on their purplish buds. And the marigolds inside the front gate are like little golden eyes and appear to be well tended. Nice day; this ugly place has its beauty.

Guangzhou: I need a break from this unbearable weather. It has been raining every day since February 22, after break. The sun just came out three days ago, so hopefully it's over—until, of course, we start sweating like pigs.

Hangzhou: There is the occasional day warm enough to allow sitting on the balcony, and nights without the (too) little space heater. I don't mind the frequent overcast and drizzle—it's warm enough to enjoy, and it makes for wonderful romantic scenes on West Lake and in the old alleys.

NORTH No reports. Maybe the weather is fine?

ZUBIN EMSLEY: Flowers are blooming. The plums started it, and now all the other trees and the tea flowers and the tulips and daffodils and a dozen others are carrying on the show. The best are the fragrant trees lining the walkway from the apartment to the classrooms. A handful of fallen flowers carried to my room every day makes for sweet dreams.

Weather Reports: Summer and Beyond

May

SOUTH Fuzhou: The monsoons are upon us.

It is spring. I know because I wake to the sound of baby birds demanding breakfast from the eaves above my windows. But by the temperature it is summer. Already very hot and humid most days.

Quanzhou: Here I am, sweating away while my Newspaper Reading Class is working on an assignment.

NORTH Xi'an: The weather here has taken an incredible turn. It seems there is a stationary high pressure system over this area, and we have had almost three weeks of solid clear sunny skies and dry warm weather.

June

SOUTH Quanzhou: The weather is scorching hot, but I'm not trying to teach, so it's bearable.

NORTH Xi'an has been a wet wonderland the last three or four days. Now we are in the midst of a humidity fog—I feel like I'm in the world's largest Turkish bath.

And in General . . .

SOUTH Hangzhou: The air drifting through my torn screen door is laden with black dust that coats everything in disappointing short order.

Nanchang: Nanchang is the dustiest and dirtiest place I've ever lived. Daily I sweep the apartment, and weekly I'm shocked by the amount of dust which gathers beneath the bed.

NORTH Chengdu: The sky is always *very* hazy. There are no stars at night. Not one. They have no hope of shining through all that pollution. I miss this the most.

Xi'an: DUST.

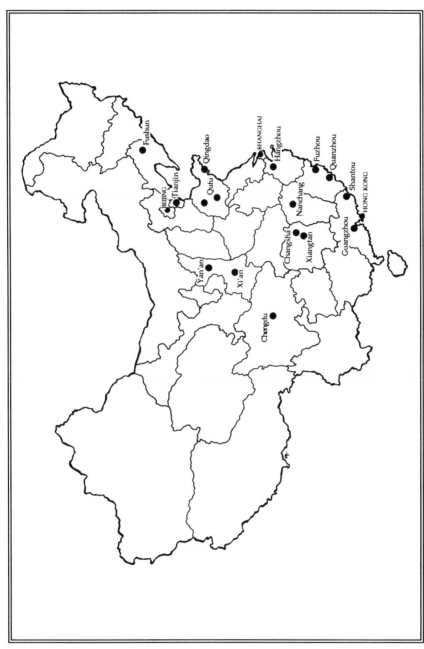

Map 5. The People's Republic of China, showing the cities from which letters in chapter 4 were written.

huoguo (**hwoh-gwo**): "hot pot," a Chinese type of fondue, where each person dips a wide array of meats and vegetables into spiced boiling water.

laoshi (**laow-shuh**): teacher.

lao wai (**laow wy**): foreigner, literally, "old foreigner," another use of the informal title *lao*.

tai ji quan (**tai gee chuahn**): the style of Chinese *tai ji* that is best known in the United States, sometimes written *t'ai chi chuan*.

wushu (**woo-shoo**): one of the general terms for Chinese martial arts, similar in range of meaning to *gong fu*.

Learning to Teach

JIM PAGE: My first class today was American and British history, geography, and current political situations. The class was third-year students. They're wonderful. I was obviously nervous as shit but eventually loosened up. I was truly a Dancing Poodle today. We had a great time. I saw some students after class this afternoon and they all said, "Good afternoon, Teacher Jim."

I have only twenty students in each class. I don't have any true English courses except one first-year Conversation class. Tomorrow I have Scientific Reading in the morning and then Scientific Writing in the afternoon. Don't ask me!

They also don't have any textbooks. I'm supposed to go to the library and copy information. The copy machine is broken and usually is. My *waiban* is a great man, but he told me to photocopy as much as possible when it works. Everyone treats the *lao wai*s very well.

MARLA JENKS: Well—I've officially finished my first week of classes, and each one grew easier as the week progressed. Overall I don't think the students are as awed and fascinated by me as I was somehow conditioned to expect. It may be because they are a geographically diverse group; I've got people from Korea, Hong Kong, Macao, as well as various places throughout China.

One class did stand up to greet me as I entered the room today—I grooved on that! But when they asked and I told them how old I was, they cracked up. I asked why they were laughing and they said, "You're so young!" Hell, we may be the same age, but I'm one up on them—I know English. I haven't had any of my freshman classes yet though. They start two weeks later than everybody else. It will be interesting to see how they compare.

MARY BRACKEN: Life here is great. I absolutely love it!! I adore most of my students. We met the other day at the bell-clock and sang English and Chinese songs. Leo, one of my students, plays the guitar. We all sang John Denver's "Rocky Mountain High" and "Country Roads." I'm constantly surprised at how much I *love* to teach. I blow their minds with the way I teach or act in class. We always laugh, and I've gotten some wonderful compliments.

One of my students wrote the following in a paper describing her happiest moment: "English, as a language, is like a bridge between China and other English-speaking countries. I hope I can get a pass to cross the bridge and set up a friendly relation. Four years is a good time for me to learn English. I hope I can get a new happiest moment after four years. On that day, I will rewrite my essay to my foreign teacher Miss Mary. I think it will be more wonderful than the happiest moment now I have."

I never had a doubt—but this sure makes it all worthwhile. P.S. One student's name is "Motor."[1]

TEDDY KELLAM: I teach 193 students, at various levels. My freshmen are the darlings, so young, eager, shy. I call them "my kids." The sophomores are the sophisticates, aware of their superior English. So I'm on my toes each lecture to keep them challenged, engaged, and entertained. Genteel and supportive are the postgrads, most of them from outside the province and even from the countryside. Through their sometimes tangled English, I can see the gentle and genuine character of traditional China. They make me feel appreciated, appreciative to be a *laoshi* (teacher) here.

The first days of class are the fulfillment of a journey that most of

---

[1] Like language students around the world, the Chinese often take English names in English class. They prefer to take names that have a positive meaning (like Grace or Victor) and will often seek out information on the roots of a name before they accept it. They also adopt names of people they admire (we will meet Jack London and Saddam Hussein in chapter 5) and even occasionally, as Mary's student does, take the names of *things* that have the right feel about them.

these writers began more than a year before. Applications, immunizations, packing, passports, and struggles to learn how to live were all set in motion so they could teach in China.

Behind many of these letters are people just out of college themselves, with little experience on the teacher's side of the podium. Those who are older may have been trained as entrepreneurs or engineers rather than as teachers of English. Primarily, these are adventurers whose native tongue is English, willing to work for a year in an environment that can most diplomatically be called "unstructured."

They come not knowing for sure who or what they will teach. Most arrive with letters of agreement but without contracts, and any agreements may well be renegotiated. Their course schedules sometimes change dramatically for the first few weeks. Even those who return for a second year have come to understand that arrangements in China are, one might say, flexible.

ZUBIN EMSLEY: The semester started on the 20th of February, and I actually knew my schedule by noon on the 21st. Fourteen hours again, but they said the teachers' class wouldn't start for a couple weeks. I was finally told last week that it won't start at all. Some of the department staff were sick, which added to the confusion. This semester is easier than the last one. It's a continuation, and I know what they know and what they can do and what they need. I've adjusted my class schedule to create three-day weekends.

G: Everything is really going well this year, though I could do with a little more anonymity. Somehow I've become a famous teacher—basically because I've been here for a year already and have had time to develop my teaching techniques. But in the first few weeks, legions of strangers were showing up to my room and classes asking me to teach them English. They just want to listen, they say, they'll sit in the back of my classroom, not say a word. (Who the hell, Alice, wants to sit and listen to me lecture on the finer points of technical writing?)

Professor Tang, in all her astuteness, picked up the opportunity and asked me to teach a night class of oral English—"How to

Survive in the USA" is the course title. She then advertised on campus, using my name, and charged 150¥ for the spare-time class. Thankfully, she capped enrollment at thirty students. But neither that nor the money stopped the ambitious. They have been showing up with my students and friends at my room, asking me to dinner, bringing gifts—if only I'll let them in my class.

TEDDY KELLAM: Re: Business. I haven't signed my contract yet. It was put on hold for myriad reasons (our *waiban* from last year died very suddenly—awful awful awful). Anyway, I wrote them a letter two weeks ago, saying (very tactfully) that I would like to request a plane ticket to the United States when I leave. The management school has given their teacher one, and I think my department should give me one for three reasons:

1. It's my second year.

2. They reneged on their promise to give me English majors only. The promise was made to entice me back, but it was made knowing it would have to be broken.

3. Last year's situation, where I took on a very difficult schedule (the fourteen different classes). In effect, I've worked my tail off for them, and remained loyal, so I tactfully requested a ticket home. But three weeks later, I have had no reply whatsoever. So, we'll see!

American teachers in China usually discover their real teaching duties when they find out where and when to appear for class. Even if they see a schedule in advance, course titles like "American Culture" or "Extensive Reading" can have a fog of mystery about them until students reveal their needs on the first day. As we will hear, course texts are often optional, out of date, or unavailable, so the field remains surprisingly undefined. When Zubin Emsley rearranges his schedule to create three-day weekends, the potential advantages of this ambiguity become apparent. But for novice teachers from America (where plans and schedules are often sacred), this open quality can be disorienting in the first term.

To give a sense of the usual range of differences and commonalities in what Americans end up teaching, here is a rough list of subjects and grade levels taught by a few of these letter writers during at least one twenty-week term:

Name	Hours	Classes
Mary Bracken	14 hours	Spoken English; listening, speaking, and writing (all freshmen except one graduate class)
Rachel Coleman	14 hours	Conversation; American culture; TOEFL sharks (university students and community adults; see her description below)
Paige Davies	10 hours	Listening comprehension; composition (sophomores and graduates)
Dal Hurtt	16 hours	Spoken English; writing; international economics
Teddy Kellam	18 hours	First term: All oral English
	14 hours	Second term: Oral English; writing; intensive reading; foreign trade English (freshmen, sophomores, postgraduates, and adults)
Joe Márquez	12 hours	Conversational English; newspaper reading (freshmen, juniors, seniors, and adults)
David Moldavsky	14 hours	Conversation; composition; American culture (freshmen, sophomores, and juniors)
Jim Page	16 hours	Conversation; scientific reading; scientific writing; American and British history; German
Doug Thompson	16 hours	Spoken English; writing; international economics
Justin Van Wart	16 hours	Oral English conversation (sophomores and juniors)
Eileen Vickery	12 hours	Extensive reading (freshmen and sophomores)
Adam Williams	18 hours	Conversational English (freshmen, sophomores, juniors, seniors, and graduates)

Of course, the reality behind such abstractions can vary widely.

MAX TUEFFERD: Here's a summary of what I've been teaching this year:

1st semester—Freshman Oral English:

- English C—very poor
- Teacher Training—better, conscientious students
- Civil Engineering (3 classes)—English is not their major, but they are OK, depending on where they are from. For example, my students from Macao were fun!

2nd semester—Oral English:

- English C (same students)
- Teacher Training (also the same)
- Listening—Mechanical engineering students (their listening is good, but they can't talk)
- British and American Culture (2nd year teachers-in-training)

KEVIN LAW-SMITH: My classes include:

- Spoken English (I entertain for an hour and do role-play stuff for the second hour.)
- Teach the Teachers (Teach them how to teach spoken English. Impossible—they can't speak themselves. So instead it's more or less an open discussion like the cultural class. We talk about gays, marriage, blacks, and so on.)
- Cultural class (Terrible book: from 1965. Chapter 16 is called "The Negro Problem." So I spend most of my time correcting their views.)

In addition to these official teaching duties, many Chinese universities ask English teachers to undertake several of the following:

- delivering public lectures in English (weekly or monthly)
- taping sample dialogues and oral questions so students can practice listening to English (especially just before national examinations)
- editing books and articles in English, often written by colleagues, sometimes by students

- organizing and attending "English corners" where students meet informally to practice speaking in English
- arranging (and sometimes discussing) videotaped movies in English
- holding office hours, both for students and for Chinese teachers of English

Voluntarily, as we will see, teachers also sometimes take on work for local businesses and nearby schools to earn extra money.

PAIGE DAVIES: We contribute two hours per week to recording tapes and editing passages written by colleagues (which we later record). This is one of my favorite two-hour blocks because often the passages are unintentionally funny, and it's like being in kindergarten again, trying to hold in our laughter so we're not "scolded."

Sample Dialogues

Man:	What seems to be the trouble?
Woman:	I've been feeling pretty rundown for the past few days and I think I'm running a fever now.
3rd voice:	Where does this conversation take place?

• • •

Man:	What time does the play start?
Woman:	At eight-thirty. We have thirty-five minutes to get there.
3rd voice:	What time is it now?

• • •

Man:	I'd like to talk to Jane.
Woman:	I'm sorry, she's out taking a sunbath.
3rd voice:	Jane is taking a bath.
	getting a suntan.
	swimming.
	watching a solar eclipse.

• • •

Man: I thought Francie and Mike were getting
                married in June.
Woman: No, that's when his cousin's wedding is.
                They're getting married the following
                week.
3rd voice: When are Francie and Mike getting mar-
                ried?
                [When *are* Francie and Mike getting married?]

•   •   •

Writing Practice

Write a paragraph based on this model about your favorite sport.

Most people like sports, and different people are interested in
different games. My favorite game is badminton. I usually play
it with my classmates in the afternoon after class. But if it is
Sunday, I play it the whole morning with my brother or sister.

I like badminton because it requires a lot of strength and gives
me a great deal of exercise. During the game I have to keep
moving my feet, working my arms, and jumping in order to hit
the shuttlecock. This is how a healthy body is built. That's why
I seldom need to see a doctor.

What's more, when I am all sweaty, I can take a cold water
shower and not feel cold in winter as well as in summer. I feel
relaxed. All my tiredness disappears and all my worries vanish.
I'm full of energy again, longing for a new day to come.

The truth about teaching in China is that, even for experienced
teachers, it is learned in the doing. This is partly because knowledge is not
something any teacher gives to a student. It is something students must
acquire themselves, with the *support* of their teachers. And it is partly
because what is expected of teachers and of students differs from culture
to culture.

In this sense, American teachers new to China have as much to learn
about teaching—about what "being a teacher" means—as their students
have to learn about English. It is a two-way proposition from the first
day. And the project is made more complex, as Marla Jenks's first letter

suggests, because both sides are trying to learn while bobbing around in that choppy ocean of difference.

Quanzhou, Fujian

Dear Alice,

Well, it's five o'clock and I just finished teaching my first class. It was challenging, and I have a million thoughts going through my head!

The class was a Reading/Listening class for second-year university students. On the odd weeks we're doing listening exercises in a language lab, and on the even weeks we go to a classroom to concentrate on reading. The language lab seems to have fairly functional equipment, which I'm happy about, but it also leads to a very impersonal atmosphere. I feel much more able to interact with the students in a regular classroom.

The classes here are two hours long, and as I walked to class all sorts of panicky thoughts came to my head. What if I'd planned too much or too little? What if they didn't understand a word I said, or else thought my class was moronic?

As the students filed in and sat looking expectantly at me, I got even more nervous. I started out going over basic details of the course and the textbooks. I told them my name and talked about my family. I don't know how much sank in, because I was rewarded only with a room full of 35 blank faces. I tried to get some responses out of them, but it was a little like pulling teeth out of a toothless old man. The few mumbles I did get were somewhat incomprehensible because of the incessant whir of the fan that wouldn't turn off.

I talked about Colorado a lot and sent postcards around so they could see Denver and the mountains. They seemed to like that. Then I played John Denver's "Colorado Rocky Mountain High," and I went over the lyrics and taught them what they meant. Again, I think a lot of it may have washed right over their heads.

For the second hour (after a ten-minute break), I moved them to a quieter, regular classroom down the hall. The classrooms around here make you feel like you're in a one-room schoolhouse. The teacher's podium is elevated at the front and center. The tables and straight-backed wooden chairs are bolted to the floor and to each other in nice even rows. It feels very formal and rigid.

I had each student introduce himself or herself and then tell me where they were from. I also let them choose English names, which they got a kick out of. Their next activity was to write their Chinese names, English names, birthdates, and reasons for studying English on 3x5 cards. I got a variety of answers. One guy simply said, "Because I have to." Most are studying because English is useful and they want to make foreign friends. One student said that she had always wanted to take English from a native speaker, and now her wish has come true. Their ages seem to be about 20-21. One student is only ten days younger than I am, and several are 18. Their level of English ranges from two years of study for one girl to fifteen for another. The average is about eight years. It's going to be a lot of work!

Marla

Behind the obvious project of learning what their students need, American teachers in China are also learning a complex new set of standards: Teachers are high status in China, and young people are low status. One should never challenge the statements of a superior, and yet each class has an elected monitor whose duties include making suggestions to the teacher. (Usually a member of the Communist Party, the monitor spearheads any interests of the group as a whole, which include organizing class banquets and outings.) These cultural "rules" are seldom taught directly, yet they lie behind many small encounters in the classroom.

MARLA JENKS: Today I had two classes in the morning; they were my oral freshmen. They're my two favorite classes because they're so eager to soak up everything I say. It's amazing how intently they listen—sometimes it's a little frightening!

Anyway, today one kid raised his hand and said, "Miss Marla, can you tell us the history of America?" I sort of sputtered and asked him to be a little more specific. We wound up talking about Christianity, Adam and Eve, Milton's *Paradise Lost,* the origins of the English language, the Vietnam War, race relations in the U.S. in the 1960s, and Robert Frost. Quite an interesting overview, huh? I forged ahead with my limited knowledge, and they hung on every word.

MARY BRACKEN: Last week, I met with Professor Tang, who told me to stay away from politics or controversy in any discussions. I was told several times, "You can discuss whatever you like outside of the classroom." One boy who asked me political questions called up the other day to apologize. Can you imagine? Someone had spoken with him, I'm sure! Just weird stuff like this lately—but nothing too problematic. A few (one in particular) of my students have opened up, and I'm learning a lot!

JUSTIN VAN WART: My status as a teacher brings considerable respect, both inside the university and out. I teach English oral conversation to 100 students in their second and third years. For half of them, I'm the first Westerner they've exchanged more than a few words with. These are bright students, as this university is one of China's top five. Through years of self-study, their English is just at the point of stimulating conversation.

I have no required curriculum; I am free to organize any activity that requires speaking. This gives me, as you can imagine, lots of leeway. We've done skits, market simulation games, debates, ghost stories, and mock advertisements. Sometimes I feel more like a camp counselor than a university teacher.

Thus far, teaching has been a challenge I can rise to, and getting these kids to loosen up has been my main objective. (And though just a few years younger than I, they really are "kids," as they are naïve in so many ways.) Getting them to raise their hands and take initiative apart from the group is a common complaint among foreign teachers. Watching Chinese professors,

I begin to see why, as there is nearly zero dialogue between teacher and student.

Every teacher is in the classroom alone, trying simultaneously to understand the rules of this game and to establish some. Most teachers manage to sort things out and, eventually, they begin to click.

ADAM WILLIAMS: My students seem to love me. Some of my lesson plans have been quite successful. Here are a few:

1. Butcher and Chicken; Spider and Fly; Lumberjack and Tree
    Have some students act as the butcher and others as chicken, etc. What would an interesting dialogue between these pairs of "killer and victim" be? (Personification is a key concept that my students really liked.) What would a tree's defense be to live?

2. My "Up" Lesson
    I explain or try to explain about fifty words or sayings that revolve around the word "up": come up, make up, up the creek, stuck up, up yours, break up, up to you, clam up, uppish, uppity, and on and on.

3. The Liar's Game
    Tell three things about yourself. Two will be true and one a lie. Have your students ask questions to decipher which one is untrue. Then during the next class, have them play the liar's game with the teacher (me) and fellow classmates asking them questions.

JOE MÁRQUEZ: My students loaded me up with sesame bread, apples, pears, and moon cakes for the Mid-Autumn Festival yesterday. I've been invited to three parties but have only gone to two. At both I was asked to perform. I refused to sing and dance, so I juggled apples—they loved it.

Classes are fine. Yang told me that my students really like me. That made me feel good. This is a great experience. I have a great time teaching. But the thing is that I really am teaching; I'm not a dancing poodle. I have yet to play one game with my students. Instead, they like my classes, I think, because I'm there for them.

The conversation is becoming more lively. I showed them a magazine called *American Photo*. It is a camera/photography magazine that I bought because I wanted to read a couple of articles. It turns out they loved the pictures. There were pictures of rock climbing, bungee jumping, diving, lions, ice climbing, rafting—all sorts of action photos. When I told the students I could rock climb, I was treated like a superhero. They seemed to feel I was extremely brave. I did not mean to sound as if I was superhuman, but since they do not encounter people scaling rock, they see it as an amazing feat.

In the photo magazine I showed them a picture of the Potala with the Dalai Lama's youngest brother standing in front. It turns out one of my students is from Lhasa.[2] I asked her to describe the Potala, but she just put her head on the desk in embarrassment. I stayed away from politics and just showed them the picture.

Whenever they come over, we talk and talk. They touch every book and ask about every music tape. Sometimes this is great, but sometimes I become a little annoyed—but calm.

PAIGE DAVIES: There's no American VCR player here that works. M——'s department dean used to have a private one in her home, but it broke. However, I'm glad I brought two tapes along. I showed one when the machine still worked. There is a photocopying machine on campus, but the departments won't pay. Either you or the students pay. However, you can type things on this funky blue paper and have them mimeographed. This is the normal procedure for exams, and the department, of course, covers the costs.

MARLA JENKS: Other than the dropping temperatures, things are

---

[2] The Potala is a remarkable palace in Lhasa, the capital of Tibet, traditionally the home and headquarters of the Dalai Lama (lit., "ocean of wisdom"), the spiritual leader of Tibetan Buddhism, who fled to India in 1959 when the Chinese military closed all Tibetan monasteries. China and Tibet have had a see-saw history of influence, but since 1951 the Chinese have claimed to control the country, which they call Xizang ("Suh-zahng") Province.

going fine around here. Today I had a really great class. In fact, I had my reading students—who are usually only marginally interested—but today we really clicked. We read a story, and when I realized their comprehension level was below zero, I acted it out for them. That got their attention right away, and soon they were smiling and nodding and comprehending! We went line by line, and at the end of each paragraph I called on random students to tell me what had just happened. They were a little dense at first, but as the story went on, they got much quicker. At one point they even corrected me when I got a character's name wrong. It was so exciting! It was one of those rare days that makes me feel like I could teach for the rest of my life!

DALE ASIS: In my writing class, I asked my students to write to the editor of *China Daily*,[3] as a writing practice. Lo and behold, three students got published. I can't help bragging about it like a proud parent. The college was so elated, they treat me like I can walk on water. (Since this is a *mining* college, they think I can walk on hot coals.)

SAMANTHA TISDEL: A stack of magazines my parents sent me for Christmas elicited joyful enthusiasm not only from me, but from my students, who literally burst into applause when I bore the prizes triumphantly into the classroom. My students constantly peruse my personal bookshelf, which is stocked with books I brought from home. They go for anything from the Bible (officially illegal) to Tennessee Williams to Joyce Carol Oates to the funnies.

G: In all, my classes ended wonderfully, especially the Ph.D. class. I remember the initial frustration in having so many students of varying abilities having such a wide array of different needs and wants. But after a month or so, the class clicked; everything that didn't work easily developed into something that did. Though busy with their jobs and research and families, they managed to

---

[3] The English-language paper of China.

find time for out-of-class project work, which they performed splendidly. In fact, the class transformed from an English class into a symposium on ethics, philosophy, theories of education. What a gift that class was. Perhaps you can understand. I have developed many friendships from among them as well; I am only now recovering from the numerous dinners.

KATIE SHOWALTER: Our newspaper is coming along well. I'm proud of them. They've done their best writing for this paper.

A Fairy in the Sky
A beautiful girl
Living in the sky
Wears seven-color clothes
Being so shy
She seldom shows up
Only after it rains in summer
She appears in curiosity
Bends her body
To see the new appearance of the earth
She seems like an arched bridge
But so shy is she
She disappears gradually
Without being noticed.
      by Ou Guihua and Huang Fei

Memorable Hometown
If I were a famous writer,
    you would be the soul in the essays.
If I were a good artist,
    you would be my creative fountainhead.
If I were a best photographer
    you would be my spotlight.
If I were an advanced constructor,
    you would be the land of peach blossoms.

I love your typical landscape,
I admire the friendly and hard-working people
    within you.
Wherever I go, wherever I am,
    you are the destination of my life's voyage.
Whatever you would look like,
    I will always be with you.
East or West, you are best.
      by June Lin

A Cross-cultural Drama

It is sometimes hard, even for U.S. educators, to understand why teaching English for fourteen hours a week in China is a heavy load. Perhaps this formula will help: Each two-hour English class requires from one to two hours of grading each week plus one to two hours finding books and mimeo stencils, preparing exercises and vocabulary lists, designing activities, and so on. Thus, a fourteen-hour class schedule actually requires between thirty and sixty hours of preparation and grading each week. Every different subject, every writing assignment, every activity outside class (such as setting up films and newspapers) calls for more time and more creative energy.

Beginning teachers have no clear sense of what "normal" is for their new profession, and they make allowances because they have to invent every class from scratch. Even experienced teachers find that in China the rules for good teaching are unfamiliar and obscure, so they watch, wait, and experiment for a while. Many teachers feel overwhelmed at the start, but they all try not to rock the boat too soon, being all too aware of that deep ocean of difference.

After all, when you don't know the rules, you also don't know what counts as a *violation* of the rules. Since everything feels odd and unfamiliar, too fast or too slow, too chaotic or too regimented, you hesitate to say "Stop! That's wrong!"

But there are finally limits. In this little three-act drama, played out by G and Amanda Myers, we see the considerations and the courage that lie behind a decision that things have gone too far—in a place already far, far away.

Act One

September

Alice:

I am a teacher. It says so in my contract. I signed it earlier this week—the salary, the responsibilities, the conditions and benefits, all these I agreed to with a stroke, a few strokes, of this pen. But two days ago I was giving a speech to welcome the two hundred or so guests to the grand opening of the New World Restaurant. On behalf of Amanda and myself, I wished the Hunan provincial officials, businessmen, their friends and friends of friends, a warm greeting and continued happiness, and other Chinese formal pleasantries. I said these things with flowers in my hand and the red appointment folder, which stated that I was an honorary general manager of this new, privately owned, Chinese first-class restaurant. Welcome to China! I accepted an invitation to lunch and ended up the new Puyi,[4] puppet emperor of the New World Restaurant, Manchukus. Imagine that.

I've been in Changsha for two weeks; the banquets are over, but the invitations continue. Gifts from the Foreign Languages Department on Teachers Day; moon cakes for the Mid-Autumn Festival; more invitations to dine at friends' family homes, students' dorms. People ask me if I am a Christian, and I respond truthfully: My religion is my appointment book.

I can, of course, recommend my life here, my students, my friends, my teachers. I have 150 students—Ph.D.s, postgrads, community adults, and wonderfully bright and innocent first-year students. My teaching schedule changed twice before my classes began. The department has thus far respected my stand to teach only twelve hours per week in the classroom with two hours of office time, and only four preparations. Though Amanda has five and doesn't seem to mind.

---

[4] The name of China's last emperor, member of the Manchu Qing dynasty, who ascended the throne in 1908 at the age of two.

The FAO is most accommodating, extremely honest and up front (or so it seems) about how things are done. They are helpful and friendly, eager to please us, and in brief doses, intercede on our behalf in disagreements with the Foreign Languages Department. It is a difficult department to teach in, perhaps because it is required to shoulder 10 percent of all the class-hours taught here. I have been consciously developing the skill of parrying off every encounter with Mr. Lu—the loony and befuddling dean of the department—which inevitably results in requests for more typing, attendance at English corners, translations. The Chinese teachers just teach their eight hours a week and go home.

With Amanda and me, however, the teachers seem kind and interested, for we are outside the game. They think we cannot understand China (which we don't!) or office politics. They are a good group of people (some of them, anyway) who would rather make money in Shenzhen (one of the SEZs). They are devoted to their students, I think, and that alone is enough to earn my respect, given the fact that they are treated by the university worse than the students. A strange contradiction.

Amanda and I don't have too many grievances yet, for all we've heard and expected. Our students are kind to us—more students, more kindness; and since they are local students they provide us with opportunities to meet and eat with their families and experience Changsha as people who know the city well. We compromise. Everything is a compromise. And if I've learned anything from my students it is this: Swallow the frustrations and take advantage of opportunity.

Write if you get time. Until next time,

G

Act Two

October

Dear Alice,

Oh, if you could only see me now. . . . I'm sitting in semidarkness (the electricity has gone out and the sun is going

down), with my 1920s typewriter. If you go too fast the letters
get tangled up, and then you must dissect the whole machine.
You have to pound with all your might to have the keys actually
make an impression on the paper. I suppose I could just hand-
write a letter but this seemed like so much more fun. It actually
seems to be working—hey, maybe I have found my calling. A
typist in China. They make good money, from what I understand.

I'm a little worried about something. Besides writing a long
overdue letter just to say hello, I wanted to tell you a few things.
Fred told me that he took the liberty of relaying some of my
difficulties with the department. This is fine, but I am so afraid
that he has given you the wrong impression of my overall state of
mind. Keep in mind that he has been trying to talk me into
moving to Guangzhou. Alice, I am in no way, shape, or form
considering transferring. I hope you're not worried about G and
me because we are, in fact, doing quite well.

Let me begin by telling you that I love teaching. It has been
one of my greatest lifetime joys. When I do feel unhappy here
(which is inevitable) I simply plunge myself into teaching and it
always makes me happy. Although I teach all oral classes, I have
my students write journals too. The journal entries have been
some of the most beautiful pieces of writing I have EVER read. My
students are a constant joy and wonder to me.

I also, believe it or not, have fallen in love with China. The
people never cease to amaze me. Every day I learn something
about history or economics or politics or people. The energy of
the city is amazing—so different from the energy of a large city in
the U.S. I have made some truly incredible friends, as well. My
closest friend is a Chinese woman from the English department
who has shown me a part of China I could never have seen as an
outsider. She has reminded me how wonderful friendship can be,
and I respect her in every way. I spend most of my spare time
alone, but when I look for company, I have only the best people
surrounding me.

Changsha is a pit. There is no denying that it is probably one of the most polluted, gray, depressing places in the world. But I must say that the two million people who live here give it a character of its own. I've never spoken to a Chinese or American who was the least bit happy about living here—but it makes for a sort of brotherhood, ya know? Everyone hates Changsha and somehow out of all its disadvantages there is actually something very likable about it. I haven't expressed myself very well. I hate Changsha. I love living here. Make sense? Probably not. It doesn't make much sense to me.

So now we get down to the nitty gritty—the Foreign Languages Department. Oh, where could I ever begin? If I gave you a rundown on these past few months, I could write a book. Although I was furious at first, I have come to realize that all the teachers are treated poorly. It is true that we are particularly taken advantage of, but none of the teachers are treated well. I'm not sure if the Foreign Languages Department knows and understands what they are doing wrong. I will tell you and I will give you some suggestions on how things might be changed, but I believe that infamous culture-gap problem will keep the department from ever truly understanding what they do wrong.

I teach six classes, each of them two hours a week. Each class has different people. Two of these classes are students grouped together according to their English proficiency. Four classes have everything from fluent to "My name is . . ." It is October 25 and thus far I have not received any class lists. My classes range in size from 35 to 55. My classes were shuffled, cancelled, rescheduled, recancelled, added, dropped, etc., up until last week. So far no changes this week . . . but it's only Monday. My nursing class started at 20. Every day new people come; now we have 42. Their level is BEGINNING, so we basically have to start all over each time there is a new student. I beg for class lists, I put it in writing, I ask nicely.

We are told that we must give lectures to the teachers in the department every week. We are also told we must give lectures to the public every Tuesday night. This is not in our contract. Do we have to do it? I would have preferred being asked rather than told. We have office hours, but I got in trouble because I (stupidly) invited my students to visit me during office hours. I was sternly informed that office hours are for the teachers of the Foreign Languages Department to use me as they like . . . translating, taping, talking, etc. If my students need to see me, they could see me on my own time. I also do tapings with G for two hours a week on top of this.

Mr. Lu is in charge of foreign teachers. I call him Lu-Nee. Alice, he is 100 percent inept. He's a fool, he's disorganized, he's a weasel, and he's a pain. He cornered me last Saturday as I was getting my hair cut to bug me about doing an English corner for the fifth-year students (there are 300, by the way). I ever so sweetly explained that I already had an English corner. I have 175 students now. I used to have 275, but I finally got it reduced little by little. I only remember half their names and there are some I don't even recognize. I have yet to receive the dates for the last day of term or the first day of next term. (I've been told we get that information within four or five days of the event.) One of my classes began two weeks late due to poor organization of the department and now I've been told that I must teach two weeks into Spring Festival. To make up for lost time. Well, we'll see about that.

Oh, I'm so sorry to be complaining so much. But it is necessary that this stop. I haven't begun to tell you how irritating it can get. I am well aware of the Chinese way, but this is far more chaotic than the train station during holiday.

OK, my fingers are bruised and my neck has permanently cramped into this bent position. Sorry this letter took on such a bad tone. Don't forget that I am truly very happy here, as is G. Later I will write and tell you some funny stories—they happen every day. Alice, thank you so much for making this year possible for me.

I hope all is going well for you.

Please drop us a letter.

Love,

Amanda

Off-stage, Alice sends a fax, and . . .

Teaching condition is getting better for Amanda and G. Some things are not under our control, but we are doing our best to coordinate. Amanda and G will write you in detail in the near future. Thank you for your suggestion!
Dean Wang

Act Three

November

Dear Alice,

Oh, it was so great to get your letter. It's wonderful to have someone in the "home office" who cares and supports. I thought your letter to Mr. Wang was good, very to the point. Mr. Lu must definitely learn that badgering the teachers only annoys them to the point of saying "No." Oh, well, culture gap strikes again. What can you do?

It's difficult because the other teachers in the department are treated unfairly also. In making these demands we are asking for special treatment. How I wish I could organize the department all over again. I find that both the students and my fellow teachers are patient beyond belief. I had one interesting conversation with one of my brightest students about this very subject. He explained that everything in Chinese life is like this, frustrating and chaotic. If one allows himself to become irritated, then he is the one who loses. Patience is definitely a virtue here. It's simply a way of survival.

Classes are going well. I have the students keep a weekly journal to practice their writing skills. Sometimes I give them specific topics to write about, but other times I let them choose any subject. One student took this opportunity to ask my advice about love.

In the university, it is generally accepted that students should not divide their time between academic study and romance. My student, however, seems to have fallen madly in love. She can't go to her parents because they will punish her. She can't tell her sister for fear of harsh criticism. She can't turn to her friends because they certainly wouldn't understand and might even laugh. But she has decided that I, being a "good model," am the one she must come to seeking advice.

She says she is so in love that she is unable to eat, sleep, or study properly. Her boyfriend shares all her interests: music, literature, medicine, and English. Should she discontinue this budding romance, which is surely unacceptable in most eyes? Or should she "follow her heart as it pulls her toward him"? (I think she got that from a novel.)

Well, having this responsibility was not what I expected, but I had been told that the student-teacher relationship oftentimes goes outside the classroom. How to handle such a touchy subject? Of course, her education was most important. So I simply decided to plunge in and give the best advice I could.

"Dear Student, it sounds as though you have a wonderful friendship with this boy; not just a boyfriend but a true friend. We learn and grow from our friends. Perhaps you could use your love to encourage your studying. It sounds as though you both value education. Don't let your love lead you away from your studies. Let it motivate you to try harder. You are an excellent student, and I would be disappointed to see you not live up to your potential. I wish you luck and happiness. And happiness should first come from pride in yourself."

Heehee, Ann Landers I am not, but I hope I gave her useful advice.

I have one absolutely fantastic class of young nursing students from the countryside. They have never been away from home, much less in a huge university in a city. They are shy, sweet, enthusiastic, warm, and always a joy to teach. We had to begin with the basics: "Hello, how are you?" But we've made great progress. Their writing and grammar are good, but many of them only studied from books—no oral English whatsoever, so even the simplest words are completely foreign.

OK. If I don't go and lesson plan for tomorrow, then it'll never get done. We both enjoyed your letter and appreciate the support you have given us. Take care.

Sincerely,

Amanda

December

Dear Alice:

Happy Holidays!

Your letter to the FAO shook up the department a little—but it will help in negotiating for classes next semester.

All the best,

G

Learning about the Students

As the letters so far suggest, attachments grow between Chinese students and their American teachers. They come to know a little of one another's lives and to care: Teddy's student brings her a flower; Joe talks with his students about books and music. But real understanding of the motives and minds of people from cultures so far apart grows slowly, sometimes at a cost to both parties.

Todd Lundgren is one teacher who was granted access to deeper knowledge of one of his students, in conversations that he says "yielded a great deal of painful insight about the way China works."

A Walk with Zhang

I am in my apartment waiting for Mr. Zhang[5] to arrive. I am curious and a little apprehensive. Two years ago Zhang, then a sophomore, was one of my students. After I returned to the U.S.

---

[5] The name of Todd Lundgren's student is pronounced "Jahng."

we often corresponded, and this last June he sent me a joyful letter saying he was happy to have heard through the campus grapevine that I was returning to teach for another year in his province.

Zhang appeared soon after my return, with some classmates. I was elated. I rose up smiling as he came in and shook his hand warmly. But he remained strangely stoic, and his hand as I shook it was as lifeless and heavy as a pump handle. His presence was infused with a seriousness I had not known in him. After he left, I thought that I had deluded myself about my "friendship" with Zhang—our American and Chinese expectations of each other had fallen with a big splash in the middle of the Pacific Ocean, and any relationship we had constructed had sunk with them.

As an American, however, I like to ask that most difficult of questions in China—why? I went to Zhang's room and invited him to dinner. He said he would prefer an evening walk. We agreed on the following night.

Just after seven, the phone rings. It's Zhang, waiting downstairs. We go outside and begin to walk down the narrow road between the stout hulls of teachers' apartments. We stroll past the Foreign Languages Building—the center of both of our lives here. We are walking at Chinese pace—about one step every second—which is difficult for me as I'm still used to U.S. walking speed.

Zhang begins by saying he has tried on the way over to think of things to say, but that he was unsuccessful. I feel for the briefest moment as though I'm about fifteen and on a date, but then I think that his is a matter-of-fact statement: He does not know what to talk about. I smile and say that, in that case, maybe we'll just walk in silence. He gets my joke and becomes slightly less solemn than before.

Eventually he begins to tell me about the decisions that surround becoming a graduate student. In China, the graduate examinations are subject-specific; students can select only one topic, and they are allowed a first and second choice of schools. Many will choose a university famous in their field as a first choice and use the second choice—usually a less prestigious school—to bolster their chances of being accepted somewhere. The test is usually a one-time affair. Students who do not succeed generally return to their homes to accept the work they are offered there. Zhang is worried about scoring high enough to gain admission to either of the schools he has chosen.

I ask him why he and so many of his classmates want to do graduate study in linguistics. It seems horribly dry to me (though I do not say this), and I wonder why they don't choose literature. He says, "Perhaps the literature test is too difficult." He and his classmates feel they have a better chance of scoring well on the linguistics exam. And he does not have to tell me that some kind of graduate study is better than none at all. It is a question of his status in society, not his subject preference.

He says he wants to go to Shanghai to study. He wants to live in a big city, not his village. "The leaders there are not very democratic," he says. "Even if I become a teacher, I do not want to teach there. It is not the place for the young man." Zhang pauses and then says that I do not know him well.

He is from "the countryside" (a generic term for any place smaller than a town), and he reiterates that it is no place for young men. Then in one quick spurt he tells me that his father drowned himself during the Cultural Revolution,[6] unable to bear further persecution; that his mother remarried out of necessity to a man who does not treat her well; and that his family is very large—he has three older sisters plus two younger brothers and a sister born to his mother and stepfather. He breathes, and I feel that now he *has* told me something.

We have reached the main gate to the university. He wants to turn around. I ask why, standing under the massive timbers of the traditional gate, its arches festooned with strings of multicolored lights like a colossal Christmas tree. We step aside from the

---

[6] A many-faceted, shifting set of purges, imprisonments, and re-education campaigns that swept, first, the Chinese Communist Party bureaucracy, then intellectuals, artists, counter-revolutionaries, monasteries—any group that could be labelled feudal, exploitative, or capitalist—beginning in 1966 and winding to an end by the mid-1970s.

bicycle traffic, and he says it may not be safe outside. I peer out at the vendors, at the vacant pool tables along the road, and it all takes on an ominous appearance. I'm not really afraid, but I know that most of the students are leery of this town at night. Some have been assaulted and robbed by the locals. Still, I coax him out saying it's only dusk, that we'll just cut around through the open market to the small gate in the back wall of the campus. Grudgingly, he agrees.

It would be possible to write a treatise as long as the Great Wall on what it means to be "inside the wall" and "outside the wall" in China. Now, outside the university wall, bicycles ghost past us, trucks thunder by, and Zhang begins to tell me of his ambitions, of his family's life in the village. Out here I feel that I can understand it all slightly better: With the fruit vendors framed in clusters of weak dusty light, the young dudes drag racing ancient motorbikes, the pool tables filling now, with the general rush of Chinese life to which I will never be privy, I get a clearer picture of what Zhang's life holds—a sense of the chasm he has crossed simply to move inside the walls of a university.

What he tells me is not all that different from what an American student might say. He wants to go on to graduate school and, in the long run, to improve his position. But he's worried about the immediate approval of his family and, of course, about money. He says he is in debt to all of his older sisters and, as they are all married, to his brothers-in-law. It is these husbands who are grumbling about where the money has gone, which makes his sisters inquisitive about what returns their investment will bring. Zhang says his sisters are divided over what he should do. Two of them support his graduate school plans, but all agree that the sensible thing to do is to first become a teacher. That way, he could work for a couple of years and save for his wedding. Later he could take correspondence courses and eventually earn a master's degree.

Playing devil's advocate (as I think he wants me to do), I ask, "How much would you have to save for the wedding?" He tells me a figure in the thousands of yuan. "How much on a monthly salary of three hundred yuan will you be able to save in two or three years as a teacher?" He nods and says, "Not enough." His biggest worry is that he is now a little old. By the time he finishes graduate school, he will be twenty-nine and perhaps will not be able to find a suitable wife. As it is, there are no suitable candidates in his village. On the other hand, if he obtains a graduate degree, he will be a much more eligible bachelor outside his village. He will have a better position and perhaps a stable career. He smiles and says in a faraway voice that, with a higher degree, he will be able to choose a prettier bride. As we walk through the small rear gate back onto the campus, I wonder how many of his ambitions are inspired by that dream alone.

The campus has darkened. As we retrace our earlier route, Zhang brings up the subject of his father's death. Among the shadows, part of him emerges that has seldom come to the university. It is a part that calls him back to his village. He is bitter about his father's suicide and says maybe he will go back to his father's home and get the details of what happened. "Why don't you just ask your mother?" I ask, and he says he fears it would greatly upset her. Then he laughs a short, hollow laugh and says perhaps he will find those people who mistreated his father and avenge his death. "Perhaps," he repeats, "I will."

Our conversation lists toward the surreal. As we come into the shadow of the administration building, the symbol of Beijing's authority on campus, Zhang begins speaking of his infatuation with the Italian Mafia, how he admires its leaders. He insists that the Mafia did not start out as a corrupt organization. At first, he tells me, it was just a group of businessmen doing business. He sees in its original leaders great courage and resolve. He pictures himself as such a leader—a leader of men.

His infatuation with the Mafia and his admiration of its leaders fit, oddly enough, with the political sentiments of many Chinese: Many feel the need for strong, seasoned, and even ruthless leadership to maintain order (and, through order, prosperity) in the country. The paternal godfathers of Zhang's vision could easily be Mao, Zhou Enlai, Liu Shaoqi,[7] and other hardened revolutionaries who fought to establish the People's Republic. The irony is that, while Zhang idealizes such leadership as centralized and philanthropic, actual mafia-style baronies have emerged in China and are trafficking drugs, foreign cars, hard currencies, and even educational opportunities abroad. Whereas Zhang sees such organizations as enhancing the power of a central authority, they more often undermine Beijing's control over provincial and local governments, which seek to profit from this illicit trade.

I don't believe that Zhang has a sense of the magnitude of such operations, because most of what I know comes from the foreign press. He is, however, certain that such black-market activity is, for himself and many young people, the only way to make real money. He recognizes that many young men resort to selling drugs, though he hastens to add that *he* would never do such a thing. But he says he is frustrated by the obvious dead ends presented by living a "legal" life. He says that to be a teacher is good, but that teachers are not respected and their pay is very low. He finds it hard to watch friends who did not attend university acquire more with less education through mysterious activities. "Why should I be a teacher," he asks, "when others have money and nice apartments?" He pauses, then adds, "Some in my village have expensive weddings—and even cars they have not rented."

The harsh realism of Zhang's assessment is new. That it was not characteristic of our conversations two years ago may be a result of his now being a senior and facing the stark limitations his circumstances impose on his future. Students are perhaps the most politicized and heavily propagandized portion of the Chinese population, yet this bewildered and stoic candor seems a sign that

---

[7] Mao Zedong was the great revolutionary leader of Chinese communism. Zhou Enlai, another early revolutionary—now considered the intellectual architect of Chinese communism—was premier from 1949 until his death in 1976. Liu Shaoqi was one of the early Communist revolutionaries who remained a leader as the Party matured.

he is descending from the clouds of idealism into the storm of life.

He seems to be trying to reconcile the reality of his circumstances with his notions of justice. Though some of his ideas are romantic or ill informed, what he says of the inequities in Chinese society and of his limited future are true and mature assessments. I wonder how many other young men and women in their nighttime of separate thoughts think similar things. How many, seeing the visible scars of the Cultural Revolution on their parents contrasted with the new "socialist" idea of getting rich quick, will be able to balance the extremes? And faced with the possibility of a future "outside the walls," what recourse will they have?

We step onto the college track to take a slow lap and watch the moon rise through the night haze, orange as the sun. As we circle, we can see Zhang's dormitory over the north wall—squares of light with black borders. I ask him to point out his room and he does: three high, fifth from the right. I yawn and he laughs his first real laugh of the night. He says rather triumphantly, "I think you are getting tired." Yes, I say, and he laughs again, incomprehensibly.

Zhang is silent for a few moments and then says that, although many of his classmates think him odd, he believes in palmistry. Recently he had his palm read and was assured that his future looks prosperous and bright—especially, he says, between the ages of thirty-five and fifty-five. Therefore, he grins, it is only natural that he sacrifice now and study hard. "I have ten years of work ahead of me. Then things will improve." I tell him that we should contact each other in ten years to see how things are, but he does not reply. I ask if he will go back to his dorm now. No, he says. He'll go back to his classroom for a few hours to study. I say I'll walk him as far as the building.

When we arrive at the Foreign Languages Building, I thank him for placing such confidence in our friendship. He is smiling distractedly, says thank you too, then protests that his belief in palmistry is true and correct. "I believe you," I say. He is unconvinced. "Here, I will show you," he says, and twists my palm upward. But here he stops, confused: The lines on Western hands are slightly different from those of the Chinese. "The living-line, at least, is the same," he says at last. "Something we have in common," I say, trying to smile away the awkwardness. "Yes," he says, "in common," and tightening his grip across my palm he says he will see me soon, looping my arm up and down in an intimate, obscure handshake.

Teachers learn about their students' lives in many ways—from long walks and short visits, from special projects and daily observation. Slowly, many begin to piece small details together, to construct a better sense of the whole.

A single English class, after all, is part of a much larger system of education that extends from preschool through the universities that train teachers. As Zhang's story suggests, students attend language class broadly aware of how it might affect their status in society and their earning potential. And they react to each lesson based on values they have absorbed during a lifetime of other lessons most Americans can barely imagine.

MATTHEW REES: The brutality of life here is the very force that binds us. This university, in the eyes of many students attending and of the self-proclaimed sophisticates of S. Shaanxi, is a farce. It is a Teachers University, and this qualification depresses and scares the hell out of many of the students. At a time when Deng[8] has proclaimed $ and private business to equal national pride, when six of the twelve teachers in our English Department vanished during the vacation (as expected; they headed south for better employment), the students are destroyed, slapped in the face by the very system they are expected to proliferate.

I am glad Patrick and I are here. The students have really opened up, feeling like a big family at times. I'm not sure what we'd do or if we'd be able to maintain any kind of educational, hopeful environment without each other. This sounds all too

---

[8] Deng Xiaoping, premier of China during the time of these letters.

dramatic, but more so it is sad. Sad that this bloody system of education, at least here, is the very force that students and concerned faculty must battle in order to receive and assist in education itself.

JEANNE PHILLIPS: I haven't heard more as yet on China's possible big cut in the number of English teachers in favor of high-tech experts. What is happening is even more of what I've written about before, the push for universities to raise their own funds. A professor here said that they will have to attract many more tuition-paying students, which means low exam scores and people not interested in teaching. (As he put it, "No one would pay money to become a teacher or professor.")

So they will develop new applied programs—e.g., in public relations and who knows what—to attract students since they have no technical and business departments. A professor in Chinese literature is currently teaching public speaking, as a step in the applied direction by his department. So journalism, advertising, public relations, accounting, survey research, etc., are likely to be more in demand by schools who can't count on hard sciences, engineering, or a business school to pull in the cash-paying students. Hotel and restaurant management and quick workshops on tourism or customer service are likely to be in demand. Two Brits just gave a three-day workshop here on tourism and trade, attended by all the bigshots of relevant organizations and of not-so-relevant ones as well.

KEVIN LAW-SMITH: Reactions to *Beverly Hills 90210:* My students freaked out. A simple episode showed gun ranges, gun shops, cohabitation, open sex (almost).

AMANDA MYERS: My nurses class is a true, true joy—a group of about forty girls between 16 and 18 years old. They are shy but enthusiastic, bright, genuine, and a constant amazement to me. They learn in the shadow of the medical students, but I find them to be incredibly motivated students with the most charming humor I have ever known. Although they often act as a group in class, they are a diverse collection of individuals eager to share and to teach me more about themselves.

These girls live nine or ten to a dorm room, their bunks in columns of three. Each has a small desk with personal treasures from home locked safely in the top drawer. They seem to have a tolerance for closeness that we Americans have lost or never acquired. Last week when I visited their dorm after class, they showed me how they practice ballroom dancing. On one of the desks, a pocket tape-recorder played the latest pop tune. The girls paired up and danced down the narrow aisle between the beds and the desks, then up the other side and around again. It was a beautiful thing, watching them with arms stiff, their faces set in concentration.

ZUBIN EMSLEY: "Janie" is a junior now. She is tall and skinny and moves like a rag doll or maybe the puppet of a novice puppeteer. She asked if she could meet with me outside of class to get more English speaking practice. But because she's used to putting her heart on paper, she gave me these writings about her childhood and school.

Childhood

I was born on 12th of November of the Chinese lunar calendar in 1975. I grew up around love. I have memories from seven years old. The first seven years, I have forgotten.

At the age of eight, I went to school. My sister was four years ahead of me. My brother was two years ahead. Every morning, our grandma got up early and cooked for us. She woke us up and we had breakfast. Sister, brother, and I would go to school after we said "Bye bye" to grandma. It was not far. On our way, brother helped me carry my bag and I sang for them.

I knew my grades were excellent, but I realized that I would lose this if I did not listen to the teacher. I was very quiet and did carefully the homework. After school, I stayed in the classroom with my friends. Sometimes I played the teacher and taught them math.

I wore glasses and one day I wrote on the blackboard. When

I faced the class they all laughed at me. I looked blank. They laughed again. I acted angry, but they didn't stop. They said my face was covered with dust. I walked to a mirror and saw my face was very white. I laughed too.

When we finished the lessons, we played "catch the chicken" on the school grounds, and also "soldier catches the enemy" and we jumped ropes. We often played and forgot the time. When we got home, it was dark.

My parents worked hard in the fields for us. Sometimes, I would go to the fields after school. My parents were happy when they saw me. I helped to do small things. On holidays, I went to the fields with my aunt, who is two years older than me. We cut the grass. There are two oxen in her home and she let me ride on their backs. We walked along the ridges. The crow of frogs, the cry of birds, and the peasants carrying two baskets of vegetables or rice on a shoulder pole—we were ecstatic with the rural scenery and we talked about our thoughts.

Schooling

When I was fourteen years old, I went to Middle School. In my mind, I changed much in this school. I had few words, and I also didn't sing and dance anymore. Perhaps I grew up and knew something. Perhaps I was afraid of people judging me. I didn't make friends with all the students.

At that time, a girl and three boys were friends of mine. They understood my thoughts. We always studied and played together. We played near the rivers and on the hills. There had to be a contest: a climbing contest or a cooking contest. We laughed and talked to the sky, we looked at the clouds walking and felt the wind drifting.

Once, we had a knowledge contest. Afterwards, we played cards in the bedroom. If a person was defeated, she or he had to stick a white paper on their face. Finally, our faces all became paper faces. We looked at each other and laughed and laughed. Sometimes, we had a little disagreement, but soon it was nothing and we played together again.

At this time, I could do work in the rice fields. In winter, the peasants were all getting ready for the next year, selecting the seeds. And in spring, they planted them. When the seeds were budding, they made scarecrows and put them in the fields. Then the rice would be harvested and the rice seedlings would be planted in May. I planted the rice shoots faster than brother but more slowly than sister.

The rice needs water, so brother and I went to the fields together and let the water into the fields. Sometimes we cut the grass. We had a contest: We threw stones. If I threw the stone farther than my brother, I shouldn't cut the grass. But it was impossible. I had to cut the grass and brother carried the basket. Sometimes, I would drive a group of ducks and go out. The ducks swam in the creek, I sat on the grass, relaxed, sang in the sunlight.

I was very busy in the summer holidays. On the one hand, I had to do my homework. On the other hand, I wanted to help parents do some work. In the busy farming season, we worked in the sun. I felt very hot. But I went on planting, not stopping. At night, we had supper around the table with grandma. She is an old woman but healthy. She always talked much. Sometimes I was very tired and the eyes automatically closed, but she continued talking. So I had to say: "Grandma, if you don't mind, I will let my heart listen to you, I need to sleep."

When I was sixteen I finished my lessons in Middle School. Of my friends, three of us went on to the same school. Two boys went to another school and finished in two years. One became a doctor and the other a worker.

A particularly poignant glimpse into the hearts and minds of Chinese students of English came to PJ as a pile of notes. These had been written to an American teacher who ultimately left his job mid-year because he could not make lessons click. He had tried teaching American rap music to his literature students and had showed violent films like *The Terminator*. The students had been silent. He saw Chinese students counted and questioned at the gates and was outraged. He grew angry with the system and with students who would not talk in class, with people whose ideas about freedom and responsibility were so different from his. One day he exploded, calling his students apathetic and accusing them of laziness. He dismissed the class.

Over the next week, students sent him notes and letters, which he shared with PJ. They give us a rare and complex view of the thoughts behind those still faces, ranked two-by-two in desks bolted to the floor.

D——,

May you be not angry any longer for yesterday's literature class. Though under such a circumstance, whoever he may be, he would have raged. It is a disrespect of the teacher, indeed. Most of us are very sorry for that unhappy doing. Some of us hadn't done their assignment just because they wanted to depend on your giving the lesson. That's a cut way and more convenient. Usually you're so kind to your students, maybe you give them an impression that you're not a hard and serious teacher. I should say they didn't do that thing on purpose.

We're terribly sorry for making you so unhappy yesterday, Thanksgiving Day.

Dear D——:

How are you!

Today your sincere words moved me and threw me into deep thought. Thank you for your kindness and frankness to us; at the same time, I felt sorry for making you disappointed with us or our literature course.

As an American, you would like to be so concerned about a group of Chinese students and do your best to give them knowledge as well as teach them how to conduct themselves. These may show something beyond your conscientiousness and responsibility. As for this point, I have nothing to say except gratitude.

However, I feel it necessary to express some of my point views about your words. Generally, your statements to us are right. But I think there exists some misunderstanding between us. Being frank, your word "apathetic" made me uncomfortable. I don't think we are apathetic about everything. It may be unbelievable for you when I say that we are just apparently "apathetic." It is due to our introvert characters, not that we believe "silence is golden" (I think you were making a joke).

I'm not sure whether you remember, I have ever said, most of us would speak just when spoken to. We are inclined to keep everything in our minds instead of speaking out. For example, we all love our parents, and feel gratitude to them for what they do for us, but we never express our feelings with words, we only use other means. Maybe it's an obstacle for us, especially studying language. I hope I can improve it.

Furthermore, we love our country and hope she will get richer and more powerful, so I think most of us want to be responsible for her growth and development. And we are concerned about what's happening in the world and hope the world is full of peace. So we are far from "apathetic."

As for American literature, most of us have great interest in it, it's just hard for you to find it. There are many reasons. I agree with you that literature can broaden people's mind, and improve their ability of thinking. However, it cannot be used as means for making a life. Sometimes people need to master one or two practical skills to make a life. That's why students spend a lot of time on something else, instead of literature. So I don't think they are wasting time. Anyway, I'd like to extend my sorrow for taking an un-cooperative attitude to your class, sincerely!

I am not sure if I make things clear and you understand me. I wish I were a bridge to connect you and Chinese students and narrow the gap between us, and I wish you enjoy yourself in China in the new year.

D——,

At first you must be confident in your teaching. You are an excellent teacher. Most of the students think so, you know. Students are passive in your class, but it is not your problem, but ours. Every student thinks it is horrible. I have tried to collect suggestions from my classmates, but they themselves don't know how to solve the problem. Firstly, most students are not very interested in literature class. They have been studying literature for three years and are bored. Only a few of them have interests in literature, of course including me.

Secondly, Chinese students are not as active as American students. It is very common that when a teacher raises his questions, few students will answer him, even if most know the answer. Silence can carry all messages, and silence is the only way to answer the teacher.

By the way, I suggest you to have a test before you explain the text or novel. After students all have handed in the papers, you may ask students to answer these questions one by one. On the one hand, students have looked through the material and know it clearly. On the other hand, these questions are not very difficult to answer and they can find topics to talk about.

However, it is very natural that Chinese students still keep silent even if you have made great efforts to make your class active. Be confident in your teaching. Every foreign teacher has to face the same problem.

D——,

I dislike literature, but I admit that you teach well. I see that you want us to talk with you in the class and you try to make the class a good circumstance. It is not realistic. There are lots of differences between American customs and Chinese customs. You are in China, not in America. Chinese students have been in the habit of listening to the teacher in class. They don't want to show everyone their own opinion, even their classmates. They think that is show off.

Most of us do not have the custom to answer questions volunteerly, which is the main problem of the boring class. So, if you want us to be more active, if you hope we participate in the class discussion, you'd better call our names. Our last American literature teacher at first was annoyed by the same trouble you now have. Later, he solved it by calling our names and forcing us to speak.

I'm sorry that we Chinese students are not active like you American boys and girls. But, you should know this is mostly due to the culture difference.

D——,

Sometimes we do not answer your questions, not because we could not or something, but because we (or rather I) do not want to waste others' time to hear my opinion. They are probably not interested in my unsystematic and untheoretical opinion. They value what the TEACHER says only.

It's OK that you keep your way. Only be relaxed.

If you want us to remember something that we should master, you might write the key words on the blackboard. Or you might say something more detailed about the work.

To D——

Today is Thanksgiving Day. We brought a fresh roasted chicken instead of turkey. We wish you to be happy.
I brought a musical tape for you. I hope you like it.

Primarily, of course, teachers get to know their students through class assignments and related communiqués, often charming and unfailingly polite.

A Self-Introduction

My name is Jennifer. I passed my eighteen birthday a month ago. The most beautiful thing to me is play, not study. I'm interested in sports, music, literature and drawing. Especially I like literature and I often write something. Another thing I often do is walking under the setting sun alone. I do be crazy about the nature and have longed for a silent and natural life all along.

I'm not so easy to approach. But I really wish others could understand me and don't care of my strange, bad temper. I have many shortcomings. I'm not a hard student. Sometimes I make fun of others and cheat others to be happy. But I am a good friend that never does bad things to get my friends in trouble, and I'm also busy in helping old men, little kids. To tell the truth, I don't know which kind of person I am.

I also like animals and I can easily make a dog become friendly with me at the first meet.

Oh, I like to eat. That's my favorite hobby.

I like you, you're very frank and have a good sense of humor. Would you like to become my friend and don't care of my short-comings?

Hunter

My name is Lu Anhui in Chinese and my English name is Hunter. I came here to study for two years, but my English is poor. In last test I was failed. I came to realize that I must study hard. But I have many problems that need help. I think with your help, I would have progress.

I like popular songs and I sometimes dance. Sometimes I like to go see a film and watch TV.

This term I have many lessons. So after class I have to go over the lessons. Those interesting things which I often did in the last year now are far away from me. Oh! There is no way to change this state!

Every year when a new foreign teacher came, I must write self-introduction. I don't know how to introduce me well. And I don't know if you can know me. Yes? or no?

An Interesting Person in My Family

In my family the most interesting person is my husband. He is very kind and optimistic. He often makes us laugh.

I remember the thing which happened on my daughter's birthday. My friends and my daughter's little friend went to our house to celebrate. At the party, we all ate the cake and sang birthday's song. Just then, my husband went out the room quietly. After a while, a man wearing a rubber monkey face appeared at the door. "Monkey!" my daughter shouted. My daughter was fond of monkey very much. "I'm Monkey Sun.[9] Happy birthday to you!" Then he gave my daughter a very beautiful doll. "Let's dance," the monkey said. Following him, my daughter began to dance. Then we all danced, too. At the party, we were all enjoyable.

Some exercises reveal remarkable depths of expertise.

Dear Dr. White:

I am writing to inquire if you accept visiting scholars from outside the U.S.

I am a vice-professor in the Department of Diagnosis. I graduated from this university in 1964. I was engaged in teaching for 23 years, and I have been doing research on ultrasound diagnosis for 18 years. I have published 25 papers. Most of them are on ultrasound diagnosis of abdominal tumors, specifically the histological examination of ultrasonically guided fine needle

---

[9] The Monkey King is the main character in the classic Chinese epic *The Journey to the West*. His name is Sun Wugong, so here Sun is a surname.

puncture for diagnostic studies of malignant tumors. I'd like to prepare myself for further research in this field.

I have passed an official English exam and now I am on government sponsorship to do research and study abroad. I'm very interested in your college of Allied Health Sciences, and I'd like you to send me an application form and some other relevant information. My documents and references are available on request.

Thank you for your attention!

Others hint at a remarkably different sense of courtesy.

Dear Teacher J——,

I've received your correction, and I would like to appreciate your friendly help once again. I told my wife about how well you're working in our department and how carefully you've corrected my paper and she was deeply moved and said that we should give your mother something useful to express our thanks for your help.

But in the end, it is human warmth slipping through the language barrier that carries the greatest meaning, both ways.

Dear Teacher:

It is the lastist class today. I want to tell you, thank you for your help. Thank you very much. I miss you. Maybe I will be the one who most misses you in our class. I never forget you forever. Because you have helped me understand many something about English. I remember when I wrote the first time. I wrote in Chinese with English word. Later your teaching has me know how to write in English. I wrote about 20 English essays and diaries. I also wrote a long letter to my niece, a college English teacher. Although there are a lot of mistakes inside that, I think I made great progress.

Dear Teacher J——,

How are you doing?

It's a pity that today I can't have your class. You're very funny and your class is really interesting. It has been a long time

*since I found something wrong with my longest tiptoe. I haven't
cared about it until last night. My friend told me there will be
something very dangerous happening to it if I don't cure it on time.
You know, I am afraid of death, everyone does. I think I'd better
see the doctor at once.*
    Yours,

                                   Nancy

Learning about Limits

Learning to live in a new country and learning to teach in one, any
newcomer faces two crucial inner questions: "Who am I?" and "Where do
I stand?"

"What does a teacher do?" and "Am I a teacher or an entertainer?" are
common forms of the "Who am I?" question that appear in these letters.
"I still don't think I'm a dancing poodle," says Joe Márquez at one point,
reflecting on his feelings about the work, "more like a juggling shar-pei.[10]
I'm still young but the wrinkles are setting in."

"Where do I stand?" implies both "How much can I stand?" (as in how
much silence that looks like apathy or how many "loony" demands from
Professor Lu) and "Where will I take my stand?" (and demand that my
ethics and values be respected). When do I stop compromising and stand
up for what I think is right?

We all learn what we think is right in two main ways—by being told
and by seeing it done. Specifically, we learn how students are supposed to
behave because teachers say to us "Please pass your papers forward" and
"Settle down back there or you'll have to leave the room!" We also learn
what is right and wrong in class when we see fellow students flunked for
cheating and when grades are lowered on papers turned in late. By the
time these teachers come to China, they have absorbed a complete set of
classroom ethics they are hardly aware of—until it collides with a very
different set in the halls of Chinese academe.

---

[10] A breed of dog whose skin falls in heavy folds, especially around the face.

These letter writers are facing other collisions outside of class; the post office and transportation systems, for instance, are rattling their ideas about how public services are supposed to work. But most people have few *ethical* problems adapting to external systems like utilities, no matter how frustrating these seem. Within the classroom, however, teachers often feel they have both the right and the responsibility to establish rules and limits. And when students violate these rules, the teacher assumes an ethical responsibility to stand firm and mete out punishments. After all, isn't that part of the teacher's role?

New American teachers often feel the most responsibility to be firm and consistent regarding grades and cheating. Here the questions "Who am I?" and "Where do I stand?" involve deeply held ethical principles, and the price of almost any compromise can seem too high.

> KEVIN LAW-SMITH: Gave a test in my Cultural class on Saturday three weeks ago—everyone cheated. They had cheat sheets, notes, books, used their friends. I busted two guys three times—they had backup notes. I spoke to the Assistant Dean—he says fail them. So there it is. I was furious at first, but slowly took it as a joke. Unfortunately the students are hounding me: "Be fair, do me a favor." I'll give a make-up to the cheaters, then if they cheat again—I'll kill them.

"Who am I?" Kevin is asking. "What would a good teacher do in this situation?"

> MARLA JENKS: I had one awful class this week, and I wanted to knock their bloody little heads together. First of all, I asked them to turn in their journals, which only half had chosen to do. I made it crystal clear that the assignments were not optional. They looked at me sheepishly, but they still didn't seem to grasp the connection between completing the work and passing the class. They've grown up with an educational system that clashes with everything I believe. Teachers in China rarely give students lower than a B, not because the students are particularly bright, but because the teacher loses face if the students fail. Thus, the success

of a student reflects more on the teacher's effectiveness than the student's intellect. Another common practice is bribery. Students bring fruit and gifts to their teachers in exchange for good grades. There's nothing shady about it; it's just the way things are done.

Furthermore, some students blatantly sleep through class. Chinese teachers just stand at the front of the room and lecture, without much concern for what the students do in the back. But I walk around and physically shake anyone who thinks it's nap time. (Next week, anyone who's sleeping will be asked to leave the room.) Additionally, I would call on some people and they wouldn't even have their books open, or they'd be on the wrong page.

Which brings me to another problem. I'm teaching non–English majors, so my class is just a required class that many of them don't want to take. Additionally, they're all at very different levels of proficiency. Some can carry on a sort of normal conversation with me, but one guy couldn't even understand when I asked "What is your name?"

After this class I was really frustrated and talked to R—— about it. I was wondering if they're taking advantage of me because of my age, my foreignness, my sex, or something. She assured me that it wasn't my fault. It's the way they're used to behaving. Luckily, my class later that day went much better—I wanted to hug them all.

"So, where should I stand? What should I stand for?" Marla wonders. "What is my role as teacher in this class and in this culture?" The questions are particularly hard to resolve when the results on tests are dramatically mixed.

KEVIN LAW-SMITH: Have my cheater class tomorrow. On the test, one guy got 15 out of 100—great. Two people got 99, though. Average: lenient-as-hell 82.

One approach to these deep questions, as with so many others in the early months, is simply to stand aside from them.

Without the raw edge
or that feeling of wanting
to punch a hole through the night.
I come to my senses
slowly
on a lazy Changsha morning.

I know the chase is on
my moves are sideways.
Stepping away
from any direct confrontation.

Many rules surround me
and I know
none of them.

Keeping my focus
as my feet stand solid,
face to a new wind.
          Todd Hamina

ANONYMOUS: Can't believe it's December already! The rest of the teachers are all terribly concerned with who will get the A- or the B+, and even who in their classes might *fail*, but I try to avoid those topics (as well as most of the teachers) and focus more on what I can learn from the Chinese.

But developing the ability to stand aside in a genuine, satisfying, and *ethical* way involves real learning, because what is happening here is a cross-cultural clash between different sets of value.

Cultural values (like the U.S. value on individual responsibility) enter the classroom as codes for ethical behavior (do your own work). Most travelers do not realize this connection. They might understand that the Chinese have different values (say, a strong commitment to helping others in the group), but they think that ethics are the same all over the world (everyone believes we shouldn't cheat, right?).

When we go abroad, we take an unexamined code of ethics with us. Then we encounter a different set of values, and the whole ethical landscape shifts. How are we to react then—fairly, responsibly, and ethically? Who are we now? And where in this shuddering world will we stand? The Colorado China Council's orientation packet tries to prepare teachers for these questions with an essay.

•   •   •

Cheating or Cooperation?
a.k.a. The Individual v. the Group

Early in my career teaching ESL in China I got a surprising story when I asked my junior-year medical students to write about "the most exciting day of my life." One girl told about her first day of school when she was six. She had been raised in the countryside, away from other children, and was shy and frightened but filled with anticipation, too. Early on her first day, she said, the teacher called on her to answer a simple math problem and she froze. She stood to answer, as Chinese children are taught to do, but had nothing to say. Then her seatmate in the two-person desk whispered the answer. Her heart soared—not only was she able to satisfy the teacher, but she had found her first friend.

I thought about this anecdote often as I watched my students whisper to one another in my classes, openly prompt speakers who faltered, and spell out words for one another with their fingers in English and Chinese on the two-person desks. This all looked like what my own teachers in America would call cheating. Yet these were bright, diligent students here, and they passed help without furtiveness, apparently as a sign of friendship.

As time went by, I came to see in how many ways Chinese learning is far more a "cooperative" endeavor than in America. When one student began to lag far behind in any class, I only had to drop a slight hint and one or two others (often the brightest in the class) would quietly change seats the next week and begin coaching the weak one. I believe this help continued outside of class. Even among equals, there was constant cooperation. I once walked in on a group of Chinese teachers of English, reading over an assignment: One read it aloud while others called out corrections in pronunciation or repeated an unclear phrase. Whoever knew it called out a translation of the phrase and the whole group moved, easily and quickly, through the reading.

I came to believe that the differences in how Americans and Chinese study are rooted deeply in core values of our respective societies. Everything in America, and this includes the educational system, is designed to foster the individual's unique talents and to develop the ability to stand alone. Almost everything I saw in China seems to me to do the opposite. I believe the Chinese might say that their core value is to shape the individual for the good of the whole.

At a simply human level, American teachers new to the Chinese classroom must realize that most groups of students they teach will live and study together almost every minute of every day for their entire college careers. When these students are freshmen, they are far from home for the first time and look to their classmates for emotional support. By the time they are juniors, they have strong ties and suffer deeply if one of their friends fails to succeed in the program. Even in classes of adult students working together for only one term, the idea that the group welfare precedes individual wants is so strong that you will see that subtle shifting of seats so that, say, an engineer can whisper a translation of your instructions to a doctor. Is this cheating or cooperation? Are these students helping or hindering the teacher?

Each American teacher must answer these questions alone, in a strange country in a dramatically different educational environment. Since most Americans have a strong moral reaction against cheating, an important step for teachers new to China is to *refrain from judgment for at least a month*. The Chinese teaching term is very long (often 20 weeks), and there is plenty of time to get through any realistic syllabus. Go easy at first. Get to know the students. Try out a range of activities—take-home, in-class, individual recitations, group projects, impromptu readings, and memorized dialogues. See what they do well and watch how they work. Remember: Students in prestigious Chinese colleges scored in the top 10 percent on a national exam. In their own culture, they must be doing something right.

In planning your teaching strategies, ask yourself frankly *what's wrong with cooperative learning*? Find out exactly why they are taking your course. (This is a very good project, either orally or in writing, for the first class. It helps everyone if you give them a long list of possible options and let them select or add.) If they want to learn English primarily to pass a test, then of course it is important that they learn to function alone and under rigorous test conditions. But what if they primarily want English to listen to Voice of America (VOA) or to talk with foreigners or to read and write scientific articles? What if (perish the thought!) English is just a required course, of very little use to them outside of school? In most situations where they might really use English, remember that they will seldom be alone. Consider that opportunities to share information might even enhance their learning.

Whatever you decide to do around cheating versus cooperation, *consider introducing it as an exploration of a difference between our cultures* rather than as right versus wrong. My writing students, for example, were indeed studying primarily for 30-minute exams. It was very important that they learn to work alone and under a strict time limit. They strongly resisted my "no notes, no talking, no dictionaries" rule, and at first I had to tear the papers from beneath their pens at the end of 30 minutes. I constantly explained that, because I was an American, my requirements were probably far more rigorous than they would ever have on an actual test in China. And I stressed that this was a game, just practice, to help them get comfortable with a whole new way of writing. I also alternated these practice exams with rewriting assignments designed to be cooperative. And I sincerely praised the phenomenal work they eventually produced under both writing conditions.

The best teaching begins where the students are and moves them in a direction that both teacher and student agree is good. But for new teachers in China, "where the students are" is often a near mystery, and agreed-upon goals can be hard to find when our cultures start so far apart. I found it helpful during the dark periods to remember how I learned my own language the first time and how I began to learn Chinese—by simply hearing it and hearing it; by having mother, father, and friends prompt me over and over and laugh out loud when I got it right. In the long run, perhaps we do not need to decide whether anyone cheats or not. We just need to talk often with one another and to listen.

Phyllis L. Thompson
for the Colorado China Council
1992

•   •   •

Ethical issues in the classroom are just one of many lessons about limits that face American teachers in a Looking Glass World. More will follow. In the face of strange limits, anyone who chooses to stay working in China must find ways to adapt—either with help from outside, as Amanda did, or by adjusting old habits and feelings to fit better with reversals of custom.

By the end of the first term, the majority of teachers seem to find paths through the ethical and organizational mazes of the classroom and to arrive at various sorts of positive pragmatism.

G: Happy New Year! Just thought I'd check in with you before final exams—pretty tough finals I might add. My students, I've been figuring out, don't give a hoot about writing, except those preparing for (and scared out of their wits by) the Michigan Test. They informed me last week that the winter TOEFL[11] exam doesn't include a writing section. Bring on the antics and dancing poodle gig, the spicy lectures about American government conspiracies and sexual innuendo in advertising. So be it; it's the end of the term.

KEVIN LAW-SMITH: Class goes by as the days do—I realize I can't change their ways or thoughts—just try my best.

INGER: The teaching anxiety is finally calming down. I've resigned myself to just going into class every day and winging it. Since all my classes are conversation (except the freshmen language lab, which has a book), this seems to be what they prefer. I stopped beating my head against the wall of lesson plans.

TEDDY KELLAM: I enjoy my teaching immensely, can teach now, but I also realize my role as entertainer, so I try to balance education and comedy as best I can. Last term was so busy, but this term I've decided to curb my "usefulness" as an English-speaking tool. I have my friends, and a zillion students, and my

---

[11] Test of English as a Foreign Language (see Rachel Coleman's letter in this chapter about her TOEFL sharks).

wonderful Mandarin teachers, and those people are my priorities. Funny how you finally pick up all the useful skills—language, assertiveness, a teensy bit of wisdom, and suddenly, it's just about time to leave!

G: Someone passed on a gem to me which I now recognize as close to truth: That in the first year, you will learn about 70 percent of all that you'll learn in China, 30 percent the second and ensuing years. They were speaking mainly about cross-cultural communication, but in fact, this may be true of teaching as well.

DAVID MOLDAVSKY: One piece of advice that I would give anyone coming over here is, always keep in mind the benefit you're getting, and try to learn at least as much as you try to teach. If you attempt to convince yourself that you're going to change China and the Chinese, then you will be awfully disappointed. China is opening itself to the West, but it's going to take a hell of a long time before there are fundamental changes to this country. We foreigners really are like drops in the ocean, making only small temporary ripples. And so I say, at least let us take in some of that water around us and learn something from it.

Learning!

TEDDY KELLAM: My own *laoshi* is Mrs. Liu, who has taught me Mandarin Chinese for over a year now. We have the classic relationship of wise, tolerant teacher and adoring student, but also a very close kinship. So I learn, the most natural way possible—by chatting, joking, gossiping, and often pouring out my heart—in Chinese.

AMANDA MYERS: OK OK—I'm being completely manic jumping around from subject to subject. Did I mention I'm studying calligraphy? It's such a beautiful art form. My teacher gave me a name stamp as a gift but says that I may not use it until my work is worthy of it. It would disgrace my name (and his, as my teacher) if I stamped a poor work of calligraphy he says. So now I'm all the more motivated to produce my first masterpiece.

P.S. A student gave me a bag of some dried fruit last week. I thought they must be dates, as I've never eaten dates before. Stayed up late one night reading and munching on them. Ate the whole bag. About 50. Turns out they were PRUNES! As if I don't have enough BOWEL problems!

Chengdu, Sichuan

Dear All:

I am sitting here in my green-carpeted flat having a bowl of noodles and a cup of tea. I'm writing with my new—most beautiful—pen, given to me by one of my wonderful students. They still use fountain pens here—and they are *so* lovely to write with. It is a pity we've essentially given them up in the West. The day, of course, is GRAY. It's so gray that you can visibly see a layer of this "grayness" only yards away. The cacophony of honking & bleeping goes on in the background. Chinese voices yell out; a flute's notes rise up from some flat.

Alive. Whatever else it is, China is greatly ALIVE. Unpretentious, un-self-conscious, She *is* a living enigma of perfection & chaos ceaselessly intertwining from moment to moment.

So much . . .

There is no such thing as a typical day here, each one seems to have a character *all* its own, but I'll describe yesterday & give you a feel. I awoke at 6:00 A.M. in pitch blackness as I do every morning, to the buzz of my tiny tinny alarm, struggled out of bed, stumped into the kitchen to boil H_2O for coffee (uh, yup: Instant. There's no such thing as French roast here!). Started reviewing lesson plans for my 8:00 o'clock class with the TOEFL Sharks, as I have lovingly entitled this group.

They are voracious & unforgiving: "Knowledge, knowledge, knowledge!" they demand. And they accept nothing but pure "meat"—anything less is frivolous & a goddamn waste of their time. They let you know it in *no* uncertain terms by snorting & staring off into space when they are not receiving the "feeding" they expect! Yes, these students are not some ignorant bunch of bright-eyed innocents. THEY WANT TO PASS THE TOEFL TEST! THEY WANT TO GET TO AMERICA AND STUDY! For some, the only ticket out is to study abroad, and to study abroad they must pass the TOEFL, and to pass the TOEFL they must have a larger English vocabulary & better comprehension skills than most educated Americans! It is a *gruesome* gruesome test—and most of them never make it. The other day one of them (the class monitor as a matter of fact) came up to me over break (two-hour class) and asked, "What is the difference between 'doctrine,' and 'dogma'?" (Omigod!) Luckily I came up with something & kept myself from being eaten alive in utter disdain, which would have happened if I had not *known* the answer ON THE SPOT.

Uh, anyway, so class prep for this one is fairly intense & I must really be on my toes. I got to class, unfurled my lesson plan, and put my Sharks to work. I made them read, identify the topic, summarize, & hit the main points of passage after passage after passage—they were utterly drained and ecstatic by the end of class: The Feeding Frenzy was over! I handed them two lists of vocabulary words, which I type up every week for them with definitions, synonyms, example sentences (only takes me about four hours a week!), with words like *hyperbole, oxymoron, nepotism*.

So I'm packing up—with a bit of an inner glow, because I know my Sharks are well fed—when one of them swims up to me, apparently not quite stuffed to the gills and demands, "What is the difference between 'egoism' & 'egotism'?" (Here we go again!) I said, "Ego is a concept created by Freud & is an essential part of our nature, therefore 'egoism' can be healthy self-centeredness. 'Egotism' is the misuse of that same principle; to be conceited." "Oh," he said sort of dreamily as he copied these new-found nutrients into his Journal of Shark Cuisine.

To be absolutely honest, I adore these students, and I think they know that, but they are certainly a constant challenge for me!

After class, I sat and talked with my best buddy, Jaffa—she &

I have become survivalist soul-mates here in Panda Land. We were then invited to a fabulous lunch by the three German doctors studying Chinese medicine—laughing, chatting; they all have excellent senses of humor & a genuine loving, loving warmth— quite contrary to the stereotypical cool, austere Deutschlander!

After lunch I had a few moments to put together some vocabulary words, then a knock on my door. It was "Lionel," one of the students from my Reading class (these are normal, happy, easygoing students). He is a real character—strong, alive, vibrant, & very vocal. He is quite an anomaly here in China, methinks! For the first time, we sat & talked like people, not teacher and student, and this wonderful gem began to shine. He's only 22 & gives the impression of being a real goof-off. As it turns out, he is a physics major with quite a proclivity for math. And as he talked, he began using quotes from Plato, Socrates, Nietzsche, & Kant! It was chilling. This young lad had a love of art & philosophy that rivalled the best, yet he wants to be a physicist. But he cannot because in 1989 during "the event"[12] he played a role that landed him in prison, & they took away his "approval" to study as a regular student. (His class is in the Language Center, which serves workers who enroll privately or are sent by their work units to improve their English; other departments serve full-time enrolled students.)

During the course of our conversation, two other students dropped by, one to drop off a borrowed TOEFL example test, the other to pick up a letter of recommendation I'd written for his girlfriend who wants to study abroad. It was now 5:00 P.M. & I had a *wushu* lesson at 5:30. So Lionel departed & I quickly changed and walked to the park to meet my two *wushu* teachers.

During TOEFL class one day, I'd mentioned that I do some martial arts & would love to study more here. A few days later,

---

[12] The student protests in Tiananmen Square in Beijing in 1989, in which military police fired on students (and others) pushing for more freedoms in China. Hundreds of protestors were arrested, an unknown number killed. Similar protests and arrests took place in several large cities in China, although only the deaths in Beijing made most Western news reports.

one of my students comes up to me in class & says, if I don't mind, he would introduce me to a *wushu* teacher. Mind? That would be great! So he takes me over to a very tall older fellow & introduces him as one of the athletic directors at our university—this is all in the classroom, one of my own students. The athletic director says that he basically teaches track & field, but if I'd like to learn *wushu* he will introduce me to Mr. L——, another athletics teacher & his colleague. This introduction happens a week later & we start lessons. Mr. L—— is the teacher and my student is interpreter!

Wushu is unbelievably hard. I thought being a black belt in *tae kwon do* might be good for something (!), but as it turns out, for *wushu* it just gets in the way. Empty your Cup. (Though actually, in the kicking, jumping, & turns, it is helpful. It is just that *wushu* uses all these intricate, to-the-floor stances & "poses" that are really the antithesis of *tae kwon do*.) Also, I have started *tai ji quan* classes (it's called *tai ji* or *tai chi* in America). It's led by this beautiful, stately old man with gray-white hair, who wears a constant expression of equanimity. He's beautiful, and so is *tai ji*—slow, graceful, elegant, & deep, and painful as *!@#?! on your thighs! So I do that Tuesdays & Thursdays, and *wushu* on Fridays.

Soooooo back at the park: We all three worked out for two hours—yes, always drawing a crowd. Any time a foreigner is doing something, people come and observe, then shuffle on. One day I went to the park to sketch the beautiful old pavilion—I felt like I was a freak show at the circus. Children, adults, everyone stopped, hung over my shoulder, peered down over the front of my sketch pad as if to assess if American art is really as good as Chinese. Many just shook their heads & turned away. Some stayed & watched. I heard snatches of *bu hao huar* ("bad picture") and *hen haode hua haur* ("good art"). Strange. Two little girls stayed with me for about one hour. They just stood above me on some steps & watched—dark shining eyes.

So, yes—crowds. We walked back toward home after our workout, and my two "teachers" (by the way, Mr. L—— is very young, maybe 23, 24, & is a champion *wushu* competitor; my student is older, in his 30s, and is much more patient & gentle), they asked if I'd like to go dancing with them sometime & to a *huoguo* afterwards. It took me by surprise. It was really a sweet gesture and indicates another level of personal acceptance, beyond just the business of *wushu*.

Got home—sore; into the tub. Raced off to dinner with Jaffa —at this *great* restaurant, the Bamboo Bar. Talked about the Universe. Got back (about 10 P.M.). Tomouki, the Buddha-like Japanese studying here, was out in the courtyard and invited us in for tea & laughter. Tomouki has a saintlike visage and a sense of humor unequaled in this compound. He knows about as much English as we do Chinese, so we always converse in this bizarre & funny mixture of lingo & body language. That wrapped up about 1:30 A.M. And that was a day.

Honest to god, life is like that every day here. There is always something going on and *always* things left undone. It is beautiful and chaotic & flowing, just like the mayhem of bicycle madness. It all works, but ONLY if you do not resist—go with the wacko flow.

With great, great Love from China. Please write.

All my love,

Rachel

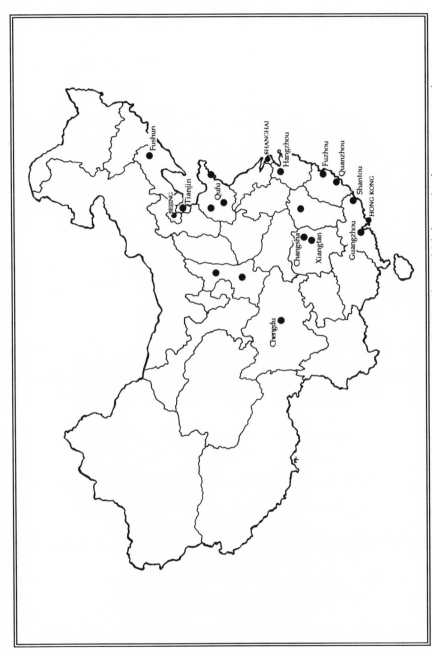

Map 6. The People's Republic of China, showing the cities from which letters in chapter 5 were written.

CHAPTER FIVE
VOCABULARY

baijiu (**by-joe**): strong rice wine, which PJ describes as "a white hard liquor in the turpentine family."

danwei (**don-way**): the work unit, which provides a job, pay, housing, and other necessities to its members. Each American teacher's *danwei* is the school in which he or she lives and works.

dim sum (**deem-sum**): a highly varied selection of bite-sized delicacies, especially popular in southern China.

mapo doufu (**ma-poh dough-foo**): tofu (bean curd) cooked in spicy meat sauce.

waishiban (**wy-shuh-bon**): same as *waiban*, the Foreign Affairs Office.

CHAPTER FIVE

Fame, Fortune, and Festivals

I was interviewed for the campus radio's special New Year's Eve
broadcast! Wow, I'm famous!

Nicky Combs

Fame

Of all the new things American teachers face in China, perhaps the
most unexpected is celebrity. Being Caucasian in a country that is 95
percent Han Chinese[1] means you just stand out!

DALE ASIS: In my local noodle stand, it is common for thirty
Chinese to gather and watch me slurp my noodles. Their eyes are
saying, "He almost eats like a human being." Every move I make
is watched by others.

MARLA JENKS: The most notable event this week was probably
the elevation of my "freak show" status to new heights! People
stare around here like I'm a creature from the pages of *National
Geographic*.

The little kids walking home from school stop, stare, poke
each other, and giggle. The university students pass by, but continue to jerk their heads around, as if they expect me to undergo
some kind of transformation and they don't want to miss it. The

---

[1] Most native Chinese (90–95 percent) are considered to be of the Han race; the remaining
5–10 percent, classified as minorities, represent hundreds of groups, including Turkish, Naxi,
and Manchu.

people in town nearly fall off their bikes as they ride by with wide eyes and gaping mouths. Even our students make fun of our appearance. Brian's think he has a big nose and hair like instant noodles. Matt's are intrigued by his blue eyes and very blond hair. Mine are also intrigued by my eyes, and they say I look like a Native American. I would think that by now most Chinese would have seen enough Westerners so that they wouldn't act as though we have two heads and three eyes. And most don't, but the ones who do stare nearly pop their eyeballs out of their sockets.

The other day, as Y—— and I walked to lunch, I noticed a girl who kept looking at me as if she knew me. Thinking it might be a student, I stopped and said hello. As soon as I took notice of her, her face lit up and she came scurrying over to me. She put her face close to mine and peered into my eyes as if something were hidden there. Then she burst out excitedly, "I love you!"

I smiled uncomfortably and stepped back to reclaim my personal space. She asked my name and shook my hand eagerly. When I asked what her name was, she told me and then wrote it for me in characters. I nodded and told her it was wonderful and again she said, "I love you!" as she scampered off to join her friends.

In the dining hall people continued to gaze in fascination. Y—— and I sat down and a group of Chinese people promptly positioned themselves for the best possible view. It's somewhat disconcerting because they fix their gaze and stare unblinking-ly—even when I stare back. It's like I'm an animal on display. During lunch I started to wave at them and they fell into fits of laughter.

Sometimes the phenomenon amuses me, but sometimes I find it so rude and annoying. It's not like there's any reason to be flattered, either. They don't stare in admiration—they think we're aberrant.

So American teachers in China suddenly find they have something in common with the Rich and Famous—wishing they could hide from a curious public. But being very noticeable can have its advantages, too.

KATIE SHOWALTER: One of our third-year students took me and K——— to a calligraphy exhibit. Interestingly, the student said she had come the day before and no one spoke to her. But because *we* were there, the director walked us through the exhibit, explained which pieces were good and which were so-so, and told us the names of each style. He explained what some of the characters meant, and how to know what a good stroke looks like. Fascinating stuff.

MICHAEL MAY: The past month has been pretty interesting. Another foreign teacher and I became actors for three days. We got to play British soldiers during the Opium War. Unfortunately, we got our butts kicked! Our uniforms went through many transitions, mainly in an effort to attempt historical accuracy. Our first uniforms consisted of Spanish conquistador pantaloons, tights, and a Trojan helmet. The crew finally opted for red modified-PLA (the People's Liberation Army) band uniforms. As my partner said, "We looked like Charles DeGaulle (me) and John Philip Sousa (him)."

It was fun in the beginning until we were forced to become real actors. "Do it smartly," they advised us. I think I caused some problems when I was supposed to show fear. "Stop laughing," said the director. But, finally, I successfully finished the scene and the director praised me. "See, you can do a good take when you want." (I was quite surprised that he didn't include "Babe" in his words of praise.) Well, I have to get back to my adoring fans; you know what it's like to be a star.

BRIAN CAMPBELL: Two weeks ago, one of my students told me that she loved me. I was speechless. I said, "Well, uh . . . you're a good student." The most personal thing I had ever done with her was attend her birthday party. So this week when another girl I had met only once invited me to her birthday party, I declined. No use getting married off to someone I can't really talk to, I figure. My ego is going to be shot when I return home.

DALE ASIS: I teach a lecture open to all students every Friday night, and I do pack them in. Last Friday, I taught them about Thanksgiving, the Pilgrims, turkey, and football games. At least 200 students were there. After class, they ask for my autograph. I feel like a rock star in China!

For its size, China has a remarkably homogeneous population. In much of the United States, "variety is the spice of life" on every street; we expect to see different colors of skin and hair, new clothes, and new cars. In China, where a single kind of shampoo and a standard loose-cut jacket can suit a huge percentage of people just fine, the variety of hair, eyes, and clothing that foreigners display is a marvel. And as Marla Jenks observes, the marvelous is sometimes a little suspect in a country that values fitting in.

Ultimately, however, the pluses and the minuses of fame as an alien seem to balance out, and teachers learn to flow pretty well into the strange places their celebrity takes them.

MATT THIBODEAU: After class last week a student approached me (he was the monitor) and said he needed to set up a meeting with me to discuss something *very* important. I was worried I had become too controversial in class and this was the "break your kneecaps" meeting with the Party members. Luckily, the *very* important meeting was to discuss whether I would be interested in attending his brother's wedding! I explained that, since I didn't know his brother and I barely knew him, it might be a bit awkward. Jack assured me this wouldn't be a problem, so we set off to his hometown. I knew I really couldn't go wrong, Alice, since I was traveling with none other than Jack London[2]—and he's not shy about telling you this!

Instead of being a one-day trip, I was kidnapped for three days and paraded about the streets of Nanjing. On wedding day, after the bride and groom had met with friends and family in their

---

[2] Matt Thibodeau's student has adopted the name of an American he admires.

"nest" (bedroom), they left for the reception, which I was told would start at 5:00. I stayed behind with grandma and the baby in the apartment. Finally at 6:00 they came to fetch me and took me to the hall for what turned out to be my Grand Entrance. Yes, the reception had started at 5:00, but they wanted to build a suitable amount of expectation for The Foreigner. Anyway, all 300 heads turned as I was ushered in *arm-in-arm* with a bride and groom I'd known for a grand total of one hour!

I hoped I could escape notice by sitting anonymously at a back table, but no, I was seated at the groom's *right hand* at the head table! And boy! They all wanted me to smoke, and while I was smoking they *expected* me to drink. I was told I *must* do a toast and a shot of *baijiu* with all thirty tables—and they were vehement on this point. I was getting a bit angry at what I "must" do, so I refused to smoke or drink anymore. Jack London became *very* tense. Finally things loosened up and I did a few "room" toasts in English and Chinese and posed in a million pictures with strangers using my film and camera. (Jack London has now demanded *his* pictures—slight cultural difference.) When the night was over Jack London looked at me and said, "I'm satisfied now; you've added *great atmosphere*."

And this, Alice, sums up the whole year!

ZUBIN EMSLEY: I was invited to the coast to visit a student's family in their village (population 250). The first foreigner since the Japanese invasion gets lots of attention. His peasant family ate like royalty that week. Every meal was a seafood banquet. Who would have thought that jellyfish would replace corn flakes? The hot rice wine with eggs helped against the 50° breeze wafting through the house and made me less aware of the open doors and glassless windows. In the next village we watched Shaoxing opera in the old Taoist temple. It was out of my world.

DOUG THOMPSON: Last month, I was approached by Hunan Radio to do an interview. They discovered I spoke Chinese and was teaching international banking and international trade. The other foreign teacher here also had an interest, so they asked her too. The interview explored what, in our opinion, Changsha should do in the area of international finance and economic development. Yesterday, we learned that the mayor of Changsha and the governor of Hunan heard the broadcast and they felt some of our ideas had merit. So we have been asked to attend a meeting of Chinese regional leaders (a development think-tank of sorts) to elaborate on our ideas. The *waishiban* is excited, and informed friends here say that it will be an important meeting.

JEANNE PHILLIPS: I've been on TV being interviewed a couple of times, in a local magazine talking about tourism, and most recently was taped for an hour and a half (to be edited down to eight minutes, I think) for broadcast as part of a new English-language program to start in the fall. Fun, but I sure wish I could do it over and say more sensible things. We are all used to being glimpsed on the evening news, since the cameras always train on us at any event, I guess to show that people come from all over the world. Entering the opera and later in our seats, the spotlights shine in our eyes. But long ad lib interviews are a different matter.

TODD HAMINA: I took part in a bicycle race in Changsha on New Year's Day and was on local news because I was the only foreigner both racing my bike *and* helping the reconstruction of New China.[3] Someone thought this pre-race interview was a gem, so I made nationwide television on the Tuesday night sports show. My ride of pride was a fourteen-year-old Yellow Wind, which was built for speed in Shanghai. It was easily the biggest piece of shit out there. The course was a lilting 18K out in the country east of the train station. The weather sucked as did my health, but since I'd already paid the entry fee I had no choice but to ride.

P.S. 13th of 126 in race, with cold + hangover.

---

[3] This refers to a polite Chinese phrase which means, in Todd's case, "teaching English."

KATIE SHOWALTER: P—— has an American friend in Beijing who's working PR, and she's also the star of the newest, hottest TV show, "Foreign Babes in Beijing." The taxi drivers know her. She did a racy, semi-nude scene, but made the director and camera crew and everyone else strip, too—which has made quite a sensation in the newspapers and mags.

Fortune

American teachers have all the *money* they need . . .

MARY BRACKEN: I was on Radio Guangdong (with my sophomore class) on April 1st. No, it's not an "April Fools'." Really! They wanted to record a foreigner's Spoken English class. I also teach five businesspeople at night, so have plenty of money. Who could ever imagine $230/month would be *more* than ample. It's strange how your expectations change after living in the PRC.

KEVIN LAW-SMITH: Signed contract last week—1,400 ¥. I get by on 400 if no big purchases like kilos of hash or pot and that opium habit is tough to keep up. Just kidding—beer is it. Trust me.

INGER: I find my stipend sufficient, especially since I make extra money at the kindergarten. Shantou is an expensive place to live, but 1,350 ¥ is plenty to live on.

. . . plus *luxuries* beyond the imagination of most Chinese.

TODD LUNDGREN: Eileen's aunt sent us some gourmet hot-chocolate packets, and the last two mornings we've made Nescafé mochas. Today's flavor was Irish Cream. Ah, decadence!

JEANNE PHILLIPS: As a gift to myself, I spent two nights at the best joint-venture hotel,[4] reveling in a bathtub full of foaming bubbles and hot water, central heating, easy access phone to call long distance, and American-style breakfast buffet—three glasses of OJ, toast, bacon and eggs are all it takes to make my day spectacular. The real treat, though, was the TV—four channels of Hong Kong TV via satellite, including 24 hours of BBC's news service. It is too brief and repetitive to compete with the great BBC shortwave news or with CNN, but what a treat! Little sleep for me from staying glued to it.

DALE ASIS: I'm going to travel to Hong Kong for the semester break to recharge. I am going to buy enough cheese, chocolate, pasta, and good coffee to last me one more term. I can't wait to have a good glass of orange juice.

INGER: I'm now in Hong Kong at Howard's dining table feeling oddly as if I'd never left this average opulence we live with in the West. Yesterday we (a foreign teacher from the U came with me) went to McMecca and were just happily dazed by the things you can get in H.K. I'm not buying much since my budget is very low.

It's good discipline living in China; there you buy what you can find since there are many things you "need," but here in Hong Kong I recognize most of the things I see as mere "wants" and have no problem resisting. Yesterday I bought Gulden's mustard and a half-price, date-expired bag of Tostitos. I would like to find a used clothing place to buy a men's suit coat to take back for the winter. We've got four more days to shop and try to remember all of the things we wanted so badly.

Even the relatively normal activities of American teachers in China often add up to full, rich lives unknown to the average Chinese.

---

[4] At the time of these letters, businesses owned jointly by both Chinese and foreign interests were just beginning to become common in China.

RACHEL COLEMAN: A couple of weeks ago, Jaff & I went to a Chinese circus (as if normal life isn't a circus?). It was amazing. Old, dingy, frayed setting. Equipment that must have been around since the Qing dynasty.[5] But the performers were stunning, talented, & indeed, death defying. After the performance we sneaked back behind the ratty curtains & were greeted with great excitement, shown all around, given tea in dingy plastic cups, & had a great "conversation" with them all (understanding not a word), as the little children (also performers) peered out from behind their parents' coattails.

Last weekend, the whole *danwei* of the Language Center and about half of all the students organized a trip to YaAn. It is a sweet, small, fresh-air town nestled up in the mountains of Western Sichuan. We went to a beautiful mountain temple & climbed & climbed; sat & drank tea in a lofty summit teahouse; and an old monk came out & read some fortunes for people off sticks selected out of a big vase. I had mine read. It was very poignant; something about harmony & success in "outside" ventures. The mountain is covered in bushes whose tea is famous all over Sichuan. So we bought tea. The next day we went to a beautiful lake & paddled around in small pedal-wheeled boats. On the way home we stopped for a great dinner and bought oranges —also famous in this area. Got home exhausted, silly, & satisfied.

Tonight there's a birthday party for S—— (Italian); tomorrow, Jaff & I are having a dinner party for four friends. This afternoon, one of my students is taking me to find sweaters. . . .

So much.

KEVIN LAW-SMITH: To give you a quick rundown of things, events, happenings: *2nd week* here went to Taishan, 6,000 steps straight up, saw the sunrise, slept that night on rocks, 6,000 steps down. Wow. *3rd weekend*, the Great Wall, school-sponsored trip —excellent, didn't have to pay for anything. As expected the Wall

---

[5] The last imperial dynasty, extending from the mid-1600s to 1911.

was great. *5th weekend*, National Day and Moon Festival—oh boy. Spent the weekend in Beijing; saw the raising of the red flag 6:05 A.M. on National Day and then at sunset I saw the downing of the flag. My day as a Commie. Of course I ate at McDonald's and, I hate to admit it, at Kentucky Fried Chicken. (There was nowhere to sit and relax at Beijing U—so many, many people—so KFC it was.) Sat by the lake, watched the row boats. *6th weekend*, big foreign student party at Tianjin University; oh boy, the bike ride back after eight beers—those liter kind. Wow. I think I got to know every wall, tree, garbage can, curb from Tianjin University to here. Won't be doing that again soon. *This weekend*, saw *Platoon* tonight at school—oooh Boy!! Also went to Danshan, mountain near here—another school-sponsored trip.

Saw a great, great movie. *Farewell My Concubine*. Amazing. Issues—homosexuality, politics, Cultural Revolution. China is really opening up.

Loving life
Food's great
Beer's cheap
Girls are short

MARY BRACKEN: Tomorrow night I'm going to (SERIOUSLY) see Paul Simon, who's playing at the stadium here. Pretty wild, huh? I'm going with a couple from Innsbruck, Austria, who've been married a year.

ADAM WILLIAMS: Over Chinese National Day/Mid-Autumn Moon festival, some friends and I went north to Inner Mongolia. It's so beautiful. In many ways it reminds me of northern New Mexico. Of course there were no margaritas, pastel coyotes howling at day-glo moons, or dolled-up tourists in white cowboy boots. Just corn, chili, and many earthen walls.

TODD LUNDGREN AND EILEEN VICKERY: We climbed Taishan, which was a truly magical experience: the fall colors, the stone steps, the sunrise, the stone steps, the 200 people with whom we watched the sunrise, the amazing views, and again the stone steps.

Climbing on stone is much different from the mountain climbing in Colorado, and our legs groaned for days.

Our other little journeys around town have been fantastic. We need only go into town to be in the heart of a historic wonderland, and only a ways out of town in any direction to see the less-frequented spots—the best places. We were invited two weekends ago to speak in the FAO director's hometown. The town is south of Taishan and is a coal-mining area. It is the best incentive we have seen to ban every polluting device, from autos to industry, in the U.S. It was, literally, an environmental disaster, and we both mourned for China and its people. The people, though, seem to bear it and are wild and wonderful hosts and neighbors.

Noblesse Oblige

Relative wealth + Celebrity status = Power, and this is a form of power egalitarian young Americans often find uncomfortable, or at least unfamiliar. Most U.S. teachers in China shy away from this power potential or remain only vaguely aware of it. But a few manage it like the gentry they have become, doing good works . . .

> ADAM WILLIAMS: I've joined a group of foreigners and Chinese students who are putting on a benefit concert for an orphanage here in Tianjin. It's an insanely dismal place. But whenever students pop in to surprise the nurses, things change. We are trying to involve as many local students as possible.

. . . and acting as patrons . . .

> JEANNE PHILLIPS: I hope to make several short jaunts to places in Fujian, with former students whose current jobs with schools or colleges give them the same long break I have for Spring Festival. Their friends will all be working, distances in the city are slow to cover by bike, and they are afraid to be out a lot late at night, so

these holidays are actually rather boring for them—hence a jaunt with me is attractive. I'd cover the minimal (for an American; not for them) costs and they would handle all the talking—a lovely arrangement for all.

. . . and "graciously" submitting to the ritual demands of their unelected position.

Fuzhou, Fujian

Dear Alice,

It has been a strange week. I suppose it's sorta funny, but I'm not sure. I have been asked to co-host a river trip that the Education Commission of Fuzhou is sponsoring. Everybody gets fifteen minutes of fame? Come to China and get two or three hours. On a boat. Going downriver.

I was excited about a boat trip on the Min River; they're showing us some interesting sights, they'll tell us some history. But today the Education Commissioner came to our house "to ask our opinion about it." Whatever that means. He has games planned like pick-up-the-marble-with-chopsticks and hit-the-gong-while-blindfolded. He wanted us to suggest a few more. And he wants us to perform, as usual. When we commented that performing was not how Westerners relaxed, he chuckled. Ha, ha.

Anyway, I was in the wrong place at the wrong time. My mistake was letting on I knew Chinese. He asked me to help him host. Everyone else, afraid they'd be asked next, cheered and clapped and said, "We unanimously vote for Katie." What do I say? It's like being asked to the prom by some guy singing to you at the top of his lungs in the school cafeteria (no, that never happened to me). How could I pass this job off? I grimaced and said "yes" (and later on "thanked" my fellow teachers for "supporting" me). The good news is, I'm a ham and I may be able to pull this off with my sanity intact. The bad news is, he wants me to come up with some humorous banter. Ya, right. This guy speaks English fine. I really think they just want to showcase a "foreign friend." I guess this'll be funny after next week.

[And so . . .] Remember the boat trip I was "asked" to co-host? (Quote marks exist because I firmly believe a "no" would not have been acceptable. Our dean and a few other big shots at our school have been knocking on the doors of teachers who've been declining invites. L—— refused to talk on a radio show, so an army jeep showed up and she was escorted to the station. Want fame? Come to China!) I had just gotten around to convincing myself that this hosting could be fun when the Education Commissioner dropped by with my script: a good four or five pages worth of cursive Chinese characters. Aiya!

I can hardly read characters anymore, let alone cursive (imagine various squiggly lines written in place of key parts of the character, making it virtually impossible to look up in a dictionary). Worse, he then asked me to help him translate some introductions to performances. Like I know the word for "hula hoop" or "wind instrument" in Chinese. Yeah, sure. Well, I do now. Anyway, two hours of translating later, I am cursing the day I decided to study Chinese. Aiyo!

I had to have our *waiban* read the script out loud to me so I could write it in a mix of legible characters and pinyin. Then I had to go through and figure out which characters should be said together to form words—a terrible, long, stupid process altogether. I guess the bright side is, that's the most written Chinese I've studied since I got here. And I learned how to say "hula hoop." Almost as important as "beer foam," really.

Anyway, then we went on the boat trip. We left the dock at 8:30 A.M. We arrived home that evening after 6:00. I saw almost nothing because I spent the whole way out practicing my lines with my co-host and translating the lottery prizes. We stopped at an island to take a walk. That was the best part of the whole trip. I really enjoyed that . . . until the Education Commissioner (name's Yang) started herding us like animals. J—— and I tried to escape and get a few photos, but he followed us, running after us to tell us the road was too difficult, we should turn back. Oh, and there's a military base here, too. Egad.

But he did manage to herd our bevy of "foreign friends" and Chinese people back to the boat. Once on board we began the entertainment. He opened the program by announcing that the performances and games would last three hours. Yes, win over your audience with the first sentence out of your mouth, Yang. I don't know one Westerner or even Chinese who has an attention span that lasts an hour.

The first game was called Pass the Pig. Like Hot Potato, but when the music stops, whoever has the pig "gets" to perform. If you can't perform, you can opt to pick up glass balls with chopsticks, hit a gong blindfolded, or an assortment of fun things. Then, whoever performed picks lottery tickets. Then we would call the lottery numbers, and those people would win a prize, such as a cannon-shaped clock, a plastic crocodile imprisoned in a glass prism, a heart-shaped plastic music box, or a clip-on tie and belt set. Then the prize winners had to draw straws. Shortest straw performed. Neat. Then the amateur performers chose an act from a list of professional performers (i.e., acrobatics or singing). So then we watched someone spin hula hoops around her ponytail, ankles, and waist, or watched magic tricks, or heard someone sing much too loudly. And this cycle just continued on and on for three hours. People were falling asleep. Even my illustrious co-host was getting bored with it. And all this on a rocking boat, no less. (Did I mention TV news cameras, also?)

By the time we arrived on land, all I wanted was a shot of tequila. I settled for a beer.

Katie

Festivals

Outside of educational boat tours and weddings with foreigners as "atmosphere," foreign teachers attend plenty of real parties in China. On the Chinese side, there is The Banquet, almost a national art form. Americans experience these most commonly in two basic types.

Banquet Type A is a public affair.

JEANNE PHILLIPS: I went with local "big potatoes" (slang is a bit behind the times) to a banquet at a new hotel opening the next day, built with Indonesian money. We went because the manager of the hotel used to be the middle-school student of the woman heading our English program. Since the banquet was apolitical, we were spared the thirty minutes of speeches beforehand, but that also meant no time to maneuver into position for the charge to the buffet.

These events always have dozens and dozens of different dishes, all beautifully presented, often in arrangements that are like pictures of animals or flowers. But there is no queue, just a rugby scrum push-shove-kick-elbow mass attack. Even at banquets in honor of foreign teachers, given by the foreign affairs provincial office in the fall, we fare badly in the plate-filling department because the host organization and friends know the drill far better.

This banquet had a new twist—they kept bringing out new dishes as old ones emptied, and had many more tables dotting the big room. So the battle would be joined anew whenever someone spotted a waiter with a new haul. Table inspection tours by our rivals alternated with their eating from heaping plates while stationed firmly in front of a table that looked ready for replenishment.

The foods at this one were unusually varied and delicious, even satay skewers of barbecued meat and *dim sum* delicacies, and the booze flowed freely. The Old Ladies I was with and I all avoided the flaming *maotai*, but the fruit juice turned out to be OJ with a heavy dose of rum, so I switched from beer to that and all the Old Ladies became quite merry and red-cheeked. Luckily the college van took us home, for we drank a lot—we stood for several hours wearing our winter coats in an overcrowded room, all conducive to great thirst.

Banquet Type B is a truly ancient Chinese ritual.

Changsha, Hunan

Dear Alice,

During the week of Spring Festival, I went to seven different banquets in the city. During my country tour, there must have been eight or so. Out of these, only one quick dinner failed to follow the pattern I'll outline.

You come in and everyone says, "Sit. Please sit. Sit. Sit," and pushes you toward the couch. A square wooden table is placed before you and covered with a tray of peanuts in the shell, watermelon seeds (either smoked or sweet on the outside), and sunflower seeds. In this season, oranges are brought out. If they're the tangerine-like one that is easy to peel, they just start stacking them in front of you and saying, "Eat. Please eat. Eat." If they're the valencias, they quarter them with a huge cleaver and pile them in front of you as above. Talk ensues.

Eventually someone comes in and announces that food is ready. For this, a large round wooden piece is often added to one of the square wood tables to make it bigger. Square or round, I don't think I was ever at a banquet with fewer than six people, and the usual number was nine to eleven, once fourteen. Some one or two people are cooking and they start bringing out the "dishes." ("Dishes" is how they translate their word for the wonderful Chinese mix of meat and spices and vegetables. "Less rice, more dishes," smiles my friend as she eats and eats. And that, in fact, governs the selection at banquets—there are very few carbohydrates. They offer you rice at the very end as some kind of token.)

"Eat," they start to say. "Help yourself. In China we are very informal. At Spring Festival the tradition is to do whatever you want. Eat. Help yourself." And they will put select pieces of the special dishes in your bowl. You eat. You drink "wine" which is *baijiu*, a white hard liquor in the turpentine family. (I have been scrupulously impolite about *baijiu* everywhere and flatly refused to drink it, even in the face of an indirect lecture about how "if you don't understand wine, you can't understand the

Chinese people." In Chengdu, a student first introduced me to the idea that the ability to consume lots of *baijiu* and still be sentient is the key to high political office; this idea has been repeated several times.) Or you drink Pepsi. In the countryside I finally put out the word that I drank grape wine, so was able to get offered a beverage I could accept. Drinking tea, because it is so ordinary, is only a barely acceptable out.

There are dishes and dishes. They are the point at which the banquet varies widely—twice-steamed pork, bamboo shoots, pork strips, pork chunks, pork fat, chicken cleavered into small pieces; in this province mutton is very special, as are squid and tripe. Happily for me, all are flavored with ginger or hot pepper or white pepper or spring onion and lots of oils of various types. One teacher told us the order of delivery of the eight special dishes for a really fine banquet: a fried pork served in sauce, mutton, chicken, lotus-nut-and-white-fungus soup, squid, twice-steamed pork, tripe, and the last is freshwater fish. The fish is last, said the teacher, because the word for it is like the word for "sufficiency, prosperity." You never eat quite all of it, so it looks as though there was too much. And there is!

Eating etiquette in general is quite shocking at first. The existence of the concrete floor with no carpets, even in middle-class homes, is fully explained by this. You politely let bones and other things you don't want (for me this includes fat, but not for them) slip out of your mouth onto the table or the floor. You spill a little bit of hot water out of your tea cup to sterilize the edge before drinking. You hawk and spit onto the floor, and you blow your nose by closing one nostril and adeptly shooting the contents off to one side of the room, then clearing the other. You wipe your hands together and sometimes on your pants to clean up. You may eat very loudly—chew with mouth open and slurp up liquids. There is a lot of gusto and enthusiasm around eating.

After the token rice is passed, the small table returns with seeds, fruit, and tea. Someone sweeps and mops the floor quickly and the cook joins the group. Talk resumes. During the before-and-after sessions around the smaller table, everyone at every moment is cracking a seed and throwing the shells on the floor. Little tottering kids take big handfuls, or their mothers crack the seed and give them the kernel. Cigarettes are offered one at a time to guests; the host takes them out of the pack and hands you one, even if you are currently smoking. The guest will take it and hold it or put it in a pocket. A treated tropical flower bud called *bin lang* is cut in thirds with the cleaver and handed around; this will get you a little high, but it also creates an unpleasant lumpy feeling in my throat. Even the smallest kids go around chewing this smoky bud. There seems no distinction between what adults and children do in most banquet behaviors, except adults sit at the central table and younger people stand around it, grabbing a little of their favorite dishes from the sidelines.

That's it. When you're ready to go, you say, "I'm going now." And you leave. Very little ceremony around this.

Fifteen times, Alice, in two weeks. I came home from the country, turned on some rock and roll, and made a cup of coffee from home. It's all I ate for two days!

PJ

The return gift for a party is a party, of course, and Americans design their own festive eating rituals in China, both among themselves and with their Chinese friends.

MARLA JENKS: The barbeque that I went to was organized by the foreign teachers as a celebration for all the people with October birthdays. We spent the afternoon roasting meat over the fire and eating fruit, peanuts, and gross Chinese chocolate. We always have a good time hanging out together.

My birthday was a lot of fun too—although it was quite a gluttonous affair. In fact, I've been eating for about a week straight. I feel like I've gained 20 pounds. I woke up to find a huge sign taped to my door. My neighbors had made it and stuck a Hershey bar on. (The chocolate had just come in from the Philippines with one of B——'s friends.) I got a rice paddy hat, two packages of my favorite biscuits, a dragon key chain because I keep losing my keys, some homemade cookies, a loaf of chocolate chip bread, and R—— gave me a begonia that she had propagated.

AMANDA MYERS: Halloween has come and gone. We had a great party. I was a witch. I made my wig out of an old mop. We are also planning a Thanksgiving feast. I'm going to make sweet potatoes and gumbo (not together, of course). Should be fun.

ADAM WILLIAMS: I finally hooked up with Kevin. He came to our raucous Halloween party (300 students). I won best costume for Botticelli's "Birth of Venus."

MARY BRACKEN: Thanksgiving was fabulous!!! I, of course, had the traditional dinner in my apartment with seven Chinese, one Jamaican, one French, and one other American from New York. I sat at the end of two adjoining tables and "Saddam" (yes, as in Hussein) sat across from me. I mean, where else could you have this? (By the way, I did not name a student Saddam. The name was given to him by his roommates.) The irony of the evening was really something. My leftovers consisted of squid and snow peas, *jiaozi*, fried rice and Great Wall white wine at the horrendous price of $2.00 a bottle. Jealous? It was great fun and unforgettable! I had take-out Chinese food in China for my Thanksgiving Day dinner, and the table looked like the United Nations.

DALE ASIS: My Thanksgiving celebration was quite memorable. No, we didn't have turkey. (There *is* one at the Changsha zoo. It crossed our minds to hijack the bird for Thanksgiving dinner.) I celebrated with the other American in town who teaches at a nearby university. We ate my last package of spaghetti and my last can of tomato sauce. It was delicious to the last noodle.

The premier American festival is Christmas. And it can bring out the party side of foreigners from many nations. Still, like everything else, Christmas is bound to be a little different on the other side of the planet.

KATIE SHOWALTER: Xmas was great. What a trip. I was awakened by knocking at my door early (OK, 9 A.M.). My students are soft, yet persistent when they knock. They tap lightly (so as not to disturb me?) but consistently for a good long time (so as to disturb me?). I crawled to my door. They greeted me with presents. Of course, I was delighted. If I have to get up early, it may as well be to receive gifts.

That night P—— took me as his guest to a banquet at the Foreign Trade Center Hotel. One of our expat friends got us on the invite list, so I felt pretty cool. But we soon discovered this wasn't your usual sit-down affair. When the welcoming speech was over, everybody pushed their way to a buffet "line." While everybody shoved and grunted, I went to look for a table in the next room. *Mei you* tables. So we all stood around, pushed around, walked around with plates of food through the whole dinner. With chopsticks, no less.

After much spitting, slurping, and sucking, we had a couple beers (Pabst Blue Ribbon—can you imagine?) and retired upstairs to a snooker table. For those of you unfamiliar with the game (as was I), it's a British game, a lot like pool. There's a whole bunch of red billiards you have to get in the pockets before you can hit the colored balls. After snookering a while, we went to a ballroom. We did a couple of Chinese-style waltzes, then they broke out the Madonna for us wild Westerners who wanted to "disco." We rocked the house 'til they closed (at the ridiculous hour of 12:00). Some drunk Chinese kid told me he loved me.

We went to yet another part of the hotel, had coffee (coffee's all over here—but it ain't very good) and gave Westerners a bad name by being stereotypically loud. Just one night's OK, I s'pose. Besides, the place was almost empty. When they kicked us out of there, we went on to the streets and found a food stand. They're "restaurants" that open at 7 or 8 at night and stay open 'til 5 in the morning. They just set tables up alongside the streets and put canvas up in case of Seattle-like weather. It's the only nightlife around. They charge more, but they'll teach us Fujianese dialect. We ate more food, and sat there 'til 5 in the morning just talking.

We actually wouldn't have done that, but one of us was locked out and couldn't get back in.

See, schools lock their dorm gates here, and if you miss curfew, you're bummed. Our school is unique in that they give us a key (although I've been lectured for staying out late, so I know they're watching). Most of us teachers have figured out how to climb back over the gate. But this particular friend hadn't found a way to get in her gate. Granted, she coulda stayed with me, but she was getting a call from her parents at 6 in the morning (the sadists) so may as well stay up. We had fun, anyway. Ever notice how intellectual and deep those late night conversations get? Good stuff.

G: Christmas here was outrageous, unquestionably more in fashion this year than last. So fashionable, the Christian church was loaded to the gills (that's an idiom; means "very full of people") with Changshaese on dates with their girlfriends, impressing them with their international insouciance. All were dressed in their finest: new suits for the men, and clip-on ties, mock turtlenecks sticking out of the collar. One middle-aged man was wearing his new Santa Claus sweater, nice polyester slacks, and wonderfully adorning his feet with furry, warm, purple slippers with cats' faces on them, whiskers and all, long and wiry. Have you eaten yet, sir?[6] Mind if I pet the kitties?

I'm not a Christian, nor was I longing for yet another rendition (this time seasonal at least) of "Jingle Bells," but I agreed to accompany my friends, help them impress the girls with their bigshot international contacts. Fun really, Christmas carols in Chinese plus a few throwbacks from the heavy missionary days, "O Come All Ye Faithful" and the like. (The few sincere foreigners in attendance haven't realized those days are gone and that money is the god now. Their voices boomed from the front seats, serious faces, setting the example.) Before each song, firecrackers were lit off. Boom.

---

[6] G's translation of a common Chinese greeting.

It would not be dishonest to say that I've received more Christmas cards this year from students, friends, any marginal acquaintances, than the total received throughout my life. I still have yet to figure out the senders of twenty or so of them. There are Christmas trees, lights and all, and a gigantic, stuffed Santa on the main boulevard, thirty feet tall. No question that my favorite gift was a small plastic *black* Santa. Where the hell did that come from?

JEANNE PHILLIPS: Christmas shopping brought the funniest outing of my stay so far—I bought three plastic Buddhas that laugh heartily when moved the slightest, each powered by one AA battery. Imagine me walking up our hill surrounded by their gales of laughter and my own embarrassed laughs. At least this time babies didn't cry upon seeing me—too strange even for tears. Surely the maddest of the crazy foreigner acts the locals have yet seen.

In many cases, Christmas is a gift American teachers give to their students . . .

MATT THIBODEAU: On December 9, 1993, Lin Yanzhi, a member of the State Education Commission's Communist Party, officially banned Christmas. Of course no students in China believe this, or at least they won't admit to foreigners it's true, because we *all* know that the Chinese people are free! (I was actually accused of being a *spy* and spreading lies for the American government by stating this. I responded that, if I was a spy, I was *drastically* underpaid!)

Anyway, the ban on Christmas has been relatively ignored by the students here in the progressive Southeast. Tonight Santa made appearances at two different Christmas parties. He was greeted by standing ovations and an almost preschool enthusiasm as 18-to-22-year-old students actually bounced up and down. They applauded madly for an anemic-looking Santa (who can stay plump living on rice?) who had taken on the square shape of the pillows stuffed liberally into red pants that had been made for a much smaller Santa. But for peasant students, this was *their* Santa—thin ankles and all. The party was designed so Santa would enter and hand out presents to the faithful. After fifty handshakes, the 51st student came to receive his prepackaged gift, and requested permission to hug Santa—Santa granted it.

Well Alice, if you haven't already guessed, I was Santa and I "ho ho'd" my way through the night. As Clement C. Moore writes in *'Twas the Night Before C'mas*, "He spoke not a word, but went straight to his work, and filled all the stockings, then turned with a jerk; And laying a finger *aside* of his nose, [and giving a nod], up the chimney he rose!" (I thought it might be more appropriate here in China for Santa to stick a finger *up* his nose!) But all the students heard him exclaim, as he drove out of sight, "Merry Christmas to all and to all a good night!"

DALE ASIS: We had a great Christmas party, the first ever for Xiangtan Mining College. I was surprised the former foreign teachers never bothered to give one. We had a real pine tree, and all my students made their own Xmas decorations. We hung stockings around the dance hall, and I filled them with fruits and peanuts. I taught them Christmas songs, and all the bigshots of the college came to our party. Probably they were wondering what the big fuss was about. And they weren't disappointed. As a finale, I dressed up as Santa Claus and shouted, "Ho, Ho, Ho! Merry Christmas!" After the party, all my students and even the leaders wanted to take a picture with Santa Claus. I felt like the Santa at a shopping mall.

. . . or their colleagues.

JEANNE PHILLIPS: We had a merry party for our Chinese colleagues, a high point of the year since we (the ten foreign teachers) fix Western foods for them to giggle over. My acclaimed contribution this time was tuna salad with mayo and pickle relish, on crackers from Hong Kong (that are like Ritz only better), Oreo cookies, and peculiar imitation potato chips from Malaysia—only the last purchased locally. I was willing to raid my precious shipped-from-home supplies only because Hong Kong is coming soon. This also made gifts of cheese and M&Ms to fellow FTs [foreign teachers] possible, and a can of tuna to one friend whose name I drew for our own little party.

I got a calendar from a new FT who drew my name and didn't know that this is the gift students give endlessly. (How do you make people feel OK when there isn't room on your walls for the tenth or twelfth big calendar showing kittens or blond, blue-eyed babies?)

The party for our Chinese colleagues had as its crux the decorating of the Christmas tree, which is a peculiar sort of too-symmetrical pine rather like a Norfolk pine (if I have the right name in mind), grown in a pot outside and brought in each year for us to put on blinking lights, tinsel from home, paper cuttings, and paper blow-up balls made by Chinese teachers. This year on top of the tree, above paper chains and Santa wax figures, went a crepe paper jack-o'-lantern left from Halloween, an act for which no one has yet claimed responsibility. We have surely the most creative and original Christmas tree extant. I love it!

Outside is a real Christmas tree—a three-story-high poinsettia covered at this season with huge blooms—lovely. And the narrow lanes still have their arches and walls covered with falls of purple bougainvillea, so all this warm, sunny weather makes walks appealing. And we still are getting fresh bananas and pineapples; tangerines are now filling the markets, and cheap!

Still, overall, Christmas can seem a little out of place in the Chinese context. Some teachers discover they have fallen out of practice with American traditions . . .

KEVIN LAW-SMITH: Wow Christmas has sprung—but still I'm waiting for the spirit to flow. I guess I'll have to wait 'til next year. As for Christmas Eve, it was the Sheraton for me and the other Americans here. A full-on buffet—Paradise in other words.

But it all got me a little too excited. Cheese. Bread. Smoked fish. Lamb tenderloin, beef tenderloin, stuffed chicken, beef stew, turkey, ham, vegetables, mashed potatoes, one glass of Dynasty wine—and I splurged for one glass of my old friend Jack Daniels and Coke. My own Christmas present for myself. But as I ate and ate and ate and ate—whoops—stop—help I can't breathe—my body went into overload digesting it all. So Christmas Eve I lay—well, I couldn't lie in bed—I sat up in bed, moaning like I was about to give birth to an elephant. I definitely learned a lesson in moderation. Next visit to the Sheraton, I'll take it easy.

. . . while others notice a certain lack of, well, um . . . let Rachel describe it:

RACHEL COLEMAN: Christmas here was uneventful. The Westerners, of course, put on a mock pretense of celebration—but this becomes quite empty when a *billion* or so others think *nothing* of it! That tells you something of the nature of great holidays, & what they are really about! I was perfectly content to go to the Bamboo Bar for a dinner of rice, stir-fry vegetable, *mapo doufu*, vinegar-sauce pork, fried potatoes, pickled radish, sweet & sour soup, and *baijiu* (this *wickedly* strong Chinese liquor—something like kerosene!) There was joy in just seeing everyone else thinking it was a normal day!

We Westerners did exchange presents, and the more diehard put up decorations & sang carols etc.—but it seemed more pathetic than authentic somehow. I gave presents to some of the Chinese staff members of the Learning Center. Though appreciative, I think they too thought it a bit odd. Really, the greatest surprise came from my students, who intermittently stopped by with Christmas cards and "Merry Christmas" wishes. One card played "Jingle Bells" when you opened it up (this is almost the Chinese national anthem—I'll explain later), & a spooky light on it glowed. This was touching (not the card!)—because my students were genuinely concerned. They knew about Christmas, that it is an "important" holiday (like their Spring Festival), and they

were afraid I'd be lonely and homesick away from family &
friends.

About "Jingle Bells": It is played everywhere here, along with
other famous tunes. When trucks go into reverse—Yes!—out
comes "Jingle Bells"! My Chinese neighbor's doorbell—yes,
doorbell—plays the whole rendition of "Jingle Bells" when the
button is pushed. And you hear it on the street—people merrily
whistling it, oblivious, apparently, that we usually limit the season
to be jolly!

China's own premier festival is the Lunar New Year or Spring Festival,
a movable holiday that falls sometime in January or February. Celebrations last for two weeks, and universities close down for a month. Most
Americans use this time to travel, though a few spend it feasting with
Chinese friends (you'll recall PJ's fifteen banquets), which takes them to
the heart of several ancient rituals.

G: My Spring Festival was fabulous. S—— and I went down to
her hometown, an isolated village four hours from Shaoyang. So
much ritual, very traditional, and I don't think I'll ever spend
another week of my life eating such amazing food. A real China
experience, no doubt. Killed a few chickens, fed the pigs, made
fires, picked vegetables, smoked meats, made *doufu*, sharpened
cleavers, worshipped ancestors, and blew off more firecrackers
than I ever thought existed.

PJ: I attended an early, reverent, vegetarian Buddhist dinner on the
eve of Lunar New Year, then went to a more traditional orgy.
The second banquet broke up about 11:30 P.M. Everyone seemed
to be going to their separate homes and no one invited me to join
them, so I assume midnight is a family thing. I've heard the
fireworks are set off to scare away demons.

As we pedalled home, kids were popping color from long
tubes over walls, into trees, from the back of their parents' moving
bicycles—lobbing red and green and white fire at one another and
at me. On the sidewalks, elaborate fountains and showers sent

bright white stars crackling up with a slow parachute falling. The air was full of sparks and bombs.

My hosts left me at my door, suggesting that I might want to go back outside the university walls to get the full effect of the fireworks. But I was full and lazy. I thought I'd just stand here on my porch, hoping I could get a sense of it.

At midnight I watch a neighbor on the fourth floor hook a long coil of fireworks onto his balcony, light it and let it fall, tumbling down in gold sparks . . . and it is swallowed in a universal roar. Niagara Falls and I am rolling inside a barrel, terrified, overwhelming. Hiroshima a nuclear roar of light and sound rising and rising and rolling drumming down on my body, my mind, my ears (save them!). It roars and roars, engulfs the city inside my university walls, inside my locked gate, inside my chest, a primal, aweful center of the world rising up. The Roar.

Ten minutes later it is down to the level of a huge crackling bonfire, the whole city sucking in air and bowling it down on the world as sound. The smell of sulphur. There are no demons anywhere around *here*. No sir.

Zubin Emsley even collected this account from the Chinese perspective, written by his student Janie.

Spring Festival

Spring Festival draws near, people start preparing for it. The children are overjoyed.

People go to town to buy the things they want for Spring Festival. The children will come with them and get new clothes. The streets are very crowded. Standing in the streets, you can see hundreds and thousands of people. Their faces are all full of smiles. When the children look at the colored clothes, they are dazzled. They pull their mothers' hands and look up at their faces when they see clothes they like. The mothers understand and buy for them.

In general, the streets, the bus stations, and the train stations are very lively. Those who live away from home will come back. There is a family reunion dinner on New Year's Eve.

People start cleaning their houses. They use a long pole to flick the dust off. If it is a sunny day, they will wash quilts, pillow cases, and sheets. They wash the cooking utensils. Sometimes the children help bring water to clean windows and doors. On New Year's Eve, the outside and the inside of houses look brand new.

On New Year's Eve, the women get up early and prepare supper. Children go out and play with friends. The grownups tell them that they can't say bad words. Because it is said that bad things will happen in the New Year if anyone says bad words.

About two o'clock the children come back in. They wash themselves and put on their new clothes, new stockings, and new shoes. Their parents warn them not to get their new things dirty. After dark, the parents don't allow the children to go out.

Now supper is prepared. There are many delicacies: chicken, ducks, beef, fish, eggs, bean curd, fried spinach, cauliflower and green peppers, cooked meat slices. On this day children can drink. The children don't want to leave their seats. The parents help them fill a bowl with rice, but now they don't want it.

Grandparents and parents give children some money and let them buy something they like. Some children will save this money and give it back when the next term starts. Some will buy good books and toys.

After supper, families sit around and talk about the New Year and watch TV. There is a Spring Festival evening party on television. There are wonderful games, a farcical play, dramas, folk songs and dances, magic, and comic dialogues. When 12 o'clock comes, people will stop and listen to the bell—they dismiss the old year and welcome in the new year. But the evening party on TV doesn't end until 1:30 A.M. The parents are very tired and go to bed, but the children are excited and can't fall asleep. They play cards or continue watching TV.

Men don't cook except for the first day of the New Year. They get up early and cook New Year's cakes and bring them to the women in bed. Some people put a coin in a dumpling on New Year's day and mix it in with the other dumplings. The person who eats the dumpling with the coin will be very lucky during the New Year.

On New Year's Day, people usually don't go out. But on the second day it becomes lively. People visit their friends and relations with presents. Generally speaking, the men go to visit with their children because the women must stay at home to entertain guests. The women only go to visit their parents, where they can have a good rest. When a child comes to your home for the first time, you must give her or him a present. Sometimes the present is a hen. Sometimes it is money. When the guests leave, the hostess gives children some candy, some eggs dyed red, and some crackers. The children are very happy.

The visiting and presents do not finish until the fifteenth day of the New Year. On the fifteenth day, there are lion dances and dragon dances. When the dragons and lions face your home, they nod their heads and send best wishes for you!

And after the great ones, minor celebrations still go on.

TEDDY KELLAM: The Chinese (students, at least) seem to really get geared up for April Fools' Day. A—— is thinking of dyeing her hair red or something, to fool them. We're planning an April Fools' Day party. We'll invite many students, as we did to our untraditional Mexican theme Thanksgiving party, and also to our Christmas party—both large galas where the five youngest Westerners made invitations, decorated rooms, cooked Western food, and made alcoholic punches (very very funny to see one's students with pink cheeks and silly grins). Believe it or not, we might play Twister!

G: Well, Alice, I'm still being visited by dozens of young women. In groups of twos and threes they've come to my office, waited for me at breaks. They come all decked out in Sunday-best polyester. It began on April 1st: I received a phone call. "Teacher G," she said in very poor English, " . . . I, I want you." Things are finally looking up, I thought. I told her she could speak in Chinese and she responded by telling me she wanted a job. Huh?

It turns out that some students were getting into the spirit of April Fools' Day. They posted notices in the student dormitories advertising for a new China-U.S. joint-venture restaurant. It said that I was looking for 25 young women to work as waitresses and would pay them in U.S. dollars. A great joke, and not just on me. I felt terrible telling those cute, shy young girls that it was just a prank, their dreams of hard cash floating away. I got some bright students, I tell ya.

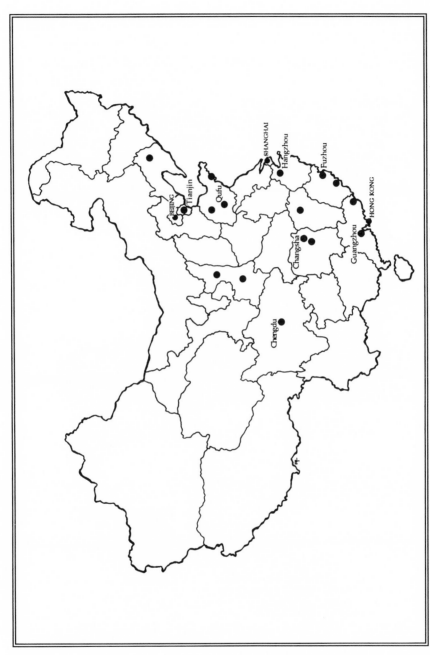

Map 7. The People's Republic of China, showing the cities from which letters in chapter 6 were written.

huoguo (hwoh-gwo): "hot pot," a Chinese type of fondue, where each person dips a wide array of meats and vegetables into spiced boiling water.

qi gong (chee gong): the internal art of collecting, storing, and moving vital energy in the human body.

Philosophy and Perspective

> I've always made it a rule never to eat blue food. I'm happy to be in a place where I can put this principle into practice.
>
> Todd Hamina, refusing a soft drink
> in China

China is different—that's obvious. But as becomes increasingly clear, the differences are not just a few customs and techniques Americans can learn, then go on as before. The differences are so many and go so deep that they amount to an entirely new system.

And like the American system, the Chinese system *taken as a whole* works. Oh, this part may be outmoded and that part may be unwieldy, but each of these defects is balanced by some other strength so that, overall, things get done. Taken as a whole, the Chinese system has managed to feed and house billions of people, invent gunpowder and paper, nourish Taoism and Maoism, and in general just take care of business for more than three thousand years.

At some point, most American teachers who remain in China arrive at this perspective. And what happens then feels quite remarkable. First, they begin to see *themselves* in a different light:

PJ: My culture shock evaporated utterly November 1st. After that I entered a new phase in which I've accepted being a slow learner, being thought silly and rude, being misunderstood and incapable of correcting it. These are new "acceptances" for me, and a striking new feeling surrounds them.

Second, they feel quite different about *China:*

ZUBIN EMSLEY: It happened about two weeks ago. It was a shift, not an instantaneous transformation. The new and continuing feeling is an attachment, an affection, a preference for this country and this way of living. They still spit their bones on the table and throw trash on the ground to my annoyance. They clear their throats and push and run the lights and blow their horns. All these irritations are there as before, but the romance of the scenes and the novelty of the faces and streets have become the most noticeable aspects. Other pleasing things come to mind: the distance from the O.J. trial,[1] the proximity to the rank water of the Grand Canal, the inevitability of my old age. Something, many things, have made a lover out of me.

An ability to feel how all the odd separate parts fit into a meaningful whole is the eventual sign of adaptation to any culture. After only two or three months, few American teachers in China have gotten that far. Perhaps for some, faith begins to emerge that a meaningful whole might exist. But for most, it is enough to arrive at the place Rachel Coleman describes, where you just let go and stop trying to make sense out of anything!

Chengdu, Sichuan
November

Dear All:

So much has happened since last I wrote. It has not been a month, it has been a lifetime. Initially, I was enamored with all & everything here—even bugs were more fascinating—they're Chinese for Godssake! Slowly as that wore off, a lot of homesickness set in. I think my friend Todd was right; "reality" sinks in at around five or six weeks, and you feel bare and naked to the stark extremes around you. Then—the next level, I am finding—

---

[1] The televised trial of O.J. Simpson, a retired American football hero who was accused of killing his wife and her male friend. The trial went on for eighteen months.

is one of pure love. My roots have begun to slowly work their way into this ancient "soil"; my lungs are full of Chinese dirt; my G.I. tract no longer processes American additives; my cells respond to a whole different world. And in this world there is great Peace, constant busy-ness, unbearable filth, & a great, great sense of secure Being.

I think when faced with extreme opposites, people will usually end at either love or hate. Because one must either accept & learn to live with, or reject & refuse to live with, the fact that no matter how hard one tries, "it" will not make sense. So one must, for the sake of sanity, give up trying—sink or swim. This is where I now am. The place of truly loving this bizarre Wonderland I've found myself in.

•   •   •

It is now ten days later. This is another thing very Chinese—something about time here—it just seems to dissipate into this constant and incredible multitude of Things That Go On. In truth, I think East & West are polar. As difficult as my life was at home, is as easy as it is here. One is constantly surrounded by choices, opportunities, importunities—People.

Within the Panda compound where I live, there is a constant busy stream of life. Parties, dinners, badminton—really strong, strong friendships & loving interchange. And outside our own little foreign nucleus, my students & the *danwei* of the Language Center have been incredible.

The *danwei* had a *huoguo* banquet when the head of the department returned from the U.S. (He'd been doing research at Yale as a visiting professor.) *Huoguo* is a kind of *extremely* spicy broth under constant flame, like a fondue. In the center of the table are myriad dishes, all raw: slices of liver; cow's stomach; pig's throat; goose feet (yes, with their nice little toenails still intact!); eel; pig brain; whole, bug-eyed, slimy fish—as well as some relatively normal foods, such as mushrooms, lotus root (really nice!), cabbage, bean sprouts, sweet pea greens, pork slices, black fungus, shrimp . . . etc.! These you take with your chopsticks, place in the molten, spicy broth, cook, remove & eat—if you have the courage! It was incredible fun. Afterwards, we all went to some affiliate school & sat around for some reason, then as inexplicably as we came, we got up & left—? "That's China!"

• • •

So I guess I need to explain this bit of survival psychology of mine. I realized *'way* back in the beginning that the greatest cause of stress, frustration, & disillusion was trying to apply logic to this Never-Never Land I was in. And I realized, if I just replaced "Why *!@#?! would you do that?!!!" with "That's China!" it worked beautifully! Every time I begin to question some absolutely idiotic, senseless rule, regulation, assumption, way of thinking . . . For instance: The housekeeper just came in. I had a burnt-out bulb in my room. So to change it—? She gathers up my frail end table & small kitchen table, drags them into my bedroom, ascends the rickety contraption like someone from a bad circus act, and begins The Changing of the Light Bulb—(huh . . . The electricity just blew. . . . So now I'm writing in the dark—"That's China!")—So in China, it's not "How many *people* does it take to screw in a light bulb?" it's "How many *tables*?"! . . . So to complete my sentence, any time I want to ask "Why the *!@#?! don't you use a *!@#?! ladder??" I just substitute "That's China!" So far it has worked miraculously.

Cheers!

Rachel

The strange thing is that, once foreign teachers give up judging themselves and the Looking Glass World, certain kinds of sense seem to emerge on their own.

EILEEN VICKERY: I just read *A Daughter of Han*. It was staggering to realize how imprisoned women's lives were and how radical the Communists were to get women out of their homes and into the workforce.

JEANNE PHILLIPS: Few have more to celebrate than the women of China. Most began this century as illiterate feudal chattel. While women in the West were discarding their corsets to struggle for the vote, the Chinese had only just outlawed foot binding, that painful, crippling practice meant to make young women sexually alluring. In the face of millennia of Confucian dogma that male dominance was both natural and necessary, Chairman Mao proclaimed women equal, famously noting that "women hold up half the sky." Now, only forty years later, the current economic boom is a cornucopia of unimagined material blessings for both men and women.

How then do Chinese women mark International Women's Day? Try a good old-fashioned beauty contest. It comes complete with swimsuits and lots of bare skin (although still no bikinis). One local touch is a skintight, slit-to-the-hip traditional silk dress. As in the U.S. there are small gestures to imply "Sex and beauty aren't all that matter"—"health" is part of the contest title, girls offer banal answers to banal questions, and there are rounds of singing and dancing. But no one doubts what the real attraction is, all the stronger for its novelty in this society that has been so prudish under communism until now.

American young women, invited to join in celebrating their gender at the festival, mutter in disgust: It's demeaning, selling their bodies, pandering to male power, blotting out significant values and real contributions. Young Chinese women counter: What's wrong with beauty? The Americans are disappointed in their sisters. The environment seems to say it all—the smoky hall with flashing disco lights, bar-style round banquettes filled with far more men than women. Sure enough, it is finally discovered that the affair is sponsored by a magazine with an ad campaign to follow. The Americans leave early, wondering how the All China Women's Federation ever got drawn in to co-sponsor this feminist debacle.

The next morning's small, highly select, formal commemoration of Women's Day by the local federation chapter is the key to understanding why that beauty contest is a triumph in the Chinese context. More women than men gather in a bright, no-smoking hall; the program is several hours of speeches to one another by federation and government officials and assorted dignitaries while tea is sipped, fruit and nuts eaten. All is dignified, polite, orderly, cheerful. Then the MC, a mature, efficient lady, breaks out in a shy smile to announce herself singing a classic Chinese ballad. Another head-table personage follows with a sort of disco-modern dance to bouncy taped music. After her, a hefty VIP accompanied by an elderly male cadre with a two-stringed instrument and bow sings Peking opera. The pleasure of the amateur performers is matched by the appreciation of their watching peers. Bill Clinton on sax wouldn't faze this crowd one bit.

The culminating event comes on suddenly. From behind discreet screens a line of more-than-middle-aged retired women begins a fast-paced fashion show. The music is catchy, changes are lightning fast, the clothes are smashing. But what dazzles is the verve of these women, their in-your-face confidence projected so intensely, so intentionally. The walk, the swing of the hips, the jacket or scarf sweeping off as the chest arches out, still poses and twirls—hours of practice show. And there's also the tiny curve of the lip that makes their expressions not haughty, but delighted and proud. It all has the grace and flow, the easy display of professionals, but with the unpolished freshness of amateurs. The wardrobe is for a lifestyle few are likely to live in China, yet they claim those gorgeous rags as their own. Whether fat or thin, wrinkled or gray, these old gals carry themselves as beautiful, and no one would disagree.

Then the realization comes: These women spent their whole adulthood in the drabbest days of Maoist socialism. For decades they wore navy or khaki Mao suits—baggy cotton, dark pants, white shirt, dark cardigans. All alike, all shapeless, modestly covered, no makeup. Equality meant androgynous uniformity. What an explosion of freedom, of exuberant sensual and aesthetic pleasure, what affirmation of self this show must be for these women. What a triumph of working and waiting.

These women are proud of themselves, confident and glad to show it. They are Chinese, and will modestly demur later, but there is no mistaking their true message. They are successful and highly competent in other roles. Now they proclaim their joy in being women as well, attractive and still desirable, delighting in femininity with strength and courage.

What then of the young beauty contestants of the day before? In growing up, they went from childhood permissiveness to the bright colors and Western styles of the last half-dozen years. They take for granted what intoxicates their grandmothers. But for them, too, the contest is fresh air and freedom, not yet primarily a symbol of male exploitation. After all, the suppression of their sex and beauty was an uglier expression of the same gender-based power. This contest is one more place to carve a success, to advance and compete, to express self and ability.

American women can hope that other options will soon replace beauty contests as attractive paths for ambitious young Chinese women. But they should hope that the older women continue to flaunt their stuff forever. And they should never snub their Chinese sisters for "letting down our side." Rather rejoice with them that they can do these things, young and old, right now. Other battles are for later times.

Even when sense and meaning are elusive, philosophical teachers find the questions China raises intriguing.

G: I finally got my hands on the video camera which was, unknown to me, usurped by its messengers for the past three months. Luckily, there were still a few unused tapes. (I don't think they are sold in Changsha.) Actually, the camera came at the right time. I now have six weeks off and will spend them in Changsha.

Either I am completely insane (as I had reason to suspect the last few days) or I am under the influence of a major creative surge. My ideas and writing are beginning to develop coherence. I'm thinking of a video called "Ghosts and Gaps." This will explore the idea that China and its people, unlike my experience elsewhere in life, are interesting because of what you *can't* see, what you *can't* learn. All the talk of history and progress is part of the regime's theater, as are temples and places of interest. Backstage the contradictions, the multiple meanings at odds with each other, the uncertainty, reveal nothing but ghosts and gaps. Schizophrenia.

Nothing political, just personally subversive—all in the spirit of fun.

KEVIN LAW-SMITH: It's as if you were walking through Sleepy Hollow—all the trees lie dormant. Skeletons of the night, of the day. At 10:00 P.M., the streets are quiet, an occasional bicycle comes clinking along through the heavy night, as horses galloped in Sleepy Hollow. The trees are gray, trunks the color of the world, blending into walls, blending into the scene, their bark polluted.

They stand all along my path not six yards apart. But it's hard to see them. Their bases are in a two-by-two-foot square, their trunks are thin with torment. No grass at their founding, just dirt like cement, hard and gray. The trees don't have the strength to lift the sidewalk, to raise the bricks like trees crack the sidewalks of Boston or Chicago. All lies level, too serene. Ghosts watching. The streets are dark—no lights, no cars, just eternal heavy dust. I can almost hear a wind, but none passes through these trees. It is bleak. My mind creates sound for the scene— the howl of Sleepy Hollow.

Still, these trees have seen it all and survived: the Hundred Flowers, the crackdown after, the Great Leap Forward, the Cultural Revolution, today's social market revolution.[2] They have seen it all. The drive to plant trees forty years ago brought them here. The trees overreached themselves and tangled with the wires of modernization. Now they must be sheared, stripped, to let us go on speaking to each other on phones.

I like this place for all I can see—see differently, contrasts. The place gives me the mind-set to explore, to look at everything

---

[2] The events Kevin lists represent alternating cycles of freedom followed by repression followed by freedom in China since the early 1950s.

openly, blank paper. Wouldn't it be amazing to know the thoughts of these trees, or the first thought of a baby as it opened its eyes to the world? I just saw a birth at a Chinese hospital. The mother of one of my students is a nurse. We went to look at the hospital, and while we were there a pregnant patient came in. I got to see all the glory of birth, and all I could think was "What is this baby thinking when it first opens its eyes? How much has it heard? What does it know?"

With or without philosophy, when these writers become able to relax a little into the differences of China, it can become a pleasure just to sit back, open up, and describe what they see.

Tianjin

Hello Alice!

When I look at the options I had in the States, I doubt anything could match the experience I've found here.

The White Flag

At some of the major intersections here you see someone holding a white flag, standing on the corner where the bicycles are supposed to stop for signals. A traffic cop in the center on a round red stand directs the flow with military hand signals and punishes offenders with mild public humiliation. On the white flag is printed "Obey the traffic regulations." If you don't obey them, you too may be required to stand on the corner holding that flag as punishment. After twenty minutes or so the offenders are instructed to pick out another wrongdoer (perhaps some bicyclist who edges past that stop line) and pass the flag to them.

A Dearth of Treasures

Many apartments I've visited with my students share striking similarities besides their small size and ubiquitous gray concrete. Vegetables are piled high on the balcony, and coal lies stacked in the stairway. Inside, the overwhelming characteristic is the absence of any aesthetic pleasures. No paintings or calligraphy; bare light bulbs, plastic chairs, and few plants. The floors are bare. Very little wood. Of course, the absence of some things can be explained by the fact that, with 1.2 billion people, there is just not enough to go around. Almost all the homes, however, display color television sets, which even during our meals are left on with the volume loud enough for the neighbors to hear. But what about the absence of anything handed down from older generations? Reason: the decade-long Cultural Revolution ending in 1976. Anything old was associated with the feudal past. Everything that might link a person to anything but the "poor masses" was destroyed. I had not realized how such an event might manifest twenty years later.

The Man Walking Backwards

Yesterday as I walked along a street on campus, I was passed by an elderly man who was walking backwards in the same direction. I stared at this oddity but noticed that other pedestrians took no notice. Strange. The backward-walking man continued naturally, and only a little cautiously, confidently placing each foot in steady motion behind the other. Beside me, my Austrian girl friend answered my thoughts: "It's a *qi gong* exercise."

Qi gong is one of the millennia-old traditional breathing and meditation exercises practiced to improve health and mental abilities. An early morning stroll at sunrise reveals many different kinds of these "oddities"—young and old alike practicing under trees and on sidewalks the slow, dancelike movements of *tai ji* meant to capture and control the vital energies of the body; or the sound of birds and waterfalls from boom-boxes beside a dozen figures with arms poised in the air, moving in unison, relaxed and strong. There's an amazing sense of a certain freedom in public here. Can you imagine walking down Main Street, USA, backwards, because you wanted to improve your body's sixth sense? And not expect to feel penetrating stares?

Justin Van Wart

Guangzhou and beyond

Dear Alice,

Xing Nian Kuai Le! (Happy New Year!) What an unlikely spot from which to write my holiday letter—from a rustic teahouse in Chengdu, Sichuan, in southwestern China. It's full of tangled bamboo chairs occupied by chatty, red-cheeked grampas dressed in their blue Mao suits, playing cards or chess ferociously with their caged birds beside them. Just over the brick wall lies a tiny man-made lake, where a young mother propels her baby through the gray water in a rented boat. At this frigid time of year, the children waddle about in thick, thick layers of red, yellow, and purple, but no matter how cold the air, all of the teeny tots have a navel-to-back split up their pants for piddling. So "pink cheeks" describes both faces *and* bums!

I'm here for a conference, but I've spent most of my time exploring Chengdu. The centerpiece of the city is an immense cement statue of Mao Zedong, his great arm outstretched to the masses. However, if Mao could come back to life and see the adjacent exhibition hall in his honor—nowadays holding a bustling free-market on the first floor, a mini–stock exchange on the second, and a gaudy amusement park with glitzy mermaid mannequins beckoning on the fourth—the Great Helmsman would certainly weep; this is *not* the China he had envisioned!

• • •

Now, a few days later, I'm back to Guangzhou, and back to my routine. My mornings are for teaching spoken English, and this week I've told great stories about my trip for listening practice. They loved the first one: As I was taking a minibus back from the train station, the vehicle suddenly sputtered and halted. The conductor motioned us out (onto the traffic-clogged bridge) and had us push the minibus up and over the peak of the bridge. I managed a glimpse around me between heave-hos—met the dropped jaws and stares of hundreds of motorists, *fascinated* by the evening spectacle of a foreign girl trying to push a bus over a bridge! Of course, the bus broke down again after the bridge, and most of us piled out slowly. No refunds, no angry words, just sighs of resignation, and moving on. Some passengers chose to sit and wait for the conductor and driver to tinker with the radiator. The Chinese are unbelievably patient.

Other students preferred the Wenshu Temple story. One evening I went walking, arriving at this particular monastery just one hour before closing time. I couldn't see much, and nearly left, until a kind woman steered me around one more corner. There, in gold and ginger robes with thin wool caps on their shaven heads, bowed about 75 monks, touching foreheads to the stony ground with each bow. Midway through the ceremony, though, the solemnity broke when the head monk bungled his chant, paused, and sent a giggle through his pupils. They finished, and filed out obediently, but I saw barely hidden grins and heard muffled chuckles all the while.

The students enjoy hearing about my impressions of China, so I shared my amusement and amazement at one teahouse tradition—the traveling ear-picker. This freelancer moves from customer to customer. Clients sit with one ear upturned, eyes closed, as the technician pokes busily, pulling out of his pocket a number of long-handled tools, each suited, I suppose, to a particular phase of the delicate job. So strangely fascinating to watch the flair and finesse of these ear-artistes as they flit about with their tongs and swabs and pluckers. Five minutes for each ear! Maybe it's lovely—I don't know, for I haven't dared to hire one. At any rate, these men are by far the most popular people in the teahouse, *always* busy.

Teddy Kellam

PJ: Westerners are usually surprised in China to find that men and men, women and women dance together as often as mixed pairs, but I remember adapting to a similar thing in Europe and Mexico. What I have found more challenging is to figure out their forms of polite and impolite touch. Once as students crowded around after class, I mistakenly touched the arm of a male student to soften a point. The whole group jumped back like startled fish: obviously a no-no. What is warm and welcoming, however, is the way women of any age will hug my arm, hold my hand when we walk, easily put an arm around my waist for pictures. I see this everywhere.

All the "romantic" entwinements we are used to seeing between men and women here appear between same-sex pairs. Standing by the basketball court, a tall young woman stands with her arm over the shoulder of a short one, and the short one hugs the other's waist. Once, in front of a temple, two late-teen boys stood in front of a lion-dog statue, arms around one another's shoulders, trying to pluck the moveable ball of stone out of the statue's mouth. Each one used his free hand so that it looked like one person, double-wide, manipulating the ball.

In class, they pull and punch one another, and no one ever draws back or seems to take offense in the slightest. Last week, I had them reading newspapers in groups of four, and one group of young men simply became a single body, arms all entwined and hanging over one another's shoulders, leaning on one another and slithering an arm across to point to an article. One kid leaning with an arm around his seated buddy was idly pulling the skin on his friend's cheek the way you might pull your own lower lip. No one even seemed to notice. My housemate joked, "Well, everything belongs to everyone here!" It's a joke, of course, but the stiff postures and the careful distance we think of as Asian only apply between the sexes and between people separated by status. "At home," so to speak, everyone's body, everyone's clothes are yours to tug and to hold.

G: In the courtyard sits an elderly couple on one of those cement slabs that serve as a bench. Every day I see them, when everyone is taking their noon nap. Apparently, they don't need to sleep, or perhaps they sleep when others work. They just sit, a few feet apart from each other, and smoke. A pack of cigarettes lies between them. They don't talk, never look at one another—their heads are turned away from each other. The man smokes with his right hand, the woman her left. They look surprisingly alike: the lines on their faces are deep like river canyons and follow the same courses along their cheeks. Their hair is the same shade of gray. They both wear blue.

I wait for the event, which happens on the second or third cigarette. Without any indecision, he takes his usual drag from his smoke and slowly turns his head toward his wife (or is it his sister?). With a delicate thrust of his lungs, he exhales a gigantic and thick smoke ring. The timing is perfect. She moves her head and before the smoke ring is halfway between them, she exhales a perfect, thin line of smoke that streams directly through the ring. Bullseye. Every time. How many years did it take them to develop that little interaction? Incredible.

Rainer Maria Rilke once advised a young poet to "live the questions" and not struggle too soon for answers. This is advice many of these letter writers find themselves following after two or three months in China. It is not an entirely comfortable way of life; as Zubin says, "The irritations are there as before." But most teachers seem able to tap their sense of humor during this phase, making it more fun to read about, if not to bear.

> Wondering at the pulses of the world
> and my dreams. I've no special idea
> of the details of the subconscious.
> I walk about screaming in the south
> centralness of this self-imposed oblivion.
> I'm the one who needs the dark,
> the fluid blackness, that dampness
> of the whole bean; I want my coffee.
> Todd Hamina

KATIE SHOWALTER: Nothing like a Monday. Hot water heater's broken. Toilet's broken. No electricity. Cloudy outside, so I'm typing by the light of an emergency lamp/flashlight. Computer's broken for the fourth time (not that we can use it without electricity anyhow). Good thing I was a Girl Scout. I've batteries.

I'm curled up in bed with my "laptop" typewriter, staring at the light (of course, it's off) above me. Actually, it's not a light, it's a bare light bulb. It dangles by a long cord from the ceiling. This cord is attached to a long board (a 5-foot-long 2x2) that runs parallel to my legs and the mattress. Except that the board and the bed aren't exactly parallel anymore. The board is drooping. I guess that heavy light bulb is weighing it down. I asked to get it repaired. After the third request with no result, I duct-taped it—that lasted almost three seconds. Finally someone repaired it (pounded the board into the ceiling with a hammer, basically) but that only lasted an hour. Someone suggested I move my bed. "Light broken? Move your bed!" I guess I could remove the light bulb so that when that board comes crashing down on me in my sleep—full of nails and electricity—I at least won't get glass shards in my toes.

Meanwhile, let me introduce you to . . .

Ten Things to Do in Fuzhou on Saturday Night

1. *Karaoke.* A favorite pastime of out-of-tune businessmen, you can enjoy their wailing from near and afar. Ever heard a rhinoceros die? Neither have I, but I can imagine the sound.

2. *Be invited to a Chinese banquet.* Here you can have your face stuffed (sometimes quite literally, depending on the persistence of your host) with all kinds of exotica: snake, frogs, turtle soup, jellyfish. Often you will be "asked" to perform. You will sing "How Much Is That Doggy in the Window?" or "Liang zhi lao hu" ("Two tigers"—a kids' song) out of tune. Your hosts will then bring out their child prodigies to entertain you with Mozart, juggling, and acrobatics.

3. *Have two rolls of 36 pictures taken of you.* You with each student; you under a tree; you with each class; you in the park rotunda, under a bridge, on a rock, in a banyan tree—oh, pardon, that's what you do with your Saturday *days.*

4. *Go to a bar in a hotel downtown, drink overpriced beer (still only 90¢), and pretend you're in an English pub.* Talk to unhappy expats, strange teachers, a businessman passing through for a few

months, another sent by his company to live here, someone "unfortunate" enough to fall in love with a Chinese person and decide to stay. All are fascinating.

5. *Happen across a karaoke bar with a live band.* Start hanging out there in the evening before the wailers arrive. Teach them Western rock songs. Play the guitar, drums, or piano. Or be a groupie (for those with no musical talent). Learn important Chinese words like "beer foam." Learn about their plan to escape to America via Bolivia or Rumania, some such country. How they'll play as a band together there and earn enough to buy a plane ticket to the States. How they'll give you a call when they get there. Laugh, but feel sorta ill now.

6. *Make* huoguo *with some Japanese students studying Chinese and play charades.* Guess the answer to each act in English, Chinese, or Japanese (pick one).

7. *Take sheets of paper, tape them on your walls, invite a variety of friends over, and paint with watercolors (or be invited to do this, as was the case with me).* Decorate the room with flowers, monkeys and bunnies, macabre faces. Write Chinese, Japanese, or Korean characters; show off that you can write Italian, French, Russian, or Spanish. Have a beer.

8. *Try to tune a guitar for two hours.* It's a cheap Chinese guitar that takes no time at all to fall out of tune. Plus, no one but the Korean student knows the guitar scale, and he doesn't know it in English. And he can't seem to find the right note on the harmonica. Give up and listen to Monty Python instead.[3]

9. *Try to name all 50 states and their capitals (get very few).* Ask yourself why you are doing this on a Saturday night in China, and go get a shake at McDonald's.

10. *Go to the English corner.* Subject yourself to students asking you "Where are you from?" "What do you think about China?" "Why are you here?" Ask yourself why you are here.

---

[3] A wacky British comedy group.

Changsha, Hunan

Dear Alice,

Check this idea for T-shirts!

Front: Logo/Colorado China Council

Back: A small list of answers to some of the most-asked questions, like

- Yes, I can use chopsticks.
- No, I don't own a gun.
- Yes, I drive a car.
- No, you can't smoke on the bus.
- I don't know. It's hard to say.

G

Map 8. Continental Southeast Asia, showing places within and nearby the People's Republic of China where letter writers traveled on vacation.

bagua (**bah-gwah**): one of several forms of martial arts that G practices.

dui bu chi (**dway boo chee**): "I'm sorry."

qi (**chee**): one of the three vital essences in the body.

Xiamen (Shee-ah-mun): Marla Jenks tells of her travels to this city, which is one of China's Special Economic Zones.

Great Adventures

When Americans in China need a break from the tedium of English corner and the weight of celebrity, they usually think of travel. After all, these are adventurers. What could be more exciting than exploring exotic tropical islands or the mystic hills that inspire Chinese paintings?

Fortunately, the month-long break for Spring Festival—the Chinese Lunar New Year—falls just when many teachers need it the most.

KATIE SHOWALTER: It's late December. I think maybe I'm ready for a holiday. Everything is annoying me. I haven't burst into tears or anything, but I did sleep for three days. Partly sick, partly psychosomatic. Everyone around me is going crazy, too. For that matter, my students want to go home. They're slacking.

TEDDY KELLAM: I went to India with A——, and just adored it. The colors, the smells—you're really "in it" as soon as you arrive. But when we got there, we were both so beat from the Christmas season, New Year's party for 300, and the four-day dash to get vaccinated, visas, plane ticket, etc., that we spent the first sixteen hours in India sleeping!

Still, although it provides a welcome break, traveling around China and environs is like learning to live abroad in general—never quite what an American born to interstate highways and jumbo jets would expect. This section begins with reports from travelers who ranged all over Southeast Asia, and it might rightly be called:

The Ecstasy and the Agony of Fireworks . . .

Shantou, Guangdong

Dear Alice,

I've been traveling over New Year even though it was not advised. And although there was a lot of anxiety over finding hotels, open restaurants, and tickets, it's turned out to have been a great vacation. My mother and her friend have had a nice time, and I managed to have the most romantic week of my life with Michael, a Brit teaching in Taiwan whom I met by chance in Hong Kong last December.

China seemed to put on all its charm for Michael and me. People everywhere responded in a friendly manner when we were trying our Chinese. Because we couldn't get train tickets to Hangzhou, we spent New Year's Eve in Shanghai, which happens to be the one big city where fireworks were not banned this year. Michael and I started out from our hotel near the train station at 10 P.M. and wended our way through the streets which became steadily more like a war zone. But it was magical. At midnight we were in the midst of all the black cats, sulphur smoke, sound, light, and happy families. The hoopla continued well after 2 A.M. when we finally reached the old section called the Bund.

The story of Michael's and my courtship is not one that fits well into letter form. (It's a two-drink story, I think.) But the outcome is that we're engaged. No rush. There will be a green-card wedding in August so he can come to the States, but we will have a real, ritual wedding in a year. We've both met each other's mothers since he was traveling with his "Mum" when I met him, and they both approve. It all has the ring of Kismet about it. I'm so happy I came to China.

Inger

Quanzhou, Fujian

Dear Alice,

So there I was standing on a bridge that crossed the Mekong River, which was a little dry. I had taken one of those great pedal carts from my guesthouse (those carts you usually see only in movies with colonials decked out in their whites speeding through the streets) to watch the sunset behind what probably used to be rain forest until the deforestation stripped it bare.

I felt a strange attachment to the Mekong after seeing so many Vietnam movies and reading *Heart of Darkness.* I thought about Kurtz's famous words, "The horror, the horror," and believe me, Alice, that's what it turned out to be after the sunset—because this was the eve of Spring Festival. I'd heard of the Chinese people going "crazy" and shooting off fireworks through the night, but nobody told me that these jubilant Chinese would be shooting them at me!! These weren't cute little bottle rockets and smoke bombs like we have in the U.S. for the Fourth of July. These were big suckers that don't just blow fingers and toes off; they take the whole hand and foot! So, I tried to get into the Spring Festival spirit, but with hundreds of "crazed" Chinese people tossing fireworks at me, I got some feeling for what American soldiers must have felt on the Mekong instead.

I took refuge in the one American-style cafe, affectionately called Joe's "Big Nose" Cafe—serving American favorites like Chicken Schnitzel. It was a great restaurant, with white-tablecloth-clad tables out in the street and comfortable wicker chairs. Of course nothing is more exciting to festival-crazed Chinese people than a whole table of foreigners sitting in the street (surely they *want* to be bombed!). So the drive-by lobbing was born.

This is the primitive form of the drive-by shooting. In the spirit of celebration, the fun-loving locals would hire pedal carts and drive up and down the street in front of our cafe so they could lob miniature sticks of dynamite at us while we were eating our schnitzel. This was quite entertaining to us for about two or three seconds, but then it became a *little* tedious. Fortunately, there were some Israelis at our table who had just finished their service in the army, so they led us in a counterattack. Some of us occupied another restaurant across the street and some went to the roof of a neighboring guest house. Then, as the fun-loving locals pedaled by we could catch them in a crossfire from three directions. The Israelis took this "fun" quite seriously, and I really don't think the locals are going to be doing any drive-by lobbings again next year . . . even if they have recovered. "Oh, the horror, the horror."

Soon after, back in China, I traveled to the capital of Xishuangbanna with Kevin. Usually this is a tortuous 24-hour bus trip, but in the spirit of true colonialism, we took the 35-minute flight instead. Thus, while most travelers arrived a bit frazzled, we jumped off the plane quite well pressed (and *sure* we'd take the bus back, like "real travelers" would). We had some fresh pineapple on a stick and a local beer. We realized this concept of "real traveler" was amazing. People would submit themselves to hellish bus rides and seedy rooms without bedding or water, all in the spirit of being a "traveler"—whatever that means. Kevin and I opted to share a brutally expensive $10-a-night room with wicker furniture and balconies overlooking the jungle—it was just so much more civilized. (And we didn't take the bus home, either.)

Matt Thibodeau

. . . and the Agony and the Ecstasy of Exploring

Jinan, Shandong

Dearest Alice,

I'm so sorry that I haven't been in touch—I've just returned from my travels—I'll try to give you a brief summary of my GREAT ADVENTURE in China. So much happened—both Good and Bad—I could write a book!

To start things off, my friends and I left Jinan on the 4th of January. We traveled HARD SEAT[1]—17 hours (OH BOY!)—and

---

[1] The four classes available on Chinese trains are hard sleeper, soft sleeper, hard seat, and soft seat. Most Chinese can only afford to travel hard seat, but foreigners have more choice.

finally arrived about noon the next day. We only stayed in Shanghai for two days—ATE PIZZA! croissants, etc. Rode (actually, got lost on) a Shanghai bus (V—— ate her bus ticket in a bout of insanity). Visited the Bund and scrambled around town to finally get a ticket out. Twenty-nine hours SOFT SLEEPER (of course) to Guilin. Next day we rode a Chinese bus to Yangshuo, a beautiful place about an hour and a half south of Guilin. The bus ride included REAL PIGS (not the human kind).

Once in Yangshuo, we checked into "The Holiday Inn," which was more like a seedy youth hostel. But we had 24-hour Hot Water (very important!) and it only cost us 7¥ per night! Yangshuo is one of the most beautiful places in the world (the inspiration of many Chinese painters). The countryside was breathtaking, and there were many foreign teachers/students/ travelers from all over the world. Western-style restaurants, Western music, the works. I felt like I had stepped out of China for a while. It was great! We rented mountain bikes and caroused the countryside every other day—Partied—Had a Blast!

It was freezing and wet most of the time. About fourteen days later we decided to head South. K—— and I decided to go to HAINAN; 13 hours HARD SEAT + 11 hours by bus + 2 hours by boat later (NIGHTMARE! HELL TRIP!) we finally reach our destination—SANYA! (supposedly the HAWAII of China—NOT!). But it was warm enough for shorts and swimming, and the beaches and water were beautiful! So K—— and I and Chuck, our Chinese companion from Yangshuo, searched for cheap accommo-dations. *MEI YOU!* Nothing cheap—except . . . tents. That's right—we rented tents at this place called "The Water Paradise"—a small park located right next to the *beach*—NICE! 30¥ per two-man tent, cold showers, lockers, a bar (karaoke all night—YUCK!), a blanket and pillows and the beach.

It was actually perfect—aside from the fact that we had to

Hard sleeper is generally considered the most comfortable inexpensive option; *soft sleeper* is most luxurious and often costs as much as an airplane ticket. *Soft seats* are rare.

sleep on Astroturf = *Sore backs*. And also aside from the fact that as soon as Chinese New Year rolled around we found ourselves surrounded by thousands of curious Chinese tourists—who lined up outside the fence to get a better view of the strange *lao wai*, take pictures, etc. Watched us all day and most of the night long.

There were approximately forty campers total—students, teachers, travelers—from all over the world. Met so many wonderful people. Romance? I'll tell you later on in the letter—I could write a book. (Ben? Who's Ben?) Anyway, THE ZOO, as we soon called it, was very nice—except when it rained and my things were soaked.

Three bad events occurred in Sanya: (1) Walkman was stolen (NO BIG DEAL); (2) there were RATS the size of CATS *EVERYWHERE* (I saw seven at least). No kidding! YUCK! YUCK! YUCK!; and (3) I was attacked one night while practicing *wushu* on the beach.

About that last event—One night about 10:00 or so I'm bored. K——'s in her tent and Chuck's gone for a walk on the beach. So I start to practice *wushu*, and a wobbling (drunk?) Chinese man is walking toward me on the beach. I think, "Looks a little dangerous" so I pick up my beer (I brought a bottle with me) and head closer to my tent. Start to practice again. He comes at me again. Pick up the bottle. Go to walk away and he starts groping for the bottle, saying, *"Pijiu, pijiu."* I say, "Get the *!@#?! away from me you creep! GO AWAY!" Then he grabs me! Starts to wrestle me to the ground. So maybe I would have used my *wushu* on him? NOT! I go for the throat! So I'm grabbing his throat with one hand, have the bottle in the other. Swing the bottle at his head; break the bottle on his head (Beer Everywhere!). He starts to run away, I'm looking around for glass to use to protect myself, and then I run as fast as I can.

While all of this is happening I'm screaming at the top of my lungs for Chuck or K——. NO ONE around to help me. It was terrifying! I run back to the tent area, jump the fence like a mad-woman. Scream for K——, she's in the bathroom. I tell her what happened. THE MAN COMES BACK! He's pacing outside the tent area on the beach—I'm scared shitless! He's throwing rocks and sand at K—— and me. She's yelling at him—calling him all kinds of names—I'm hiding with my Swiss Army knife behind the tents.

So finally Chuck comes back. We tell him what went on. He gets a guard and goes searching for this guy on the beach. They chase him, catch him, bring him back. He's groveling at my feet, *"Dui bu chi, dui bu chi"* ("Sorry, sorry") for 20 minutes! I'm standing there (with my knife) thinking, "GOD THIS IS TOO WEIRD! I can't handle this!" So we take him to the guard station (it's about midnight now). Chuck's interpreting, and says, "Do you want to send him to jail?" I think "CHINESE PRISON? What would they do to him?" So we fine him and let him go. RIGHT DECISION? I don't know—whatever. . . . So that was Sanya—I had a super time otherwise. We flew home on the 31st.

Back home—I still have the traveling bug, so attempt to buy a ticket (on my own) to Shanghai—actually Hangzhou. (My *waiban* was not available to help me make the purchase.) So after two hours of bike riding, I still can't find the booking office. Ride to the train station, find some help from a man who could not speak any English, get a ticket (HARD SLEEPER! almost impossible to get here). Go for dinner (my TREAT). This man—who seemed *so honest*, friendly, etc., ends up ripping me off—500¥! and my watch (another Long Story). So next day I change $, thinking my train leaves at 6:30 P.M. NO! 3:30! I find out at the last minute. End up missing my train (BIG nightmare story), crying at the train station.

Next day Mr. Lu helps me get a ticket—NOT hard seat, NOT hard sleeper, NOT soft—NO SEAT! I stand, squat, lean, cry, for 17 HOURS! Water is dripping on my head. I'm surrounded by a FLOOD of FILTHY SLUDGE. No Place to Sit—So Crowded— ALMOST DIED! Finally get to Hangzhou. Hangzhou is GORGEOUS and so is the reason I went there—PHILLIPE, a French physicist (student) whom I met in Sanya (Major Romance!). Six-foot three, green eyes, speaks French/English/Chinese/German— Tall, Dark, Handsome, studies thermodynamics. What more can I say? As far as Ben is concerned, I've received two letters total (I've sent at least thirty or so). He was supposed to visit—No. Completely ignored my bills (which he promised to take care of) etc. So he's a BIG LOSER in my book now. Besides, there are so many more *INCRED-IBLE* fish in the sea, Alice! Why settle for less?

Miss you!

Love always,

Kristen Wood

Changsha, Hunan

Dear Alice,

Here I sit on a temperate spring afternoon. First I must apologize for not keeping in touch better. Rest assured that it is only because I'm too caught up in things and basically just having a ball. Spring Festival was the most fantastic experience of my lifetime.

Fred and I began in Thailand—the island of Ko Pna-Ngan. It was paradise, with a plethora of foreigners to satiate THAT craving! I met a *fantastic* woman from England and a loony freak teacher working in Qingdao (one of the crazies that somehow are attracted to China. WHY?). Anyway, the four of us relaxed and played for about six days on the island, but once we had a chance to snorkel, play volleyball, fish with local fishermen, hike to waterfalls and generally catch up on our R&R—we were ready to begin new adventures.

Of course there's no way to write about all of them, or even to describe one or two in detail. To begin, we took the train down through Malaysia to Penang, then a boat to Sumatra, then a ten-hour bus ride from hell to a large lake, then a boat to an untouched mountainous island in the middle of the lake. It's a very isolated spot. The island is about five miles in diameter. The villagers are mostly Christian, so they don't mix much with Sumatrans outside the lake boundary. They're mostly farmers, a few monkey poachers, and fishermen. Alice, it was absolutely gorgeous. If I tried to put it in writing I'd surely fail.

The colors were spectacular, the people were so friendly, and the tropical mountain jungles were like nothing I could have ever imagined. The people were "Batak," having their own language, customs, *beautiful* wooden huts like this:

Built on stilts, no nails used in construction. Grass roofs.

We decided to go trekking into the jungle for a few days. We were warned of tigers (but they don't attack humans because there's so much to eat in a tropical jungle), of monkey poachers, and of *large* snakes (we saw a 15-foot+ snake skin of one proud farmer). Fortunately, we met with none of these evils, but we did get attacked by swarms of bats, I got land leeches, and I got stuck in quick mud. How theatrical to be pulled out of quick mud by having my friends toss me a free-swinging tree vine! We fulfilled a lifelong dream of mine—watching bands of monkeys playing in the trees above us. Clear as day they jumped and flew through the air, sometimes falling fifty feet before casually sticking out their arms and grabbing a vine to swing to safety. They screamed at each other, and the treetops arched under their weight. It was fantastic!

We ran across only one person—a lone coffee farmer on the peak of the mountain. (It was a five-hour bus ride to a village nearly at the top, and then a seven- or eight-hour hike to this peak.) He let us sleep in his loft above his water buffalos and 400-pound pigs. I watched two water buffalo go at it. Of all the animals to see hump each other, the water buffalo *must* be the most incredible. It was SO BIG! The farmer served us anteater for dinner and wild boar for breakfast. I suppose that's not all that different from bacon for breakfast!

Another highlight: The return boat trip to Penang. Got caught in a huge storm—felt like I was going to wind up on Gilligan's Island. We were radioing for emergency help but the waters were too rough. I reckon all 150 people on our boat threw up. I, of course, was one of the first. I was so sick I couldn't lift my head, so sick I *had* to pee in my pants because my legs were too weak to carry me to the W.C. Our boat was late arriving in Penang, allowing us *barely* enough time to fly in a taxi to the train station to catch our train to Bangkok (and then our flight to Hong Kong). No time to get food or rinse my clothes in a sink—I had no other clothes—my only other shorts were the ones I was wearing when I got stuck in quick mud. Needless to say, I *reeked!* As the temperature soared I only began smelling worse and worse. Ha—I loved it. It was all fantastic. I only regret there wasn't more time.

Love,

Amanda Myers

TODD LUNDGREN AND EILEEN VICKERY: We hiked the Tiger Leaping Gorge, north of Lijiang—probably the most remote place either of us had ever been. And we ended up doing it twice: Snow blocked the pass between Daju and Lijiang, so no bus for *five* days. We laughed and turned around and hiked back to get the bus from the other end of the gorge.

The bus rides in Yunnan were the scariest traveling, and probably the most unpredictable, we've ever done. Mountain roads—the Burma Road—and they turn off the engine to save gas going downhill. Pray the brakes hold. Never saw a guardrail.

We were gone from home just over a month and, if not for teaching commitments, we had the money and energy to travel much longer. We went soft sleeper the whole way back, and the Beijing train was the most elegant traveling ever. Clean, no smoke, and doilies on the cushions. Hard sleeper was too cold and *smoky* on the way south. So we decided to do our bodies a favor coming home. Luxury!

ZUBIN EMSLEY: In a little market on a dusty street on the other side of the Mekong, the Dai women laughed with me at the difficulty of buying bananas while the vegetable seller took our picture with my camera. Early in the morning in the cold mist of the Menghun market, the Hani women took me to heaven: Polypro shirts and Goretex coats next to leathery bare feet, silver headdresses, and sparkling eyes. Sewing my torn pants in the sun in a nut grove just beyond the monastery and the village on stilts. Running in the humid darkness across rice paddies. The chickens below us at the bamboo guesthouse get up at 5:30, so I'm heading out as the women are bouncing toward the market on piles of vegetables in wagons behind the garden tractors. I had some peace and ease there. I didn't curse the rain that trapped me in the pottery factory for two hours at dinner time.

DALE ASIS: I'm back from my China vacation, but it's more like an endurance test. Getting from one place to another is an accomplishment by itself. Nothing much has changed here, except the corner store now offers BOTH Coke and Pepsi. What next, Perrier and wine coolers? Things are moving too fast here in Xiangtan.

Because, as Dale Asis says, getting from one place to another is often an adventure in China, even short trips can be filled with tension and surprise.

INGER: I took a week off around the May Day holiday and went to Taiwan to see Michael. What a nightmare getting there. Not only was I anxious about seeing Michael again (and making sure we hadn't temporarily lost our minds in the splendor of Shanghai and environs), I also had a tight schedule—taking the overnight bus [from Shantou] to Shenzhen, then trying to get over to Hong Kong early enough on Saturday to get the Taiwan visa before the consulate closed at noon.

What should happen, of course, but that the bus broke down and there I was, sitting for four hours in an immobile bus, figuratively wringing my hands and thinking the whole journey was going to be a disaster. At 3 A.M. they finally got the bus on its way, but we got in late Saturday, and the consulate was closed.

I had been brainstorming ways to salvage my trip. Since my

airplane ticket was nonrefundable and I'd have to buy a new ticket if I waited until Monday to get the visa (office closed on Sunday), I decided I'd buy a roundtrip ticket midweek to return to Hong Kong and go right back to Taiwan in one day. (It's a complicated story, sorry.) You don't need a visa to go to Taiwan for less than five days, and I was not wanting to spend my first weekend in Hong Kong instead of with Michael. So I boarded my 5 P.M. flight Saturday and hoped, even though my ticket showed an eight-day stay, that they would believe me at customs in Taibei that I intended to buy a new ticket to cut it into two four-day stays.

O.K. The climax. When I got to Taibei, I went to the Immigration Office and proceeded to spill the above story so that they'd let me through. After I got through my rush of words the lady looked at me and said, "Wait, so you want the fourteen-day visa?"

"You mean I can get a visa here?" I asked, stunned.

I could, and did, and to top it off, instead of waiting two hours in Hong Kong and paying HK$250 for the rush visa, they gave me this fourteen-day single-entry visa in two minutes and it was free. Nobody had told me about this at the consulate, at the travel agency, and no one who had been to Taiwan ever said anything. From that point on, my visit went smooth as silk.

Taiwan is an interesting place. Even though Michael tried to persuade me, I still like China better. But we did visit Alishan for two days, and it is gorgeous. Taiwan is beautiful once you leave the cities.

The aftermath of the visit is that I'm now on the last leg of the year and Michael and I had all of our doubts about our engagement erased. It was a positive trip and has made things much easier over here.

Sometimes even local travel can be a nearly transcendent experience.

Quanzhou to Xiamen, Fujian

Dear Alice,

It's Sunday night and we just got back from four fabulous fun-filled days in Xiamen! I can't face grading papers and planning lessons yet, so I'll re-live the trip in this letter.

An Inauspicious Start

The five of us started out on a three-hour bus ride. (If you look on the map, the distance between Xiamen and Quanzhou would be forty-five minutes in the States. But in China the journey takes three hours on a good day and six hours on a bad one.)

Tensions were a little high at the beginning. Y—— and I forgot to bring the phone number of the woman we were supposed to stay with. And all five of us neglected to bring our guidebooks. We all have the same Lonely Planet book,[2] and each of us figured somebody else would bring it. Then, after we got off the bus in Xiamen, idiots on a motorcycle almost ran over Matt's foot. Matt was so incensed that he spit on the guy. Well, that made the guy mad, and I was sure there'd be a rumble in the street. I had visions of the PLA dragging Matt out of China by the feet. At that point I wondered if we should scrap the trip and head home, but it's a very good thing we didn't.

Romantic Hours on the Island of Gulangyu

After we regained our composure, we headed for the ferry pier and took a boat to the nearby island of Gulangyu where we stayed one night. The island was fantastic! There are no cars or bicycles allowed, so the whole place is much calmer and mellower than the mainland. It's not very big either, so it can be easily explored on foot. In the late 1800s the island was settled by Europeans, so the buildings are multi-storied with red tile roofs and columns around

---

[2] A travel guide preferred by most English speakers traveling in Asia on a limited budget.

the front porches. The villas are enormous and are tucked in among large trees that are draped with moss, and there are large poinsettia trees all over the place. It feels like an Italian village on the Mediterranean. I couldn't believe I was still in China! There are some nice beaches also, although I'd think twice before swimming in China's coastal waters.

We checked in at the Gulangyu Guest House, a huge old building that looked like it could be Tara from *Gone with the Wind*. The price was decent and the rooms were spacious, sort of clean, and dimly lit. They had very high ceilings and Matt's and Brian's had an old English fireplace that excited Y——.

We decided to split up and explore on our own for a few hours. I headed for the beach and found a great rock where I could watch the sunset. It was spectacular. The sun was a giant fiery ball striated with gradually deepening bands of red, and I just watched it slide into the ocean. There were a few Chinese people on the beach who were naturally more interested in me than in the beauty of nature, but I tried to ignore them. However, a man and two women, who all looked to be just a few years older than me, approached and asked if I'd like to take a walk with them. Since I had nothing better to do, I decided to go.

Small Talk at a Small Table

Unfortunately, my Chinese was only slightly better than their English, which should give you some indication of our level of conversation. We walked to the top of the highest hill on the island and surveyed the scene below. I kept smiling and nodding and saying, "Gulangyu is very beautiful" because I didn't know what else to say. After we got through with the hike we wound through the main streets of the village, and they insisted I have dinner with them.

The guy picked a street vendor who was cooking at a little cart on the corner. On the pavement beside the cart were four tiny tables with plastic stools around them. They were literally the size of the furniture found in kindergarten classrooms in the U.S. We squatted at one table with our knees under our chins.

The guy ordered, and when the food started arriving it just kept coming. I don't know how the roadside vendor could produce such an amazing variety from his cart, but we had great crab, snails, fish, vegetables, fried noodles, and lots of other stuff too.

The guy wanted me to have a chugging contest with him, but I knew if I did that we'd be there drinking beer all night. Besides, I think a guy loses face if a woman can drink as much as he can, so I stopped drinking and let him think he was super cool. After dinner I didn't know what the proper etiquette was. I tried to pay, of course, but they wouldn't take it. Then I thought I should buy them a gift but I wasn't sure what. And by that time I was late to meet the other four. Our parting was a little awkward because I felt like I hadn't upheld my end of the deal, but I thanked them as profusely as I could.

Our "Villa" in Xiamen

The next morning we managed to contact B—— and got the number for the woman we hoped to stay with. We called her and set up a meeting time for that afternoon. We then spent the morning wandering around Xiamen. It's busy and crowded and dirty, and there are a million shopkeepers selling lots of tacky cheesy junk—just like here in Quanzhou. But in Xiamen you occasionally find a store selling something Western like a Bic razor, margarine, or Vaseline Intensive Care lotion—that's what makes it such an exciting experience.

At 1 P.M. we met Mrs. Liu, who led us to her house. We climbed a long set of cement stairs, walked through a wrought iron gate, and looked ahead through an archway of trees at the most beautiful villa I have ever seen! It was about four stories high with large white pillars in the front and a set of stairs leading to a huge porch that surrounded the house. In the front there were gardens, hedges, and a fountain. The house actually belongs to some Filipinos who weren't there; Mrs. Liu lived in a more modest house next door. We stayed in the Lius' little house, which was actually quite nice by Chinese standards. We sat and chit-chatted with her a little. (Actually, C—— did the talking because she's fluent in the local dialect and Mrs. Liu spoke no English. The rest of us just smiled and nodded a lot.)

She showed us to our rooms, furnished with real Chinese beds, which were elevated wooden slabs covered by a straw mat. The frame was made of thin iron bars and the whole thing was shrouded in mosquito netting. It was far from the most comfortable thing I ever slept in. The bathroom was out the back door and consisted of a cold shower and a toilet. There was no sink, so when you brushed your teeth, you spat off the balcony and hoped no one was walking below. At night they locked the back door, so you had no access to the bathroom. Mrs. Liu helpfully pointed out the bedpan for use if we had to relieve ourselves in the middle of the night. I actually did wake up at about 3 A.M. and had to pee like a racehorse, but I chose to lie there and suffer for five hours rather than revert to the 18th century and pee in a pot.

A Glorious Vision from Home

After Mrs. Liu showed us our rooms, she asked if we'd rather have noodles or rice porridge for supper. We assured her she'd already been too generous and that we were going to eat out. So we hopped on the ferry. Suddenly, from across the harbor, we saw the unmistakable neon of a Pizza Hut sign beckoning. Matt's jaw dropped open, my eyes filled with tears, and Brian and the others yelped and hugged each other. At that moment we really gave the Chinese people something to stare at. We could not get off the boat fast enough.

I never imagined that a fast food restaurant could possibly mean that much to me. It's kind of frightening, isn't it? It must seem strange to you, since there are fast food joints everywhere you turn. But it really had a calming, reassuring effect—it made me realize my real world still does exist somewhere.

It turned out that it was opening night and we were among the first people to eat there. Everything was perfect. And I swear, that has to be one of the most sanitary buildings in China. In terms of cleanliness, it beats all hairdressers, dentists, and hospitals hands down! It was pretty funny to watch the Chinese people try to deal with knives and forks and pizza. It was a whole new world for them. The wait staff was a riot too—they tried so hard to please us. The restaurant was incredibly overstaffed, and there were usually about five waitresses hovering around our table. I had garlic bread, salad, minestrone . . . it was amazing.

An Awful Spectacle

After dinner, we walked outside and saw that there was a martial arts show taking place in a tent next to Pizza Hut. Matt and I were intrigued and paid the 5¥ to get in (about US$1). The others thought it was too expensive and wandered off.[3] I was a little apprehensive at first because there were huge guys out front in long robes with waist-length hair and strange beards, and they all held primitive-looking axes and long spears. They looked like they'd love to sink their blades into a couple of foreigners. But we bravely ventured in to see what it was all about.

It was a small canvas tent, and the audience was perched on long bamboo poles facing the front "stage." The floor was all dirt, there were only a few lights focused on the stage, and the air smelled strongly of incense. The audience consisted of about 75 men and maybe five women. I don't know if people were staring at me because I'm female or because I'm foreign. Probably both.

The first act was a guy who stuck a red hot poker on his tongue and let it steam and sizzle. The second act was a woman magician who was not particularly impressive. Then a woman did a little nightclub tease dance. She looked like an eleven-year-old girl would look trying to do the same thing—awkward, with no choreography to the routine, and dressed in a skimpy outfit that was more tacky than seductive. To top it all off, she had on a big pair of bug-eye sunglasses. After her came the evening's most impressive act. The guy held a piece of newspaper in his bare hand and, through some invisible force, created spontaneous

---

[3] Remember that these teachers are earning roughly $250 a month in a place where $1 is the price of a decent meal.

combustion. Then he pushed a nail through a board with his thumb. The whole scene was ridiculous, yet at the same time strangely eerie.

Impressive Institutions

Our next day was spent exploring Xiamen University. Matt and I wanted to find people to talk to. The first guy we encountered was fifty-something and was there studying Chinese. He had nothing good to say about China. He did take us to his room, though, which was in the tallest building on campus. It was very nice, new and clean. We stood on the roof and looked out over Xiamen, Gulangyu, and the ocean toward Taiwan. It is a spectacular location.

On our way out of the building we met another foreigner, from Germany, who was also studying Chinese. She was probably a couple years older than us and her English was flawless. (Apparently her Chinese is good too, because she's dating a guy from Taiwan.) She gave us a package of cheddar cheese from America that she didn't want. (I don't think anybody eats cheddar cheese but Americans and the English.)

We then left the university and explored a nearby temple, which was crawling with Buddhist monks waving incense and giving offerings of fruit. The place was also crawling with Chinese tourists who took pictures of everything.

Gourmet Delights

We decided to walk home along the beach, which was absolutely beautiful! I don't know how we got gypped out of a beach in Quanzhou, but theirs is great! The walk home turned out to be much longer than we'd anticipated, but there was plenty to see on the way. We walked through a market where two women were fighting over the price of produce. The shopper then overturned the vendor's apple basket. This threw the vendor into a rage and caused a lot of excitement among the onlookers. I'm sure someone "lost face" in the scuffle, but I don't know which one. I never can tell about those things.

Halfway home we bought a few bottles of German beer and some crackers and we sat on a pier and ate our cheese. When we finally got back, we decided we needed a last supper at Pizza Hut. The two of us split a large pizza and a pitcher of beer. I haven't done that since last spring at Roma's, and it tasted so good. (Right now you're probably thinking "No wonder she's gained weight!") All in all, I managed to go for four days without touching rice— quite a feat in this country.

One More Trip Back in Time

The next morning I went off on my own again to explore more of the island, and I wandered smack into the industrial zone. I felt like I had walked into the middle of the Industrial Revolution. I walked into the electric light bulb factory and peered into some open doors. Rows of women were lined up at tables, each performing some task. In one door was a group of people making touristy souvenir candles. I asked if I could take a picture, and they were more than happy to oblige. Then they invited me in to show me what they were making; they were all grinning and were very proud of their work.

When it came time to go, we did not want to leave Xiamen. But our hostess asked us to return, and we all felt we had had a much-needed break from the monotony of our daily lives.

Marla

"I'm Fine, Really—Only My Legs Were Amputated"

Excitement, risk, suspense, and the unknown—these are the elements of adventure. And as we have already seen, foreigners can find them around every corner in China.

MARLA JENKS: The excitement for the weekend has been an ongoing search for the source of the rotting rat stench that refuses to dissipate. Last night I was investigating the bathroom when I encountered three massive spiders. One was huddled in a corner, so I stood on the toilet to pour a pot of boiling water on him. B—— was on backup with a broom, and Y—— was standing on a chair in the hallway shouting instructions. Our small army thus managed to conquer the immediate spider threat, but the search for the dead rat continues.

Sometimes this real-life drama can be dangerous.

ANONYMOUS: I was attacked two weeks ago with a Chinese friend—three men and a knife. But my friend knows *wushu*—got the knife away. They pushed us over the fifteen-foot wall into the river—ugh. But our money wasn't stolen, no injuries—and a lesson, *well learned*. I'm much more careful at night now. It's good when lessons happen like this. My life continues to be interesting in this way—good and bad things both! Please don't freak out about it (as my mum will be certain to do *if* I tell her!) —but it's a good thing to be aware of, isn't it?

STEPHEN: This year, I have been involved in three encounters—attacks, might be a better description. In two I was able, with a little patience, to "talk my way out." In the other, I was physically attacked and, not being afraid of my attackers, was able to frighten them away. Maybe I've been here too long; I've become too hardened to the reality of the place. Maybe I am too active for a foreign visitor, explore places where I shouldn't be? My observation is that this is an explosive time in this country's development. There is some danger here, and the government has other things on its mind than protecting a few foreigners.

Most adventures that foreigners have in China involve subtler risks. One common encounter with the unknown takes place when they enter the ancient, complex system of Chinese traditional medicine. Its elaborate constructs have accreted through millennia, presenting any newcomer with a wilderness of interconnected, semimagical mazes. For foreigners from any land, Chinese traditional medicine usually appears first as an alien system that, glimpsed briefly, is easy to chuckle at.

MARY BRACKEN: Things sure are different here. As I often tell my students, in America, we walk dogs—you eat them! In America, we feed pigeons in the park—you eat them! In America, we kill rats—you eat them!

The underlying theme here is, of course, that the Chinese "eat them." Now it's winter here. You probably have mistletoe hanging in your window or door—they have dog. It really adds a new dimension to "How Much Is That Doggie in the Window?" They eat it, of course, and say it helps them keep warm.

JEANNE PHILLIPS: Hot and cold foods here are classified by essence, not temperature or spiciness.

TEDDY KELLAM: Winter weather never deters us. Dog is eaten here because it makes your insides warm, and in fact, my tolerance for the previously bizarre has grown tenfold. In Guangzhou, they believe that eating a certain part of an animal will enhance your own corresponding body part. For example, a friend with liver problems eats cow liver daily. Chicken feet supposedly make you run faster. Eat fish brains before an exam to make you smarter. My friend and colleague A—— has asked her students whether fish *lips* make you a better kisser. Only giggles in response!

But jokes and chuckles can mask nervousness in the face of a great unknown. For Americans comfortably in their own land, the workings of Chinese medicine (most famous for acupuncture and acupressure) are mysteries on the sidelines that can be explored or not, depending on one's taste for adventure. For Americans living in China, however, it is their own medical system—white-coated doctors, office visits, and pills or shots to reduce symptoms fast—that has pulled off to the side, becoming a rare prerogative of the elite. Chinese traditions of medicine are everywhere.

This ancient and intricate system becomes crucial for teachers in China who must enter it to find vital support for their health problems. As Jeanne Phillips will explain, it is not easy to dismiss a medical tradition that has worked for billions of people over thousands of years, especially when intelligent people all around you subscribe to it. And yet, if your body and your inquiring mind were both matured in the United States, how will they react to this strange new world of care?

. . .

A Simple Primer to Traditional Chinese Medicine

Historically, Chinese doctors were paid when their patients were healthy, giving preventive medicine precedence over any other practice. Instead of gauging success by the eradication of acute symptoms as they occurred, successful treatment was measured by a patient's continued lack of disease. Only then was a physician viewed as competent, proving his expertise in keeping a patient harmonious with nature.

Qi, *Moisture, Blood* The Chinese think of the body and its functions as a miniature planet with corresponding parts and functions. The sky or atmosphere, rivers, and landforms are synonymous with *Qi*, Moisture, and Blood respectively. *Qi* is the life force of the body. It is the energy of life given at birth that must be fed and protected to sustain a long, healthy life. *Moisture* is the liquid vehicle for moving energy to nurture and lubricate the body's tissues. *Blood* is the substance that builds and rebuilds the bones, tissues, nerves, and organs of the body.

Five Organ Networks The universe is further organized by the five powers known as Wood, Fire, Earth, Metal, and Water. Traditional Chinese medicine theorizes that each of these powers is associated with an organ system within the body: Wood = Liver, Fire = Heart, Earth = Spleen, Metal = Lung, and Water = Kidney. These organ systems can be thought of as networks that generate, circulate, and store *Qi*, Moisture, and Blood to create a balance and to create health.

Yin and Yang Traditional Chinese medicine is also based in part on the theory of yin and yang, the two basic and complementary principles that combine to create balance. The harmony of yin and yang is the metaphor for the equilibrium in all functions of the body and one's life. As reality is not a static thing, neither are yin and yang. Like a teeter-totter in a child's playground, the balance is achieved through the flow of energy—of *Qi*, Moisture, and Blood—back and forth in response to outside forces. Overemphasis of one function or activity (too much weight on one side of the teeter-totter) creates stagnation, imbalance, or a blockage of the flow. Illness is perceived as this loss of balance and the curtailing of the flow of energy.

Methodology In contrast to contemporary Western medical treatment (which tends initially to address symptoms), Chinese doctors start by taking the overt symptoms of a patient and then working backward to find the underlying cause—similar to psychological analysis. Using the traditional Chinese approach, the doctor will first assess the state of the internal functions of the body and the effects of the patient's lifestyle by examining the condition of the pulse, skin, nose, tongue, breath, smell of perspiration, and so on. By listening to the patient's responses to several questions, the doctor can evaluate the vitality of the *Qi* and the quality and movement of Moisture and Blood. When a diagnosis is made, the doctor will treat the patient using a combination of therapies to correct the balance of yin and yang, increase or regulate the *Qi*, and reduce the congestion of Blood and Moisture. The doctor will also address any problem with an organ system or between organ networks. Finally, the doctor will coach the patient about how to rebuild or strengthen *Qi*. This whole-body, whole-environment approach is the central theme in achieving or reestablishing health and building defenses against disease or disharmony.

Herbal therapy is a common technique here. The preparation of the individual herb and its combination with other herbs is essential to its healing properties. Depending on the problem, the patient, and his or her lifestyle, it may be better to use a fresh herb, a dried and aged herb, or a combination of herbs that are either soaked, boiled, steamed, or baked. The recipe will be exact to effectively convey the yin or yang properties and the necessary balance of constituents to induce equilibrium in the body. Chinese medicine usually dictates the use of formulas—combinations of herbs blended together in specific proportions. A single herb does not have the synergistic effect of an exact combination. The ingredients in the formula are balanced to emulate the balance sought by the patient.

• • •

Jeanne Phillips' adventures with Chinese traditional medicine began because she has a history of acute asthma. She passed the word in her work unit that she wanted to become established with a doctor in advance, "so that any acute episode would have a context surrounding the potential midnight rush."

Fuzhou, Fujian

Dear Alice,

The spry, sharp dean of my division, a wonderful woman in her seventies, said she would find me a doctor. She had a family friend come to see me, a retired professor of Chinese medicine who had also had training at one of three top-notch Western medical schools in China.

I knew the examination would not be very Western when I was told to meet him in our lounge. It consisted of examining my tongue, which showed indentations where my teeth pressed against it. This meant that my *qi* was low. *Qi* is a very difficult concept to grasp, encompassing one's store of vital energy and more. It is the target of *qi gong* exercises and is related to breathing and essential spirit. I clearly don't understand it enough to explain it at all, although I've encountered the concept often, especially practicing *qi gong* in past years. Anyway, this evidence signified that my asthma is of the deficient *qi* type—deficient in energy and function.

Then the doctor took my pulse, at length and from both wrists, and told the dean a lot of things that never got to me. He did tell me that my pulse was irregular in rate and strength and showed my heart was not good. (He may have been picking up on the signs that led to a sonar visualization last summer at work. This showed everything is fine; the sounds are anomalous.) He then wrote out four prescriptions:

One is for pills. I think I'm supposed to take three to six of them three times a day, though I compromise and do three, twice a day. They are made from human placenta and sugar and should build up my general condition.

Some other pills that look like buckshot are to be taken a large handful each day, divided into two or three batches. These are to correct problems with liver and kidney that are likely to be caused by Western medicine that I take (especially steroids) and that he disapproves of. Contents are herbs yet to be identified.

Another is a liquid named in quasi-Latin, roughly meaning nucleic acid and hydrolytic compositions. No other contents listed. An insert describes it as a tonic, able to strengthen resistance to diseases (especially colds), cure chronic bronchitis and sleep problems, and generally reduce any symptoms. Most people use it to reduce frequency of colds.

There is a sort of belt, like an old-fashioned hernia truss, that is the Chinese equivalent of our skin patches. This delivers medicine slowly through the skin from an impregnated cloth. It is to increase my strength by balancing my yin and yang and to get more yang to my kidneys (which need that) and liquid to my lungs. I can't discover what the ingredients are.

The belt and the liquid are supposed to be good for my *qi* deficiency and my blood deficiency and can also help weak limbs, slow the aging process, help reduce weight (I wish!), unblock blood vessels, and thin out thick blood so it flows faster.

Finally, there is a potion to use in the event of an acute asthma episode, the sort one needs to go to the emergency room for. This is to be prepared by a friend in advance and frozen by me in one of the square aluminum lunch pails—done so it forms a thin layer, quick to defrost. *In extremis*, while I wait for arrangements to go to the hospital, I am to remove the cooked part, defrost this on my electric room heater, then stir in a final paper-twist of mysterious powder and drink. Since the Chinese discovered epinephrine in herbs several millennia ago, I assumed that this was a key and relevant ingredient, but apparently not. The three main ingredients are:

- ginseng—very precious and good for stomach and spleen, gout, constipation and diarrhea, kidney inflammation, weak sex ability, frequency of urine, gasping, and weak nerves, all related to *qi* and cold (in the technical sense).

- *dong qing*, or Spring Worm–Summer Grass—another generic tonic whose name delights me and is made of various herbs.
- *san-qi*—made of a half dozen energizing herbs.

Somewhere in there are Earth Dragons—worms, dried and said to be great for asthma but dangerous for pneumonia. Anything called Earth Dragons has got to be powerful and good. There are reputedly over fifty rare natural herbs in this emergency tonic— but when I'm in Hong Kong I intend to get an epinephrine kit to replace an expired one I brought.

This is the official ingredient list:

1. belamcanda (English) or blackberry lily
   Belamcanda chinensis (Latin)
   Caution: not to be taken by pregnant women
2. Chinese ephedra (English)
   Ephedra sinica (Latin)
3. apricot seed (English)
   Prunus armeniaca (Latin)
   Function: reduces phlegm, relieves cough, eases gasping
   Caution: overdose poisonous
4. dry earthworm
   Function: antiasthmatic, very effective
   Caution: to be prescribed carefully in the case of intestinal diseases and pneumonia
5. ginseng
6. Solomon's seal (English)
   Polygonatum odoratum (Mill.) Druce (Latin)
   Function: eases lungs by promoting the secretion of saliva and body fluid, good for tracheitis
   Caution: to be prescribed carefully in the case of chronic enteritis
7. the tuber of dwarf lilyturf (English)
   Ophiopogon japonicus (Latin)
8. schisandra (English)
   Schisandra chinensis (Turcz.) Baill (Latin)

Function: relieves cough, eases gasping, reduces phlegm
Caution: not to be taken in the case of high fever and
asthma
9. licorice root
10. *zi he fen* (Chinese)

At this point I ask myself: Why this long tangent on contents
of traditional Chinese medicines?

I guess because so many people think they contain ancient
wisdom. I'm sure many do, while others are analogues to our
decades of bleeding and leeches to cure everything. The catch is
to know which is which. The claims for all of them are absurdly
encompassing, promising to cure illnesses of every sort. The other
characteristic that shows in my digression is that one takes huge
quantities of Chinese meds. They are deemed superior because of
their slow and gentle action, usually without risk of negative side
effects (though my friend who looked up all these ingredients to
translate did find many cautionary notes, including one against
using a main herb with asthma). They are thought to cure basic
causes in a preventive fashion—in contrast to harsh, overly
powerful, and rapid Western medicines that simply reduce
symptoms and do nothing to cure or prevent illness, nor to improve one's overall health and condition.

This latter sermon I've heard a lot and brings me back to the
point, in a way. The big event of early November was a horrendous allergic reaction that eventually stripped me of every inch of
skin from my scalp to the soles of my feet, even including inside
my ears. The swelling and itchy red wheals kept me in bed for a
week and peeling for weeks after. For that episode, it was the
college's consulting physician who cared for me. She gave me a
lot of pills, some eye drops, and a comforting salve.

Chinese friends and colleagues were wonderful in coming by,
bringing flowers, treats, and cards (and not waking me to deliver
them since I was sleeping most of every day), but we never settled
the preoccupying issue—what caused it? I'd been taking antibiotics for a few days for a small cold, and I wondered if it was

possible to develop a severe allergy over time (I now think a common U.S. antibiotic was the culprit). My Chinese physicians simply said I shouldn't take that sort of thing at all and advised me to stick with the long-term benefits of their traditional prescriptions. So I couldn't get any alternative antibiotic to take.

Another point is that the *guanxi* net requires that I use these special and prized resources of my friends and colleagues and bosses. To demand to see another physician with primarily Western training would be the scooter episode all over again, only a thousand times more serious and insulting, because of the status of the people involved, their age, and close affection for me. The fact that their ideas don't fit what *I* feel I need doesn't fit into the equation easily. Then the best way to help me is to convince me of the error of my ideas.

So the aged dean ventures to a far-away pharmacy to get the special herbs and lends me her electrical ear-stimulator (which cures everything from heart disease to hepatitis to asthma). And I still have no orienting appointment with an ER physician at the provincial hospital, no alternative antibiotics to take, and no way to test my allergic response to the ones I brought, e.g., with a scratch test. I do have an appointment with a reliable doc in Hong Kong, located through the remarkable help of Denver friends and their friends in Hong Kong—so the whole world is *guanxi.*

•   •   •

I did finally manage to see a Western-style doctor here. He is the doc for the mayor and governor and travels with them, like our Prez and the Queen take their own MDs. He gave me an antibiotic and decongestant to work on my cold and laughed softly at the meds the traditional Chinese doc had given me. He too pushed me to get off steroids, so as soon as the cold is gone and I can breathe again, I will.

Jeanne Phillips

Looking for adventure? Come to China! At least Jeanne Phillips ventured into the maze of Chinese medicine with a background in health care and some experience evaluating medicines. But to someone who is young and has never experienced a hospital on any continent before, even Western medical practices can seem like the great unknown, especially reflected in China's Looking Glass.

Changsha, Hunan

Dear Alice,

The zoo opens at 6:30 A.M., even on Sundays. The housekeeper throws the door open, slaps on the light, and noisily scuffles in with three thermoses of hot water—one for the ten-year-old singer with kidney disease, another for the dramatic thirteen-year-old who shouts at night for his mother on the cot at the end of his bed to prop up his behind so he can defecate, and a third for me, the rare beast on loan from the U.S. I was brought in one day for emergency surgery for appendicitis and left on display in the 21st ward for a week, like an albino tiger, a special attraction.

A prize catch, with bright blue eyes and oversized snout, I drew the crowds. Peasants from the countryside, workers—in fact any visitors to the zoo that day would spill into the room, blankly stare at the phenomenon of the age, a foreigner in a Chinese hospital. Perhaps they've read about people like me, seen pictures on TV, but here is one live! Almost human, with an IV and all. Can he speak? You think he can use chopsticks? The safety of the crowd grew with numbers, and so did its boldness. Occasionally, they'd send a child over in an attempt to solicit a response; instead of talking he'd reach up, touch my big nose. In fact, one brutish ten-year-old didn't just touch my nose, he grabbed it like a knob, tried to wrench it off my face. The crowd laughs and I sit there, nowhere to go. But in my mind, I shout obscenities in the local dialect.

At 8 A.M. the nurse brigade would come on, surround my bed, fluff my pillow and the only new sheets in the hospital; they reassure me they are available should I need them. By 8:30, the floor is brushed of banana peels and cotton swabs, spot-mopped.

Ready for the unit of doctors—the famous surgeon and his students, many of whom are my students. We chat in Chinese while they redress my scar. They are happy to hear that I like this zoo, as common as it is. The crowd moves closer—he can speak Changsha dialect!

The days continue in the same manner, though by the second day I can easily move about and the IV is lifted, to my relief. Finally able to eat. Three of my students were designated to prepare meals for me, bring them to the hospital, and feed me—though again, I could eat myself. But did I mind? Three young females serving me like the emperor. At night I'd dream of pharaohs and the gentry of the Tang dynasty. Five months ago I would have felt the weight of my liberal education and guilt in having women serve me. Alice, they'd even wash my feet.

Appendicitis is a common disease and a simple surgical procedure, but one would think I had a cancer or other noxious ailment. Groups of students would stream in all day, each bearing yet more bags of bananas and apples, biscuits, to pile on the heap of food that continually grew more embarrassing. Too much. In a Western hospital I'd be going home after a few days, a home most likely more comfortable than the hospital. But here I spent seven days entertaining the 150 students I have this semester, the 150 from last semester, all my friends, acquaintances, and university administrators. They said I was there to rest. So instead of resting, cogitating, or reading Somerset Maugham short stories, I was concerned about my messy hair. Actually, it was interesting, and is—might I say it?—fun. In the end, that is.

It was a Wednesday morning when I woke at 3 A.M. with stomach pain. I assumed it was from the food I had eaten at a restaurant the night before, but I had no diarrhea. The pain was bearable, and I met my friends at 5:30 A.M. to practice *bagua*. In the habit of youth, thinking myself strong and resilient, I assumed it would pass. I even taught class at 8. But by noon I knew there was a problem and I commandeered some students to help me get to the emergency room for an examination and a blood test: sure enough, acute appendicitis. I would need surgery soon.

What followed can be described as nothing less than chaos. Was I going to be put into the hands of the university for emergency surgery? Who was going to take responsibility (that wonderfully Chinese conundrum)? And under whose knife was I going to lie? The FAO was terrified, uncertain whether they needed approval from the American embassy in Beijing. Word spread quickly (what's new?), and the emergency room filled up with my students, administrators, Party hacks, and any stray idiots drawn to the buzz. As I sat hunched over in a chair, unable to control anything going on here, I could hear the wails of emergency patients now ignored because of the chaos, because of me. I just sat in pain, for three hours, not accepting the decision just passed: I would have surgery, NOW. The first time in my life as a patient in a hospital or to have surgery, and it was going to be here, in Changsha. Aye, yi, yi.

And so it goes . . .

Back home now with a week to rest before I resume my teaching duties. I was given two weeks by the doctor and briefly considered heading to a beach in Thailand. But as I walk down the street now at my natural fast clip and see students, whom I like and who have no classes until I return . . . a week is enough.

One surprising message lies buried in many of these tales of adventure: Even at the outer limits, support sometimes appears like magic. Amanda was fed and housed in the jungle by a generous farmer; Inger was rescued in Taibei by Immigration. As G's story implies, sometimes China can offer too much support! But Jeanne Phillips has explained elsewhere that exchanges of help and companionship are "the heart and fuel of the society." In her final medical adventure, when a cold became bronchitis which became a second bout of bronchitis, we can begin to see why.

Fuzhou, Fujian

Dear Alice,

A few glimpses of being a patient here, and you'll understand why our vice-president thinks I should *stay* in China so when I get sick with asthma and bronchitis, I would get good care. She worries how I can ever manage in the U.S. Her concern really shows the incredible caring, generosity, and warmth of Chinese friends.

The young woman from our Foreign Affairs Office spends every evening and night with me. Until today I've been hooked to IVs 12–15 hours a day and one can't move around much with one on, so she does a lot of fetching and moving. She also gave long back massages and slaps on the back to help me cough all night the first nights, she watches IVs, etc.—a very empathic, attentive young woman (the "die for you" relationship of a previous letter). She has a very good sense of humor so we understand each other comfortably. It turned out, all the workers on this floor thought she was my *daughter,* so now I'm hunting for a photo of my ideal Chinese husband who'd be her father!

Then *all* day, one of the young English teachers is with me, in rotation—to order meals, rub my back, help move IV to W.C., bring cloth and pan to wash up with, etc. Nurses do technical procedures, and that is it. All patients have a family member with them as much as they need, to provide all other care. I order my meals from a menu and they come on a tray (but I provide cutlery, enamel bowl and plate, and wash up myself). Most patients' relative or helper takes the enamel cup and bowl to a central cart of pots, selects from that, and carries it back to the room; some also cook with a hot plate.

Anyway, the young teachers are marvelous with me; we read and listen to BBC and talk and eat the oranges and cookies visitors bring, and they make me add more layers of clothes. They are more my mothers than my daughters. The dean comes almost daily on her way home and at 73 gives the greatest back rubs of all. She also pushes food and layers of clothes. (It's been rainy and cold, with no heat of course—but sunny and beautiful today.) Others drop by often, so I never feel neglected and will find living in my room alone very strange for a day or two, I'm sure. It is learning to accept all this devoted care, given with never a complaint or hint of inconvenience, that is the ultimate lesson in humility!

So—I have the best MD in Fuzhou (who climbed a tree to pick and bring a kapok flower to me), marvelous TLC, lots of meds, and soon will be well and back to where I was last fall, before the first cold started all this.

Love,

Jeanne Phillips

Dear Jean,

I'm very very regret to have heard that you'd to stay with so many "lovely" nurses and "kind" doctors. Have you adjusted to the Chinese hospital and the special smell of that hospital? Do you feel better? I really dislike the hospital, so I truly hope you can feel better there.

Sue had told us that you were sad for you couldn't go to school to meet us. We, too. However, Chairman Mao had told us: "Health is the base of working." So, we all hope you can take all the doctors' good advices—OK? Hope when we meet again, we can see a healthy happy fat lady again.

Yours,

Grace

Of course, on any adventure it never hurts to have a sense of humor!

Changsha, Hunan

Dear Alice,

Thanks for the recent letter—actually, letters—and your concern for my health. I'm fine, really. The infection that resulted from the original surgery wasn't as bad as expected—only my legs were amputated. But I have a wheelchair of the highest quality (made in the USA, you know!), and the university has taken pains to build a ramp up to the foreign languages building. How lucky can I be?

Take care, Alice, and hold on to your appendix.

Leglessly yours,

G

Fortunately, Alice has traveled enough herself to know when *her* leg is being pulled.

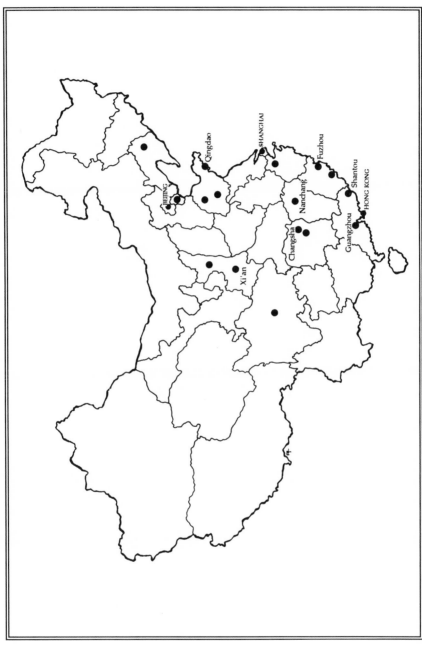

Map 9. The People's Republic of China, showing the cities from which letters in chapter 8 were written.

gong fu (gong foo): the pinyin spelling of *kung fu*.

tae kwon do (tie kwan dough): a Korean martial art featuring kicks.

Culture Shock

A. Well—you win your bet! After much deliberation, I have decided to stay another year! It took me quite some time to come 'round to this. When first I'd come back from spring vacation I thought, absolutely, NO WAY. That trip put quite a dent in my "China experience." But after being back a while, I felt that (1) my work here is not done, and (2) going home now would be wrenching. I've only just begun to get a feel, begun to understand, begun to live without constant comparisons. We are not done with each other, China and I.

B. J—— is leaving too. I don't think the department was too pleased with him—his language. He used a lot of slang and sarcasm in his everyday speech, which he didn't change when he taught. The students, the teachers all thought he was making fun of them. They couldn't understand him.

C. I love my life here, I love the Chinese, I love my university. I'm at a time in my life where I'm emotionally up and down, confused, anxious, etc., etc. The identity crisis is probably over, but the focus of my life now is looking for my gifts—what can I give to the world (i.e., *what will I do?*). Being in this environment, in China, well, it is difficult to step out of myself and look. But I think that seeing how people live and love here, what they know, what they emphasize, what they see—it affects my decisions and my growth. It's very subtle but it's there, and it will endure.

D. You probably knew M—— was, well, in his own world even before he came here. He has been on a personal self-exploration of his philosophical nature and has, at times, sat for days in his room alone reading and thinking. Most of us have adjusted to his swimming farther and farther from shore. He does generate some great conversations. But his teaching, his responsibility to the school, has been unbelievably neglected.

Two of these people stayed to teach in China for a second year; two of them survived for a year but did not adjust. You can probably tell which is which. But what creates the difference between them? The most likely answer is "culture shock," but not in the way you might think. It is the people who *adapt* to China who most directly confront and ride out the waves of confusing emotion called "culture shock."

Culture shock has been described and studied by many experts. It is characterized by such emotions as anxiety, anger, even despair, and generally sounds like something any wise person would avoid. But those who understand it best agree that going through culture shock is an essential part of learning to live well in another land. One experienced intercultural trainer, L. Robert Kohls, sees it as so common and so nearly inevitable for long-term sojourners that he calls it "the occupational hazard of overseas living."[1]

Now, granting that culture shock might be inevitable, why should it be *necessary* for those who want to adapt? The reason comes from basic human psychology: people resist hard changes. To fully accept that they must change, they often have to sink into temporary shock to marshal their resources.

So far in these letters, we have heard about many differences between the United States and China—different values, different rules, different assumptions. We first heard the rustling of unfamiliar "customs and mind-set" behind transportation and utilities. We saw some Chinese treating teachers like exotic talking birds. Ethical differences appeared in the classroom, and many things "mother taught" in America began to look out of place in China. Could it be that Chinese mothers teach their children something else? Obviously, they do. Why haven't these writers simply adopted Chinese customs, ethics, and mind-set and moved on?

One reason is that ethics and values are hard to see (and equally hard

---

[1] *Survival Kit for Overseas Living*, 3d ed. (Yarmouth, Me.: Intercultural Press, 1996), p. 87.

to explain) because they are tangled up with behavior. Even a Chinese mother might find it hard to say what value lies behind pushing onto the bus or exclaiming that an unripe pear is delicious because "that's just the way we do things." Psychologist Peter Adler points out that most people in any country are relatively unaware of their most important values and attitudes. In fact, he says, it is only when conflicts arise—as when our values collide with those of a new culture—that we are forced to become aware of them.[2]

Adults in a new land like to think at first that they can choose which behaviors and values they will adopt. But the range of options for those who stand between two cultures and the lines of force pulling this way and that create a nearly hopeless muddle. As we saw in classroom lessons about limits, choice *is* possible. But sorting it all out takes time and—let's be frank here—who wants to go to all that trouble?

Most people resist changing their customs and mind-set. Habits of life and mind are built up very slowly through years of living in the home culture, and they feel comfortable, natural, almost inevitable. After learning the American way so well, who wants to be forced to learn a whole new set of—*everything?* Inwardly, most sojourners try to ignore early hints that this might be necessary. It takes something very big or very persistent to force them to admit that they have to take on this remodeling job, partly because they sense that things could get nasty. After all, psychologists call the moment of accepting the job "disintegration."

Roughly, here's how it works:

1. *You grow up learning your own culture.* In America you learn to look both ways crossing the street, what clothes to wear if you want to be "in style," that owning a TV is normal, and how to eat with knife and fork. All this and more. Children and adults who learn well are able to understand what things mean. For example, they come to know what it "means" to own a bike or to pay (or not pay) taxes.

2. *You also grow up learning who you are in the culture.* Are you a brain or an athlete? Do people who look like you fill most of the places

---

[2] "The Transitional Experience: An Alternative View of Culture Shock," *Journal of Humanistic Psychology*, Fall 1975, p. 14.

in a board room? in the welfare lines? Are you "Most Likely to Succeed" or "The Odd One"? You develop a sense of your strengths and weaknesses and of how people usually react to them. By the time they're teenagers, most people have a feel for who they are in their culture and can make a pretty good guess about what others think of them in most situations; they can understand the meaning of a scowl or a wink.

3. *You go to China and discover that everything you learned is wrong.* Experience slowly forces you to admit that Chinese culture is different in its very bones. As Marla Jenks said, "I'm sure someone 'lost face' in the scuffle, but I don't know which one. I never can tell about those things." And obviously people are reacting to *you* differently than they ever have before. Finally, one day . . .

4. *A voice deep inside whispers, "You don't know what's going on. You are going to have to begin all over."* This is the moment of culture shock.

What "disintegrates" at this moment is Meaning. All the well-known meanings of the surrounding world and the meaning of your own actions drop away, and life gets very uncomfortable for a while. In his *Survival Kit for Overseas Living*, Robert Kohls lists the following symptoms common during culture shock: anxiety, homesickness, helplessness, boredom, depression, fatigue, confusion, self-doubt, feelings of inadequacy, unexplainable fits of weeping, paranoia, and an unusual degree of physical sickness (p. 92).

PJ gives us an account of how she felt passing through this phase.

Changsha, Hunan

Dear Alice,

When I first came to China I got frustrated by the "idiocies" of this country, and then I "matured" and just let them roll by. To me this felt like drifting. Drift. And it was basically comfortable, sort of Zen. But I'm not the kind who can just drift forever, or rather, the drift was a fake. I mean, deep down I still believed that some of this stuff was idiotic. At some point my "tolerance" and forgiveness collapsed, and something inside me hollered, "That's enough! Stop doing that to me!" My sweet, centered drift slammed up against the hard rock. This year it was the way they don't plan anything—canceling plane reservations without explanation, changing around my class assignments. But it could have been any Chinese habit I found "too different"; it just had to come when I was close to the edge.

I got furious at everything—the way they walk, the way they politely pull my sleeve, all those firecrackers at a wedding next door. I stormed around and, fortunately, in China I had room-mates with loud rock and roll tapes, and we used to dance insanely some nights. It just had to come out, or I would have taken it out on my lovely, innocent students, my Chinese friends. Anyone could see they didn't *mean* to offend me, and yet I took offense. It was so hard not to lash out at them, but . . . Really, they were not the problem. They were just doing what everyone here does. *I* was the one who was out of step. I even took the *weather* as a personal attack—shook my fist at the sky, "Why are you freezing me like this?"

One imaginative friend had given me rose bath salts when I left the U.S., "to use on a really bad day." I wept as I wrote her on one of these days, "A *really* bad day is when there's no hot water to use the bath salts a friend gave you for a really bad day!" It is funny now, but it was a hard, hellish place to be in for a while.

Then eventually I started to really accept "this is how it is here." Not secretly judging things idiotic, not taking offense, but simply acknowledging the way things are. Then I could sincerely consider Why? There are more than a billion people in China living this way, and the culture has lasted more than 3,000 years. My country can't say as much. And I've found that some things I thought so holy and normal are pure foolishness in this place. Like being "independent." They think it's conceited (how could we possibly think we *can* do everything alone?) and also that it's stupid (why try to learn everything yourself when there are so many able and willing to help?). It took me two insane trips "by myself"—in which I eventually had to solicit help from strangers who happened to be unnaturally good-hearted and honest—to learn that in this country, I wasn't being self-reliant, I was being proud and foolish.

That sort of realization makes you look deeper at everything. Why do they walk and ride so slowly, and constantly ring bells and honk? Maybe because they are reading the whole situation, getting a feel for the flow, and trying to communicate their own intentions to others doing likewise. I've been knocked off my bike twice, both times by friends nudging my handlebars with theirs and throwing me off balance. At first I was inwardly outraged—"What are they trying to do to me?!" But now I think *I* was out of line, that they assumed I would "read" their movements and flow out of the way a little. For all I know, *they* were thinking "Why is she so stubborn?!"

When you stop automatically assuming that your way is right, it's like opening a door from a small room. At first you might be confused by what you see next door, but at least you are looking around. And eventually you can start walking through their room, trying to understand why they assume *their* way is right. It takes a long time and I'm no saint, but during the moments I manage to look at China the way the Chinese do, it really starts to make some sense. (And my old little room can look pretty strange from their side, too.)

PJ

"I got furious at everything," PJ says, and "I took offense at so much." Many people react this way when they realize that they have no idea what is going on and that most of their actions are being misunderstood—that is, when they finally accept that Chinese people assign different meanings to a smile or a touch, to artwork and hot water than Americans do.

In a world upside down, every hint about what things mean has disappeared, and old clues to the self are lost. There are no clear answers to the questions "What's going on?" and "What am I doing?" To an adult hired to teach English in China such losses are, to put it mildly, unsettling. And opening the door to the questions behind the loss catapults most people into culture shock.

This is the moment to remember what Kohls says: Everything is going well! After all, the world has stopped making sense. A little confusion and anxiety are in order; homesickness and weeping are appropriate. These are *reasonable* responses to the profound and disturbing realization that, at the age of 23 or 33 or 43, you have to go back to square one and learn how to live life from scratch. Wouldn't any normal person feel depressed or tired in the face of such a huge project?

Many people find the dissolution of meaning so unsettling they look for ways to ignore it. Quotation B at the start of this chapter shows the sarcastic teacher erecting a wall of cleverness and slang to protect himself from having to ask "What's going on here?" He has a smart crack to describe everything. And those who can't understand him simply become material for more sarcasm. In quotation D, the philosophical teacher avoids the "What am I doing?" question by drifting high above it (and above practical questions about how to teach), taking comfort in a rarefied world of abstractions where he is not doing anything. Some teachers break their contracts and go home. PJ and the writer in quotation C, on the other hand, slam right into the hard questions and wrestle with feeling confused, frustrated, and hurt. Why is this better?

It's better because the moment that meaning is lost is a time of great openness to the world. Life without meaning is nearly intolerable for humans. So as soon as old meanings fall apart, the search for new ones starts. PJ calls it "opening a door from a small room" and "looking around, trying to understand why they assume their way is right." This is where adapting to a new culture really begins. Those who avoid asking "What's going on?" seldom discover an answer. They are doomed to remain unaltered Americans in a basically unknown world.

For everyone living in a new culture, the disintegration of culture shock forces two basic decisions. First, each person must choose whether to learn new ways or try to hold on to old habits and identity. Second, sojourners must decide how to explain the problems they have in China. Will they blame everything on Chinese culture, its awful people and senseless systems visiting themselves upon innocent foreigners? Or will they look for reasons in the place between cultures, where America and China somehow fail to mesh?

Often these two crucial decisions—to learn or to hang on, to blame or to look for reasons—are made unconsciously. Most people switch back and forth a little at first. But on balance, each person develops a general tendency, one that grows out of personality and experience with other deep transitions.[3] Even when the decisions are unconscious, however, they can often be read between the lines of these letters. For example:

1. On Wednesday, I had a huge dinner with the other English teachers + officials. It turned into a game of seeing how drunk they could get the foreigner. What a nightmare. At one time, I ventured out to use the local bathroom (which consisted of a brick wall) and fell into a large unmarked pit. It was definitely taller than me. Fortunately, there was more humor than pain (just a slight abrasion on my thigh). No squatting for a while! Part of the experience, right?

2. I've had quite a lot of time for introspection this week and I've come to the conclusion that anyone who voluntarily comes to live in China is absolutely out of their head. This has got to be the most backward, illogical, chaotic, filthy, God-forsaken place in the world. When I'm alone with nothing to do but think, my distaste grows.

3. The Chinese are very strict with him, tell him his Chinese is poor, excoriate him for not knowing how to write Chinese. He takes it all in stride, banging on his guitar and howling late into the night. I think he has trouble sleeping sometimes, as I not infrequently wake up at 3 A.M. to one of his tunes.

4. The Colorado crowd had a really good time together. We ate, and ate well. Kentucky Fried Chicken, Singapore hamburgers, a little black market, the Mosque, and talking for hours.

---

[3] Adler argues that culture shock has features in common with all important transitions and prefers to call them all "transition shock." Thus, becoming a parent, changing jobs, or losing a loved one can all raise the questions "What's going on?" and "What am I doing?" and force us to reevaluate how the world works and our place in it. All in all, this seems to be a good thing for people *if* they choose to adapt, and each transition experience can help build skills for handling the next one. If transitions could be given difficulty ratings, however, crossing cultures from the United States to China would still probably rank as a 10.

5. What a time these last months have been! I do miss my "freedoms." Things that were odd or strange at first have become downright annoying. One of the foreign students and I are changing the words to the ad "Come Back to Jamaica" to "Come Back to Guangzhou" to fit our experiences. He was hit several times by the gate guard one night. Trippy country!

6. Another reason this university reminds me of high school is the blatant cheating on exams. Yesterday, we all proctored an exam for the entire sophomore class. We walked around, patrolling the classroom, intimidating students. It was fun in a way to be in the teacher's position, but actually I wish we didn't have to treat them like children. It's their choice—they earned our distrust!

7. He was just confused, tired, and way over his head here. We all feel that way sometimes, but with him it started the first month he was here, and he never recovered. One woman who's still here said that last year *everyone* tired quickly of being in China. Recipe for disaster—especially if you fuel that opinion among each other, which is easily done.

8. In our building were two boxes of something they left behind which said in red marker "FAO—Keep your Hands OFF!" The FAO said that they quarreled all year, and when she was unable to purchase soft-sleeper tickets for their departure trip, they became very angry. She tried to explain that there truly were no more tickets available. But they told her that she was treating them differently from the other foreigners.

9. I often feel passionate here, and get myself worked up into quasi-poethood. Alas—moments of philosophical grandeur are quickly leveled when I do something silly, like getting chalk dust all over my bottom during a lecture or getting lost for a whole hour just trying to find where I parked my bike.

Can you see the differences here? Reactions 1, 3, 4, 5, and 9 suggest that people are trying to learn and to look for reasons. Reactions 2, 6, 7, and 8 suggest that people are trying to hang on and to blame.

The "hanging on" reactions were probably easy to identify, but were any of the "learners" surprising? Do eating American food, banging on a guitar all night, or writing musical satires about the town you live in sound like constructive paths to adaptation? Done occasionally these *are* healthy, because they help relieve the stresses of culture shock without blaming China. After all, anyone who spends months or weeks—or even an hour a day—asking "What's going on here, and what am I doing again?" deserves to return now and then to familiar ground, to let loose the cynicism, exhaustion, and momentary despair that occasionally rise up in the passage between worlds.

To weather the worst days of culture shock without blaming China takes many small acts of courage and clarity. These quick flashes of strength can easily go unnoticed in letters where they are surrounded by thundering frustration. At first glance, for example, the following letter from Megan seems to reveal only how intense the search for meaning in the midst of disintegration can be.

Hangzhou, Zhejiang
Mid-November

Dear Alice,

I wanted to write you and express some of my frustration with these people! I am finding myself saying "I hate these people" very often, and I feel terrible about it. I just really don't like a lot of the fundamental aspects of their culture. I can't get used to all of the pushing, shoving, spitting, etc. But more important, I feel like I can't trust anyone and I feel like I am going to go through this whole year and not have a close friendship with anyone.

I always think I have made a new friend, and then they come up with some tack where they need my assistance. I am so tired of people wanting to be with me for the sole purpose of practicing English or because I am a foreigner. As a person who is used to being surrounded by close friends, I find this hard to deal with. I have made a lot of friends with the other foreigners, but with all the Chinese people I know, I have a superficial friendship because they want something from me. I also get frustrated with feeling like I am forever indebted to someone if they do something for me. I have always felt that you do something for someone because you want to, not because you have an account of favors with them and need to pay up.

There are a few exceptions. We have a neighbor who is really nice to us and cooks for us. Also, I like one group of my students a lot. But conversations with them are always the same, they all say the same thing. Which leads me to wonder if some of them might be thinking differently but are afraid to say so. Is this correct? Or are they all so concerned about getting into the Communist Party that they won't say anything except the Party line? (Many of my students are currently taking the entrance exam.[4])

I am having such a horrible resentment toward these people and I don't like feeling that way, so I am writing to you to see if you can help me sort it out. I feel like I am becoming a racist or something of the sort, and I keep trying to ignore that—but sometimes I can't find anything that I can respect them for or anything that I like about them. I know these are terrible things to say, and I am probably reacting so strongly because I just got back from a really frustrating weekend in Shanghai where I couldn't stand the crowds and crowds of people.

I would like to hear what your reactions to these feelings are. I really need some suggestions on how to erase this image I have of Chinese people. Also, I hope I have not offended you, as I know your passion for learning about the Chinese.

I hope all is going well.

Love,

Megan

---

[4] Becoming a member of the Communist Party today requires passing tests and undergoing a character review.

P.S. Our *waiban* has not gotten any better. It has taken two months of asking and he still has not given us our heater. He keeps saying it is being fixed! He is *very* unhelpful and I think whoever comes here next should be prepared to do things by themselves and not expect much assistance from him. He is useless! When we asked him the last time about the heater, his response was "Just put on more clothes!" He said that as we stood there in five or six layers of clothes! The other people in the office have been a lot more helpful and have more interest in us, it seems.

Megan's letter expresses many of Kohls's classic symptoms of culture shock—anxiety, boredom, confusion, self-doubt, paranoia. She is struggling hard to make sense of the world and her feelings about it. She is scrambling around in the place between cultures where things fail to mesh, turning over every stone.

What makes her scramble constructive is that she considers her own reactions to China as part of the problem. Is it the Party exams, she asks, or my frustrating weekend? She does not issue blanket denunciations of this "backward, illogical, chaotic, filthy place," but rather asks, "Is this correct? Can you help me out?"

The ability to laugh, eat, sing, and ask questions in the midst of cultural confusion is what psychologists really mean by the phrase "tolerance of ambiguity." As Megan's next letter shows, one or two of these apparently simple skills plus a sympathetic ear can help sojourners begin their move into cultural reintegration relatively fast.

Hangzhou, Zhejiang
Early February

Dear Alice,

Thank you for your wonderful Christmas card. I was really happy to hear from you—and your words made me feel better. I wanted to write and tell you I have gotten past those terrible feelings and am much happier and a lot less frustrated.

I met a guy who is teaching near me and we had dinner one night and I just unloaded everything on him. After I got it all out, I felt so relieved. Also he listened to it all, and after everything he just nodded and said, "I hear you." That was all I needed—to know someone else had felt the same way. He then gave me some words of advice that someone told him when he was having the same feelings. He told me that some people don't have any signs of culture shock until about three to five months after they arrive, and then they hit a point of total frustration and depression. Then they pull out of it. I guess that's what happened. Compounded with this was the fact that I didn't have anyone to talk to about it, so I felt even worse. But once someone told me they had had the same anger and frustrations and that eventually it would go away—it all seemed not so bad.

It also helped to write you and to hear from a person who's experienced with China that I was normal. I really thank you for your letter. All of those feelings have gone away, and I find myself really happy here. I have made some good friends in the foreign community which also helps. My students have been a lot better, and I know I am going to have a hard time leaving them. This has all been such an incredible experience. I have learned a lot about myself.

I hope all is going well with you—and thank you again for listening and caring.

Happy Chinese New Year!

Love always,

Megan

P.S. The *waiban* has been a lot better, and we have a heater, now!

A teacher working in a foreign land is a walking paradox—within one individual there are two answers to every question. Is it good to be an independent, self-reliant traveler? "Yes," says the PJ born in America; "No," says the PJ living in China. The time of transition from well-worn U.S. answers to newly learned Chinese wisdom is full of false starts and mistakes. Learning is hard. So it is no sin to take a break from this hard work now and then, to belt out the blues or dance out frustration, to eat home cooking, and to talk it out with others who can help make sense of things again. Culture shock is an emotional reaction, says Robert Kohls; it is not going to be *reasoned* away.

The important thing is to survive and to keep learning. Teachers who are successful at both continue to engage their new world, though they know how to take breaks now and then. There is a difference between taking a weekend vacation and sitting "for days in his room alone," between composing one satirical song and turning to sarcasm every day. Samantha Tisdel sums up the advantages of trying to balance engaging the new world with taking breaks from it particularly well.

SAMANTHA TISDEL: The Chinese are insular; you can never become one no matter how long you stay, study, try to integrate. Thus sometimes it is tempting to flaunt your differentness, feel the abrasion of their difference against yours. It is a wonderful, scratchy feeling. Nevertheless, some of my best times here have been when I've entered their world, if only for a little while.

- Discovering a traditional teahouse on a lake in the heart of old Shanghai and drinking early-morning tea out of a cracked clay cup, surrounded by old Chinese men with unfathomable creased faces. They warm their gloved hands on their teapots, play chess, argue, smoke, meditate on the cold fragility of the winter morning light filtering through dusty panelled windows to fall on the worn flagstone floor.
- Spending the night with some mountain peasants in their traditional stone cottage, drinking and eating and talking with them deep into the night while perched atop a *kang*—a high platform heated from underneath with hot coals or bricks—then curling up on the *kang* to go to sleep.
- Shopping at the local farmer's market, a huge covered patch of dirt with long rows of wooden tables on which the farmers display their goods. . . . Fisherwomen and

men with their catch of the day spread before them, . . .
booths with steamed buns, dumplings, fresh noodles, sacks
of grain, sausages, pigs' and chickens' feet, buckets of live,
squirming, edible insects, . . . fresh sides of beef and pork
hanging in a row on hooks, . . . and to complete the
collage, rub in all shapes and sizes of Chinese folks, from
crinkle-faced grandmothers to bare-bottomed babies.

Still, although it may be a character flaw on my part, after a
lengthy excursion into this world, all my senses have been
assaulted and it is a relief to get back to my enclave, my foreign
ghetto. I can take a hot shower, blast Big Head Todd on my
stereo, lie in bed and read a book, drink some instant coffee.
Immersion is thrilling, but exhausting.

Samantha's exhaustion management plan worked so well for her that
she not only worked through her culture shock and adjusted to China, she
returned to teach for another year.

Many scholars agree that those who survive best in a new land include
people who immerse in a passion—something they probably could not
practice so naturally back home.

STEPHEN: The school has been a very good base from which to do
research into *wushu* and the history of military arts in which I am
interested. I have been able to meet several knowledgeable people
who have helped me greatly, and I have started to compile
information for what I hope will be a book on the history and
development of *wushu* in China. Well, anyway, I'm just getting
to know people who are talking to me. I need another year *at
least* to absorb what is here for me to learn—maybe more.

JEANNE PHILLIPS: Over Spring Festival I plan to go, incredibly, to
the only city I've already visited twice this stay, Quanzhou.
During Lantern Festival (fifteen days after Lunar New Year) it has
a colorful display with lion dances, lanterns, and I THINK,
performances of their very, very famous puppets. I've become

very interested in these but have never seen a real performance, only admired the puppets and their costumes as high craft. Indeed, I'm half-tempted to invest in a collection of heads for hand puppets, gowns, and full marionettes, thinking I could later sell them at a profit in the U.S. after lending them for an exhibit or two—then reality and the state of my treasury impress upon me the insanity of that impulse.

The hunt for information and sources about puppets is addictive. First I found one shop and got an idea of the range of prices, quality, and the age of puppets available. Then I found a shop with a helpful owner who showed me books and told me something about the famous head-makers. She also told me of a locked-up collection of puppets in the Provincial Museum in Fuzhou. So getting access and photos there is my current project —not easy. (I've heard that one Taiwan collector-millionaire paid a lot just to see and photograph them.) At least the search is fun and challenging, even if nothing more comes of it.

G: I remember hearing that martial arts was something of a disappointment in China. I guess that depends on where you are and what alleys your feet take you in. I'm training with a teacher who is very knowledgeable and kind. I teach him English (which is as necessary as my Chinese tutor!), but my black belt helps, and I have at least some superficial knowledge of the Taoist principles upon which his internal art is based.[5] After learning, finishing the outward form the other day of his most popular practice, he told me that I learned very fast, much faster than he expected; he asked me what I really wanted to learn. (He knows many styles of *gong fu.*) I told him that I want to learn the essence of his fighting form—I want to learn how to develop internal power the way his grandfather's grandfather learned. I knew I was getting in way over my head.

---

[5] The Chinese martial arts distinguish between internal and external forms, saying that most practices have both. *Qi gong* is an internal form, something that happens primarily inside the body; fighting forms that feature hits and kicks start with externals.

He looked me in the eye, and his face became serious. He was considering it. I was scared. In truth, it reminded me of the Mark Salzman–Pan Qingfu "eat bitter" conversation.[6] My teacher said it was very, very hard, very ancient. "How can I teach you that when I haven't even taught my son yet?" he said. "There isn't enough time." What if I stay more than a year? "Perhaps. I don't know who is going to work harder—you or me."

I made no commitment, neither did he. But I can feel that we share a similar spirit, and sing duets in English in our spare moments. He is wonderful. But I have to be careful not to get too attached. Anything can happen here, so unpredictable. I guess I'll take it one day at a time, learn what I can and be happy for the chance. That's how I tend to live my life here anyway: don't expect too much, and consider each day a gift. And Alice, my backpack is filled with gifts thus far.

But passions need not be exotic to do the good work of keeping sojourners engaged while they juggle all the new things they are trying to learn.

JOE MÁRQUEZ: Xi'an is great. I'm finally going out. I was very nervous at first. My apartment was like the womb, and my reluctance to speak Chinese was an umbilical cord that could not be severed, even with my Swiss Army knife. I have since been born and am out and about.

I am closer to the foreign students than the other teachers, because of age and things we like to do—drinking beer and watching Chinese TV. We are now watching a program called *Beijing Man in New York*. We watch it every night. I'm not homesick.

TEDDY KELLAM: I often spend my late afternoons tutoring,

---

[6] Mark Salzman taught English in China and wrote an account of his year in *Iron and Silk*. He tells there how his martial arts teacher Pan Qingfu ("Pahn Ching-foo") warned him that to become good at these practices he must work very hard and learn to "eat bitter."

meeting with students, and then playing volleyball with two neat guys, former students, patient volleyball coaches, and good friends. They live in the twelve-story dormitory that houses most of my students. So as I climb the stairs to their floor, I am greeted by thirty or so familiar faces on the way up. I tend to be tardy anyway, and after umpteen mini-conversations, I'm usually pretty late for my volleyball appointment. Months ago, I'd be met by expectant glares, but now they understand me, sometimes even racing in *after* "Her Lateness" arrives!

Our volleyball games on the sand playground are full of typically Chinese chaos—with two concurrent volleyball matches on each side, dozens of toddlers digging around us in the sand, and a twelve-year-old-boys' banshee soccer game blazing right through us periodically. And of course, there are always spectators who gather to watch a non-Chinese (me!) in action, flopping about!

Any deep foreign experience asks travelers to shift their idea of how the world works and who they are in it. Moving from the United States to China, teachers may shift from being poor to being rich, from smart to dumb, from feeling grown up to feeling like a three-year-old. But they are also shifting from being someone ignorant of Asia to someone who knows a little, from speaking English to speaking a second (or third!) language, from the kicks of *tae kwon do* to the low stances of *wushu*. In China, Americans are learning to live and navigate in reverse. To learn well, they must first break down and lose their bearings for a while, but in the long run they are gaining both options and insight.

Facing the temporary breakdown and double vision of passing through the Looking Glass does not always feel good. For some, it involves too many days of gloom and anxiety to inspire ecstatic poetry. But those who have not worked through culture shock are often surprised to learn that almost everyone who comes out the other side is somehow grateful for the experience. As Inger says, "Happy isn't everything."

INGER: Things here in dirty old Shantou, as I affectionately think of it, are pretty quiet at present. My class schedule is bearable this semester, and I feel like I've come out from a tunnel. I began my last class yesterday, bringing my total up to 12 hours a week. As usual, they just threw me to the wolves with no good explanation of what was expected. When they pull stuff like this, however, I no longer feel guilty for not being the most wonderful teacher in the world. I'll do my best, but I'm scaling way back on the anxiety and the unproductive efforts at trying to be more "professional"—whatever that means. My attitude may not be the most positive for the situation, but it puts me much more at ease. After all, if they're not happy with me what can they do? Send me home? Fine. They can't push me too far because they have no authority over me that I don't concede.

Don't worry. I'm not going around leading rebel students to occupy the dean's office (as if there were any rebel students around here). I'm just learning about the abuses of goodwill and how to protect your own personal space. I'm learning a hell of a lot more than Chinese over here.

O.K. I'm not having the wonderful experience with teaching the Chinese students I kept hearing everyone talk about. I like the students, class goes fine, but I would not call this an enjoyable year. It has its moments and I'm very glad I came, but much of what I'm learning I'm learning because I'm in exile. I would still encourage people to do this and have no regrets about coming. I'm just saying it's not the happiest experience. Happy isn't everything; other emotions are important too: anxiety, self-doubt, loneliness, frustration, anger, self-pity. It's an unequaled opportunity for self-reflection, learning to face these things head on, without distractions.

Merely *surviving* for a year in a foreign culture can be interesting. Actually *adapting* to that culture can inspire profound new alignments. The questions that culture shock poses do not come up just once or twice during a year teaching in China; they return on different levels. Teachers are constantly pushed to dismantle and rebuild their ideas about the world and themselves, based on the reversed reflections in Looking Glass Land. And this can lead to what Peter Adler calls "a progressive unfolding of the self." What begins as a journey to another land becomes also a journey toward the self, turning up new soil and planting seeds from China deep within.

DAVID MOLDAVSKY: China has been a real learning experience. I've made many friends and they've afforded me a chance to see the world through a perspective very different from the one I grew up with. It's been a tremendous growing experience for me, going from being an American college brat to being a teacher trying to fit in and survive in a foreign culture. I think this year has done more for me than twelve years in corporate America would do, simply because when one is put in an adverse or difficult situation one really has to consider what's important and how to make sense of the mess (which China sometimes is).

It hasn't always been fun here, but it's made me question myself and my values. I know that there are some ideals which are intrinsically bound to my psyche because of my upbringing, and trying to compromise them in order to stay afloat in a foreign place is indeed very difficult. One thing is for sure; I definitely know myself better—my strengths and my weaknesses and what I want in life.

G: Living in China is an intensely emotional experience, forcing us to think in radically different ways than ever before, to feel ourselves and our world from the inside. Because I have chosen to touch the fire of Chinese life, I have not only learned a great deal, I have actually felt a greater range of human emotions. I won't leave China a jaded and cynical man; China will hold me in its grasp, possibly forever.

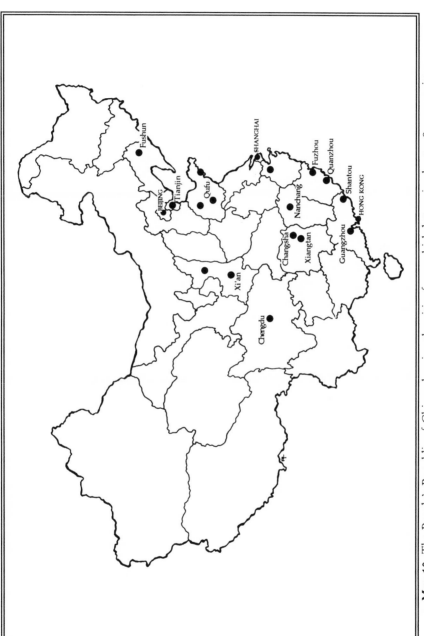

Map 10. The People's Republic of China, showing the cities from which letters in chapter 9 were written.

hukou (hoo-koh): the Chinese permit system described here by Rachel Coleman, which registers most of the urban population.

lajiao (lah-jiaow): hot pepper.

waiguoren (wy-gwo-ren): foreigner.

wenzi, zhanglang, tiaozao (wen-tsuh, jahng-lahng, tiaow-dzao): the mosquitos, cockroaches, and fleas that plague Inger.

Feels like Home

RACHEL COLEMAN: Hard seat is indescribable hell. No sleep, staring faces, gray, grim lights, & garbage piling up on the floors like a stockyard. I've never been *so* happy to get back to anyplace as I was when that train pulled into gray, polluted, chaotic Chengdu—Home!

And so it is for now. My home is this amazing land where nothing is like "home." But I have really come to love & cherish the people & life that surround me.

TODD HAMINA: Changsha food is great, I'm so fortunate. Took off to the south to visit Yangshuo (beautiful). But the food was so bland. It was great to get home, but greater still to be happy that home is Changsha. Sure it's filthy, but the people are wonderful and the food is mighty.

I'm quite happy to be in this Coal-Soot-Reeking, Diesel-Belching, Bicycle-Bell-Ringing Industrial Town.

What does it mean to feel at home? In a way, it means that things feel real and make sense. It means that you are basically comfortable in the place and familiar enough that you can get what you need.

Shantou, Guangdong

Dear Alice,

Well, the year is winding down to the end of my exile. Don't wince. I'm very happy I came to China, and I call it my "exile" with a certain melodramatic satisfaction. Like Tom Waits sings, "I never saw my hometown until I stayed away too long." But I have made a home for myself here and have been remembering back to my first month when every time I had to go out of my room was like a foray into enemy territory.

I feel quite comfortable here in Shantou, indeed, in China. It's great to become so familiar with a country that you're confident to travel or to attempt communicating your needs in the native language. Both Michael and I hope sometime in the future (jumping way far ahead) to come back to China or Taiwan to work again.

The Chinese is going well. It's nice to have enough vocabulary down to begin tackling the grammatical constructs, and I am also beginning to work on my characters. Yesterday I was buying something in one of "my" shops and there was a big group of Russians (seamen, I think) who were having trouble with something. The storekeeper knew I spoke some Chinese so he asked me to translate, and it was quite fun. Learning language is such a slow, insensible progression. It's nice to think back to when I first came and realize I *have* made progress.

Since there's not much else to do I've been cooking a lot. The vegetables are so lovely. Each time I go shopping I get so caught up that I come home with my arms loaded. I made some really nice salsa. It would be better with tortilla chips, but I'm developing a taste for salsa and saltines.

I've finally got enough time to begin my exercise/dance routine again. It loosens me up and feels good. Besides, Michael is in really good shape and does a lot of yoga, so his example is kicking me into gear to pay more attention to my body.

I can't do a thing, however, about the damn mosquitos teasing me as I write, the cockroaches that still startle me when they crawl out from under the stove in the kitchen, or the fleas that the cat has left behind in my bed judging from the bites all over my lower legs (*wenzi, zhanglang,* and *tiaozao,* respectively). This Double Prawns Brand Herbal Oil that the guy at the store said was the best for *wenzi* bites doesn't seem to do much good at all, other than staining your skin in a comforting manner like Merthiolate used to. When I move out I'm going to get a giant can of bug spray and fumigate this place in preparation for next year's teachers. Thank the Lord for mosquito nets.

Inger

P.S. Who needs pizza when you can get *jiaozi*, fry them at home, and eat them hot with garlic-chili sauce and vinegar?

Daily "Routines"

When teachers start to feel at home in China, life becomes full or lazy in ways they can handle. What they do begins to feel like a choice they make, rather than a strange mystery visited upon them. As their skills and attitudes adjust to local custom, the routines of life seem like a normal round of dull hours and good days, and small losses do not shake the foundations of the world.

G: I love this dirty little crowded city. To say that it is dirty is true; however, it is misleading. One learns to live with a different value system here, and hygiene concerns are not so important to me. My fingernails are usually grimy, as is my body—especially from the greasy but wonderfully diverse cuisine. I ride my bike in narrow streets, marvel at foreign smells and at blank stares. "Hello!" I hear from passersby.

There isn't much to recommend to friends or travelers, except perhaps the hot-pepper and garlic chicken I order everywhere. Or perhaps the man who directs bicycle traffic with his red flag, whose smile reaches me through the crowd on the boulevard as he says, "*Waiguoren*, stop." He taps me on the butt as I ride by. We share a laugh at least once a week. I don't know why; he's just a nice old guy with a million-dollar smile. Then there is the Xiang River, which at times seems to flow upstream. I walk along the bank without a lover and sing songs to myself I would never have sung at home. All I can recommend to friends and travelers is— Changsha. In a crazy way, one is more free here.

DAL HURTT: White Cloud Mountain is within a five-minute walk. A good place to escape from the "gapers"—you know, the locals whose heads can rotate 180° while their lower jaws drop to the ground. Other than the complete loss of privacy, I'm pretty well acclimated to the environment.

Guangzhou, Guangdong
(Somewhere between running to and fro
or possibly in circles)

Dear Alice,

I am busy. Boy am I busy. Even university graduation, thesis time could not compare to this! An example: last Thursday, I taught from 8 to 10, then taught privately (for free to a Thai Chinese lady—one of my charity acts!) from 10:30 to 12, quickly cooked lunch, played ball from 1 to 2 with a Japanese friend, met with a student from 3 to 4:30, volleyball from 4:45 to 6, helped a girl with application letters 'til 6:30, then hosted visitors from 6:30 to 7, then gave midterms in my room (7–9:30), then students came over (9:30–10:30), then ran over to my teacher's (10:30–11:30) to meet a friend of hers. This is typical. (Oh. I forgot to mention that I swim from 6:30 to 7:00 A.M.)

A lot of it—in fact, most of it—is fun. For that, I'm wildly grateful. But there are so many people in my life—it's over-overoverwhelming. For example, I have two Chinese lessons each week. A middle school teacher is my tutor, also becoming a close friend. But it's the classic case—busy Westerner sacrifices "intimate friendship" with a Chinese for lack of time; if I spent the kind of time with her that I'd like to, I'd be ignoring something else. Life is never slow here, unless you want it to be.

It's not that one person slurps up my time or my resources—just 370 students from last year and 180 from this year; and if only half of them have a request for me just once during the term, it's enough to keep me running. The advantages? Celebrityhood. The disadvantages? Last night I hosted three in a row until 11:15

P.M., and I heard myself grumbling silently, "Go away. I need to sleep" while simultaneously nodding, "Uh hum. Uh huh. Yes, of course."

I just don't have enough time in the day, but I can't refuse to visit with all of these sweet sweet people—they're not asking for much at all—on an individual basis. (Of course I do refuse the irritating "English leeches." This year, it's Jimmy Brown, a law student who shows up everywhere. I half expect him to be sitting in my bathtub when I wake up in the morning.) But I don't want to be anything but welcoming to most of my "darlings"!

Okay, "bitch, bitch, bitch"—I'm just explaining, not complaining! Anyway.

Thank you for the recommendation for the magazine job! How thoughtful, wonderful, helpful, and sweet that was! I took the job (well, no contract yet, but I plan to help them), but my God—they have a file of hundreds of places. I didn't know Guangzhou had that many places. Plus, they want a list of twenty events each month for a Monthly Events column—near impossible!

1. There are hardly any interesting events besides business deals going on here.

2. The Chinese don't plan ahead! I have about twenty *potential* events which *may* occur around a certain time, *possibly* at one of two places—not to be confirmed until three days ahead of time!

Guangzhou is just not organized like Shanghai or Beijing; even my newspaper reporter pals can't give me information more than five days ahead of time. As one told me yesterday, "In China, they only let the public know about events one or two weeks in advance." Grrr! I'll do my best for them, though. At the very least, I'll do the gargantuan job of updating their Guangzhou static file.

Also, I'm going to work for Procter and Gamble part-time teaching English—I really need the $ very badly. Won't cut into my work for the university—just curtail a few of my social engagements. It's about an hour away by bike—but my beautiful mountain bike was stolen.

Love,

Teddy Kellam

G, who taught for two years in Changsha, stayed in China for a third year but moved to Guangzhou. His attitudes about dirt and food remained well-adapted to Chinese systems, and his approach to bicycle ownership matured.

G: I just bought my second new bike in three months. It's the last new bike I'm going to buy in China—so far I've owned five here—because I'm planning to install a ten-megaton anti-theft device imported from Xinjiang Province. To show, however, my humanitarian sensibilities, I'm preparing a warning sticker, written in four languages, to cover the entire top bar. It reads: "Touch this bike and your balls will be blown off." And instead of leaving my bike anywhere on campus, I don't care how safe, I hump that heavy beast up to my third-floor apartment.

As these letters subtly suggest, part of the routine of living in China is actually its *difference* from life elsewhere.

MARLA JENKS: Life is pretty slow and unstressful here, but I'll give you the blow-by-blow of a Sunday in the life of Ma Lan. (Ma Lan is my Chinese name—*Lan* means orchid and connotes beauty and purity; groovy, huh?)

On Sunday morning I usually roll out of bed around nine, throw on a shirt and shorts, and head to an apartment upstairs for the weekly church service. Nobody here is a pushy missionary, all are from different denominations, and there's no pressure to attend if you don't want to. I've found that it's kind of fun to get together with everyone, have coffee, sing songs, discuss some Psalms or whatever. It's a comfortable, relaxed atmosphere and it makes you feel like you're not quite so removed from the familiar. The "service" lasts roughly two hours, and then we all troop down to the dining hall and have lunch together. That's fun because we order a lot of good food. There are usually about fifteen of us who participate in this Sunday activity.

In the afternoon we just relax, read, sleep, write letters, etc. It's much too hot between about 12 and 4 to do much but sit indoors. For the Chinese people, everything shuts down between 12 and 3 and they all sleep—it's amazing how easy it is to follow their example.

The weather gets a little cooler around five, and that's when I like to go running. There are a couple of tracks on campus. One is covered with coal (which you inhale as you run). I try to stay away from that one and use the other made of regular dirt. In the center of the track, and all around it, are lots of dried up weeds. It looks like an old field from which the hay has been half-heartedly harvested. As you run you can hear and see rats scurrying about. There are usually several groups of boys kicking soccer balls around and staring at me.

For dinner I might go grab something at the dining hall or eat something at home. All over campus are little kiosk shacks where they sell fruit (apples, pears, bananas), ramen noodles, cookies and crackers, juice, soda, rolls, pastries and ice cream. A lot of times I buy food there rather than battle the dining hall scene. On Sunday night I plan for my Monday class and then sit around some more. I have tons of time on my hands and I've done a lot of reading. I wish I knew how to knit or something. Maybe I can take up Chinese calligraphy.

JEANNE PHILLIPS: What else have I been doing? Grading exams, of course. And going several times to see the ballet (choreographed by a friend in the Fujian company), which won all sorts of national prizes in a recent competition. (I tried to help this guy get a visa to study at the Martha Graham school, but the U.S. wouldn't let him in; they were sure he would stay. Not as a dancer—he is shorter than I am! But visa clerks ignore such points.)

I've lunched or dined with former students and heard about

their romantic hopes and fears and approved of a couple of boyfriends. Alas, one lovely young woman I know very well is in love with a guy from the far northwest, on the border with Siberia—she who has never seen snow or naturally formed ice.

An old friend, the Dragon Lady, a psychologist retired from LA, has returned here impulsively from Norway, thinking it easier to live out her final years in her old hometown than with a daughter in Oslo. But she is finding the power outages, cold, water stoppages, and the absence of easy transport all discouraging. In her late seventies, she is as stubborn and imperious as ever; she is now writing her memoirs and I am finding an editor to fix her English.

I also enjoy getting to know my freshmen students, in outings at a nearby park and kids' playground (seesaws and swings are great icebreakers and equalizers) and long talks in my room. They bring their favorite street food and I share out a little precious cheese (frozen since September). They brought me a huge get-well card when I was ill, then later asked if I liked it and told me how much it cost. They also told me that my room looked a little better—less disorderly. So much for the stereotype of Chinese indirectness and politeness.

I've put in time stewing about getting vacation airline tickets. The agency has put everything onto a fancy computer network that has made the difficult now impossible, and the rules keep changing. Currently, one can reserve and purchase a ticket only seven days in advance, one way only. At 8 A.M. on the appointed day, one is told the tickets are all sold. So the back door is essential. I do have a plane ticket to Shenzhen, thence by train to Hong Kong, for one-third the price of a Hong Kong ticket—so I add my bit to the corruption. I think a lot of the problem is the economic boom, which has increased air travel by business people tremendously. New planes on order will take years, and meanwhile, when you go somewhere, you have no idea whether or when you can return.

As you can see, every day is full. A short walk or an errand can turn up an abacus factory that also makes wheeled things you use to massage your back or feet; a quick lunch while shopping uncovers a *dim sum* place. What fun!

KEVIN LAW-SMITH: I love sitting down and going on a trip in my own mind's fields. It's fun playing with writing styles—nice to have the time to do such playing.

- Reading every classic—*Brothers Karamazov*, "Metamorphosis"
- Saw the Chagall exhibit in Beijing
- Bought mondo art history books
- Reading Chinese poetry (translations)
- Reading Buddhist text "On Pure Consciousness"
- Applying to too many jobs in Hong Kong
- Waiting to hear from London School of Economics

Self-exploration all the time; studying less than before I hit a wall. Training for Great Wall Marathon May 29th. Joined a great club here—I'll keep you posted. Folks coming May 27 or so.

No worries here—too excited finding out about myself in this void of time.

G: Yesterday I took the GMAT exam.[1] What a grueling test—five hours. I walked out of the test in a daze and still had to ride my bike two hours back home. It wouldn't have been so bad had I slept the night before.

I arrived at the Foreign Language Institute on Friday night, planning to stay in the guesthouse (where I was assured to get a room). But all I got was the inevitable series of *mei you*. The school is in the middle of nowhere, up near the airport. So instead of trying to ride back, I thought I'd just bushwhack somewhere on that lush campus. But luck was on my side: A housekeeper I chatted up—yet another person from Hunan here—offered to set up a cot for me in a boiler room. I went for it. The mosquitos ate me alive, the heat was unbearable, and I real-

---

[1] A standardized exam for prospective graduate students. GMAT scores must often accompany an application to U.S. graduate schools.

ized I would have been better off camping out in a field of frogs and snakes.

Oh China, why do you make my love for you so difficult?

In fact, once China has become "normal," the way things used to be can seem quite out of this world!

RACHEL COLEMAN: I flew to Hong Kong to meet my brother. Yikes! Though I had originally flown in to Hong Kong before traveling to Chengdu, I'd only spent part of one day & a night there. Now, in comparison to China, Hong Kong looked like a Gleaming White Steamer Ship approaching a shipwrecked sailor (me)! It is *so* strange, but after you've been in China a while, you begin to adapt, adjust & fundamentally compromise—so "normal" becomes a wholly different animal. Hong Kong was CLEAN, efficient, logical. People did not jostle & shove their way past you, hawk & spit incessantly, and squeal *"Lao wai!"* as you walked past. Now, as strange as it may sound, all of that seems *normal* to me.

Hong Kong was like some kind of up-grade Paradise; not normality but an elite heaven where I wandered around stupefied by simple things like elevators that worked (!), transportation that left & arrived on schedule, menus I could read, and electric billboards. I've never before thought a subway was something of beauty, but I was almost in tears. And people lining up in queues to wait to board—"My *gawd,* how civilized."

Bureaucracy

Bureaucracy is the norm anywhere in the modern world, especially in a highly centralized system like China's. Being able to handle red tape is a crucial skill for routine living in the Middle Kingdom. As one of our correspondents says:

DALE ASIS: The teacher who wants to come to China should be

able to figure out the keeper of keys in a complex web of bureaucracy. If the teacher wants to have a video class, one department has the videotapes, another department has the VCR, another department has the television, and another department takes care of the keys to open the classroom to show the video.

In any bureaucracy, the most delicate negotiations for all players are those about money. During the period of these letters, a nationwide salary increase was mandated by the Beijing government, to apply to all foreign teachers.

Foreigners to get 50% pay raise

Foreign experts and teachers working in China will get a 50 percent pay raise later this month that will be retroactive to January 1, an official said yesterday.

The pay raise is intended to compensate for the drop in purchasing power due to inflation and the unification of the dual-track foreign exchange rate in January.

The raise applies only to the nearly 10,000 foreign experts and teachers working in the cultural, educational, media and publishing fields.

All foreign experts and teachers will receive retroactive raises for the past three months later this month.

(From *The China Daily*)

Getting this raise from their individual universities provided many foreigners with opportunities to try out cross-cultural negotiating skills. In such discussions, contracts are particularly sticky items, because the Chinese do not see them the same way Americans do. In real Chinese negotiations, contracts on paper are not seen as binding (an attitude shared by every nation that has been subject to a colonial power). The only thing that really counts is trust between the parties.

Chinese who work with Americans and Europeans, however, have learned that contracts are valued in the West. Therefore they often provide them and sometimes use them as tools in the negotiation process. Such proceedings have a different ebb and flow from the American kind, however, because they begin with a different set of unspoken rules.

DAVID MOLDAVSKY: The *China Daily* printed an article about the new salaries for foreign teachers. We have yet to hear from our *waiban* about these raises but hopefully they'll come through.

Changsha

Dear Alice:

I've been patient and diplomatic with the FAO for almost two years. If I have something to discuss with them—usually information or a very minor request—they greet me with smiles, pretend to be solicitous, and get me out of their office as quickly as possible. "Yes, we understand," they say. "We'll see what we can do." Then of course nothing happens. They like it that way; and I'm sure they think I'm a pushover—that's why they like me. Doesn't matter whether or not I'm a good teacher, or whether I contribute my mouth free of charge for the entertainment and education of the students and university community. Just don't cause any trouble for them, don't make them get out of their chairs (the tea is too hot, the newspaper too riveting). Don't threaten to go see the president.

They're uncomfortable when they see any of the four of us sitting in their office. So last week we brought some fire to put under their seats when we all went together for a little visit. Hi, Mr. Wang, you got any tea? I'm thirsty.

We brought our homework with us: copies of the articles from the English-language *China Daily* and *Business Weekly*, documenting the government's decision to raise the salaries of foreign teachers and experts by 50%. We also brought a copy of an editorial in the Chinese daily paper. They were explicit: The raise would be given at the end of March and would be retroactive to January 1.

As usual, Mr. Wu, the co-director, suddenly can't speak English. Mr. Wang doesn't know anything about it, but assures us that we deserve the raise. He'll see what he can do. Let's call the provincial FAO, I suggest; they might know something. I brought the phone number with me, just in case Mr. Wang's address book was eaten by a pig. He says, getting a little nervous, that he has a meeting with the president in ten minutes. Great! Let's ask him to help us, Mr. Wang. But since we have plenty of time, I could just use your phone here and call the FAO while we wait. The people at the FAO, he said, cannot speak English. That's OK, Mr. Wang, I'll speak Chinese.

We had another request. We wanted, like all the foreign teachers before us, a key to the gate that surrounds our house. When we come home after 11 P.M., we have to climb over the fence. He explains calmly, the smile never leaving his face, that the fence is there to protect us; the university is responsible for any of our belongings that are stolen. We told him we will relieve him of that responsibility, and I pull a contract out of my pocket, prepared earlier. He stutters, looks at the contract (pretty professional and prepared on K——'s computer). He says that the real problem is Mr. L——, the director of the University Guest House, which is also enclosed by the fence; he won't allow it, utters Wang. No problem, Mr. Wang, we asked him earlier. I pull out a second contract from my pocket, agreed to and signed by Mr. L——. Wang's smile is relentless, but he is squirming in his chair. He says he'll have to ask Mr. Tang, the vice-president for Foreign Affairs—unfortunately, Tang is at a conference in Shanghai. Oh, no problem: I saw him this morning, he must have returned today, I tell him. Come on, Mr. Wang, let's go upstairs to his office.

The real problem, Alice, is that this year is the fifth anniversary of the Tiananmen Square Massacre and the university is paranoid. They are, two months before June 6th, watching us very carefully, keeping a closer record of students coming and going from our house. I got wind of a big, secret Communist Party members' meeting last week and the result: members will be on guard 24 hours a day in student dorms and will patrol the campus at night. The last thing they'd allow at this point is more freedom for foreigners.

The north and south campuses now have only one entrance each. The others have been closed; piles of debris and construction material obstruct access to the now-locked gates. So I have to walk the long way to class, past the hospital. A few days ago, I walked through there and saw a man standing on an overhang that looks onto both the entrance to the south campus and the students' dorms. I was early, so I thought to check it out. I went into the building, went to the second floor, climbed out the open window to the overhang. He was middle-aged and holding an umbrella. "Hey, nice day, huh? What are you doing up here? Getting a bird's-eye view of the campus?" I asked innocently, smiling.

"You're not supposed to be up here, Teacher G. Go back in and close the window," he responded, surprised to see me.

"Lemme just get a look. It's such a nice day and these buildings are beautiful from up here." The buildings are gray, dirty boxes. We just chatted. He knew me and had attended one of my university lectures, though he didn't understand English. He kept his eye on the stream of people and seemed bored. "Looks like you're looking for someone," I said. "Are you checking out those women in short skirts?" He laughed.

"OK, you have to go in now, it's dangerous up here, you might fall off."

"How long are you planning to stay up here? You're not thinking about suicide, are you? Don't do it. It's not high enough; you'll end up in that hospital over there."

He was laughing, almost lost his balance. "I'm just standing up here, OK? I'm a teacher, but I have no class today. I'm practicing *qi gong*."

"How can you concentrate with your eyes on the stream of people?"

"Teacher G, you have to leave now."

So much for answers.

G

DAVID MOLDAVSKY: When I went to the post office on Tuesday to post a letter to you, I was stopped by the *waiban* folks and they gave me you-know-what—the long-promised raise. It took a lot of talking and arm twisting to get them to pay. We finally told them that, if we didn't have the money Wednesday, we would go downtown to the provincial *waiban* office and clear up matters with them. But then, what do you know, we got it at noon on Wednesday. The people in our *waiban* said that they couldn't pay us until they got papers from the provincial office, and the provincial office needed the papers from Beijing and so on up the line. Anyway we got the money.

STEPHEN: Your question concerning the teachers' pay here: The FAO was reluctant to mention the pay increase but came up with the money when the teachers got together. Common practice here is to hold out as long as possible before doing anything concerning money. We did receive back pay to January 1.

INGER: I think I told you in the last letter about the raise. That *China Daily* article was a thorn in the *waiban*'s side since I'm sure every foreign teacher in the country saw it. My school gave me my raise in short order, but the teachers at the University had to agitate quite a bit more, especially to get the retroactive part.

Those who live long-term in China also sometimes learn that, although mastering the ways of the bureaucracy is broadly useful, it does not necessarily sow seeds of harmony and goodwill across the land.

STEPHEN: I'm not sure if I told you that I am not staying a third year. There seem to be mixed feelings about it. The department wants me to stay and is doing everything they can think of to get me to change my mind. The FAO, though, seems to be doing everything they can to make sure that I don't stay or even want to come back.

I think I have become too independent for them. I have learned how the system works, even without the use of the language. I have developed a little *guanxi* of my own, and I am able to go around all the problems that the FAO can put in front of us when we are trying to get something done. I guess other schools have the same problem, that the FAOs are trying to capitalize off the foreign teachers, in a con man sort of extortion, overcharging and downright lying and stealing when they can get by with it. When we catch them at it, they laugh and apologize and say that they just made a mistake. They make huge mistakes, and often.

I have become independent of the need for any help from them. I have also helped anyone else who doesn't want the headaches that dealing with the FAO often entails. I try to keep a low profile, but they know that I have knowledge; a little knowledge is a dangerous thing.

Long-term sojourners also learn that, like everywhere else in the world, the veneer of much Chinese bureaucracy is sometimes thin.

JEANNE PHILLIPS: The economic reforms have changed many attitudes. Friends who formerly would never think of getting paid for many requests now lecture colleagues that the province must pay for things it wants translated when it has a delegation going abroad. No more doing expert work for honor and patriotism. One of my ex-students has a T-shirt and sweater shop on the side; one of her shirts says *Peristroika*,[2] which everyone thinks is a peculiar English word. But *peristroika* Chinese version and the Economic Reform ("reinforced by Comrade Deng on his visit to the South earlier this year" as the line in every speech goes) are most evident.

Fuzhou has a large square which has become more rectangular over the years as the south side acquired indoor free-market boutique shops to replace the street carts and tables under plastic

---

[2] A Russian word meaning "opening," introduced to the world in the speeches and conciliatory policies of Russian premier Mikhail Gorbachev.

awnings. Then a new bank, now a flashy chain department store, "Sincere," full of imported goods. Most symbolic of all, under the giant statue of Mao that dominates the square and inside the hill on which it stands have been built a warren of "free" (i.e., private) shops, mostly full of clothes made for export or bought in Hong Kong or Taiwan. Our prospering young grads in their new joint-venture high-salary jobs look as fashionable as any Denver yuppie.

There are still plenty of billboards extolling one-child families, urging proper payment of fees or obedience to traffic rules (nonexistent), but the largest billboard I've seen (most of a block long) shows an Asian man hitting a tee shot on an empty and lush golf course—presumably soon to be developed and why doesn't your firm invest?

Still, it is the Chinese version. I may have bought my silk aviator-style jacket from a shop under Mao's big toe, but his picture adorns most taxi rear-view mirrors and many shops' glass cases right next to the cash box. Mao seems to function as a sort of St. Christopher medal, a semideity to bring good luck and protection to one's cutthroat capitalist business.

EILEEN VICKERY: Thanks for the emergency crisis cards. We are assuming that one of the natural disasters that could beset China is Mr. Deng Xiaoping's death. We just read in the *China Daily* that Deng walks three kilometers every day and even occasionally goes swimming. Then we read in our *Newsweek* that Taiwan has already drafted condolences. Who to believe?

Portraits

For most people, the essence of feeling at home in a place is having friends there. In the pressure cooker of a foreign land, many teachers find they make friends more quickly and bond with them more deeply than they ever have before.

We have already heard of many Chinese friends—Teddy Kellam's volleyball buddies and G's singing *wushu* teacher, for example. We open this section with a more detailed picture of the variety of expatriates who can also make up a foreigner's friend network in China.

KATIE SHOWALTER: China attracts colorful people. I've mentioned all these people in my letters, so let me describe them.

"The Adventurer"

Ours is "dad" age, has three grown daughters, is divorced, has a Ph.D., used to teach kids, and is looking for business ventures here (preferably a joint-venture college or vocational school). Most recently from the U.S. east coast. Very outgoing (party animal in his youth—heck, still is), kind and generous, loves the adventure of China. Loses his temper at taxi drivers, managers of street restaurants, and security guards who let the air out of his bike tires because he parked, unwittingly, in the wrong place. Tall, big, balding, and wears a baseball cap we made for him that says, "I'm tall, I'm big, I'm handsome, I'm poor" in Chinese. Teaches college students at a teachers' college here.

"The World Traveler"

Also in the "dad" category, has three grown kids, is divorced (but has a partner who came to visit twice; she has red hair and is quite successful in business). He has a Ph.D. and comes from Sydney. Used to be in school administration quite high up, but Australia is restructuring and his job was eradicated. Since he didn't want to move down the ranks, he decided now would be a good time to have a new experience. Is having a great time in China. Reserved and dignified, but has been seen cutting loose more than once here (went crazy dancing on stage for a performance the foreigners were asked to give). Well-traveled. Grooves on 1970s tunes, has been learning to paint Chinese style (good at it, too). Doesn't speak Chinese. Teaches graduate students at a teachers' college. He'd do any favor for you, great to talk to.

"The Entertainer"

About my age (24), no kids, just graduated with a master's in Chinese history, studied in England as an undergrad, knows

Chinese. He's here to teach, and decide whether China is his thing. From Chicago, Vermont, and New York (in that order). Bought a drum set here, loves to play any instrument, and has a beautiful singing voice. His "class background" is suburbs, successful parents, wealthy high school. Intelligent, logical, loves to debate, extreme extrovert, often manic. Likes musicals (did many in high school and college), is an entertainer by nature. Has been described by many as "intense." Will do anything, provided it doesn't require being uncomfortable for too long. One of the most polite and generous people I know, except when he is ranting about Chinese bureaucracy.

"Two Artists"

Also my age, or a year younger. She's here to teach, then home to the U.S., hopes to go to grad school. Art and Asia are her specialties. Good to travel with because she's organized and rallies people and is interested in culture. Not shy, but not really outgoing. Morning person. Easygoing, experienced traveler.

He graduated from college recently, studied Chinese. Likes to read fiction and short stories, likes to write. Avid music buff (stuff like Frente). Easygoing, yet uptight—strange mix. A bit cynical, yet accepts people as they are. Does get upset with posers (image-oriented people). Tries not to be too "normal." Blonde and scruffy.

"The Athlete"

Crazy Korean. Had a birthday party recently, turned 20—except we just found out that that's in Korean age. He's actually only 18. Which explains a lot. Comes from a traditional family. Father has his life planned for him (five years in China learning Chinese and acupuncture, two years in the army, five years in the U.S. studying English). Very disciplined and conscientious, has a black belt in *tae kwon do.* Sorta naïve; can't figure out why the Korean woman here ("The Princess") isn't like his mother. Likes running about like a crazy person (I mean, he's athletic and likes dancing, but really is hyper), so he decided to quit smoking so he could breathe.

"Woman of Mystery"

"The Princess"—don't know where the name came from, but it suits her. Also Korean. Early thirties. She was a reporter in Korea, but her husband didn't like her to have that sort of work (late, long hours, weekends, drinking, etc.). But he does want her to work. At some point she met someone who told her a lot about acupuncture. She became interested—she "likes mystery." So she packed her bags and came to China to study Chinese and acupuncture. She left her son in her mother's care. She studied English literature in college, so she comes out with the funniest things sometimes, like the word "passionable." She's very intelligent, directed and in control. She looks and dresses ten years younger than she is (black miniskirts with boots, for example) and enjoys male attention. Wants to be accepted for who she is and finds that difficult here where the Japanese and Turkish male students tell The Athlete to "control his countrywoman."

RACHEL COLEMAN: Kunming is in Yunnan & I found it unmemorable for the most part, except for its beautiful old-style houses & courtyards (not all gray concrete) & an *amazing* Chinese woman we met. At 24 years old she had had a successful business in Beijing, lost it all due to thieves & government policy & had struck out on her own to see China. She had with her a baby rabbit she kept inside her coat and a puppy she had saved from being butchered & eaten.

Pets in China are illegal (in cities, anyway), because they consume food & are therefore considered a waste. Also, people do not "travel" in China long term, only for short vacation stints—to quickly get somewhere, snap photos & return home. In fact, what she is doing must be illegal.

Everyone in China has a permit to reside in only one region & city & *danwei*. Without a permit (called *hukou*), you cannot change jobs or take up residence in any other city. Without *hukou* you are an illegal citizen in China. Even the Chinese did not believe it. In one place they asked her how a Japanese had gotten a Chinese residence card. "Where is your work unit? Who is in charge of you?" they asked. None. No one. Somehow she manages—gets work in each place she goes, stays a while, then moves on.

She was amazing, strong & vital. She'd taught *herself* perfect English and was beginning to teach herself Japanese by talking to her new pup only in that language. She let me read the autobiography she was working on. Too much to tell, and things I cannot reveal, but needless to say, it was full of tragedy & brilliant spirit, just like her.

But people are not the only "friends" American teachers make in China.

KEVIN LAW-SMITH: In the far corner of the institute near the dormitories is a student restaurant—my usual haunt. One enters through a makeshift metal door. Five booths in the restaurant, gray floor darkened by a thousand students a day.

In the center is a small metal barrel, hot coals at its base. On its lid sits a pot of water steaming in the air—our heat in this restaurant. A sad pipe leads CO_2 fumes out the window. On the right are two trees. Two sisters of desolation. They were abandoned by nature and now their bases live in a restaurant. Through the roof they must grow. When it rains, water runs down their trunks to the restaurant floor.

I order a delicious plate of chicken and peppers and eat it with cold rice, drink a cold beer. My hands are freezing. I see the steam from my breath and my hot plate of food. Alone I sit with two other students, also alone in this realm. We all stare at the dismal TV screen—reception is poor but the squeals and shrieks of ghost actors blare forth the sound of Beijing Opera. We breathe on our hands for warmth. As I eat, Marlboro, Sprite, and Coca Cola keep me company, peering at me through the stand under the TV. (America is everywhere.)

The server—pudgy, dark, old Chinese face—wears plastic wellingtons, five layers of dismal clothing, and the white jacket of a restaurant worker. She squints at the TV, smiles with approval.

She is at home in all our memories of a Chinese paddy field worker. I eat. I drink my cold beer and wonder why they built this shack around two lonely sister trees. They merely stand, but they continue to exist—and keep me company as I eat.

G: Even after a brief dose of lovely Kunming, I still look forward to going back to Changsha. I'm addicted to the *lajiao*, which I've been courting like a woman uninterested in my advances.

A few months back, I noticed that I was experiencing a unique discomfort. Though I had never had this ailment before, or talked with anyone about it, I knew that I had hemorrhoids. Amazing, I thought, don't hemorrhoids result from sitting too much? If I were a truck driver, maybe, but not me. Whatever the cause, I remained in denial for a month. Maybe if I ignored the problem, it would disappear—how's that for problem solving!? It got worse and still, in my puritan, American way, I was too embarrassed to tell any of my friends or students (who, of course, are all doctors).

Finally, I had to do something. I decided to go to the clinic, even though I could not communicate my problem adequately in Chinese, short of dropping my trousers. (The few medical dictionaries I consulted did not list a Chinese name for hemorrhoids.) But I had to go.

I was hustled to the nearest doctor, who was female, and we took care of the requisite paperwork. Then she asked me what the problem was. I was in desperate hope that hemorrhoids were so common that the most minimal body language would communicate my distress. So I pointed to my butt. At that moment, a wave of shame came over me. Since I have had little need for medicine in my life, I somehow felt ashamed to need help. Was it that I considered myself young and strong, and needing medicine for such a place on my body meant I was guilty of some indiscretion?

The doctor did not recognize my need. Why should she? She thought I was asking for an injection and sought help from another who could speak English. In the confusion, a crowd gathered. Words were tried out, no one really understanding.

Through the din, I shouted, "Not my buttocks, my anus, anus!" To my horror the word was passed around: "Anice? Anice?" I laughed. The humor was undeniable, even though I was now face to face with a bodily conservatism that was new to me. They, all doctors and nurses, wanted me to drop trousers right there! So clinical, so simple, and I turned it, unwittingly, into perhaps the most humorous emotional barrier I've encountered in China.

I pulled a young male doctor into another room, pushed out all the others, and finally remedied the situation. Big adventure, Alice, especially for a small problem. Upon handing me the medicine (which is no Preparation H!) the doctor asked me if I ate a lot of *lajiao*. Yes, of course. "Well, stop eating it—it doesn't like you so much as you like it." "But doctor, I'm addicted to it—besides, everything has hot pepper in it." He suggested I move to the north!

Real Life on the Other Side

Adaptation—what does it mean? It means, in the deepest sense, that China has become real. The roads and the classrooms, the people and the food are not just exotic surfaces that will soon be replaced by their *real* American versions. The Chinese way is, at least for now, the way things really are.

> G: Nothing can replace that first year, the shock, the excitement, the frustration of ignorance and illiteracy. Yet I am beginning to see that there is also no replacement for the second year: The complexity of relationships and how they grow (very valuable in the Chinese context where tremendous value is placed on how long you know someone); experience in teaching, living, communication. The sheer naturalness of it all, the intense familiarity, even if still at a distance as a foreigner.

As G implies here, adaptation does not mean that teachers cease to be American. They continue to live the paradox of two answers for every question. But as they discover that they are developing two selves, they also develop the ability to choose which self they want to be—though they may have to fight to get some of their choices heard!

> JEANNE PHILLIPS: I suppose my long identity as a psychologist (rather than anthropologist) is the reason, but most of the time I insist people here are just the same as in the U.S. or anywhere else. Shocking though it is for someone who co-authored a book on behavior modification, I tend to dismiss a lot of behavioral differences as superficial style or just temporary. Then something small startles me.
>
> The other day, the dean of our division, a vital, quick-witted 73-year-old, came by to scold me for not taking good care of my health after hospitalization. It turns out she had come by my room at 8 that morning, knocked softly, got no response but heard my radio on, and so went out on the balcony to look in my windows to see what I was doing! (I was sleeping, luckily alone in my bed, and wearing something on my body, having gone back for an extra forty winks.) But this behavior from a highly educated, refined gentlewoman reminded me that culture does matter!
>
> So, too, did the consternation of our Chinese hosts on the trip north when I wanted to sit and rest while they and my friend walked up some hills to see local sights. I had to have a temper tantrum to be allowed to wait ALONE, since it was inconceivable to them that anyone would prefer to be alone in a strange place with nothing special to do.

It is another paradox that American teachers who adapt to China become simultaneously more conscious of their American identity *and* more able to accommodate Chinese ways. And for teachers who come to feel at home in China, the perspective slowly shifts from amazement at the reversals of Looking Glass Land to more nonchalant acceptance. Days fill with meaning—with plans and frustrations, with bureaucrats and friends, with work and play. And the United States, that place still called "home," retreats into the distance and becomes a little harder to imagine, although still alive in the mind.

RACHEL COLEMAN: Life here really is amazing—much more so than in my wildest dreams I'd *ever* imagined. "Back home" is almost a dream. My way of life here is so, so different. And so full. So full of Spirit, this place!

TEDDY KELLAM: Life here is not hard for me. I have a spacious apartment, a big bathtub, a TV and phone, a bicycle to run errands, a comfy salary (as long as I don't translate it to U.S. equivalents!). I have oodles of friends and work and favors to do, a busy, busy, exciting life. I have wonderful A—— and Edward, Miss Liu and Xiao Li and Xiao Wu who all know me very well! You can't hide your true self here! I have letters and faxes from home to keep my spirits up. I have crazy, dynamic Guang-zhou—progressing in leaps and bounds economically. If I could, I'd spend whole *days* glued to the window of a minibus, just watching it all zip by. I have my university campus, shrouded in bamboo, a tranquil envelope amidst the chaos of the city. Here boys pedal their Flying Pigeon bicycles with girls on the back, holding their books. Here, I can hold hands with my friends as I walk along; my head is full of lilting Chinese love ballads (although I don't know the words—I hum!).

You see, I'm in love. Not with anyone, but with my China. Never mind the breakdowns, the cross-cultural blunders, red tape, xenophobia. It's *all* worth it. I still love it here.

JEANNE PHILLIPS: There are always new things to learn, do, see, understand or misunderstand. I think one is *never* an "old China hand," only on the way to being one.

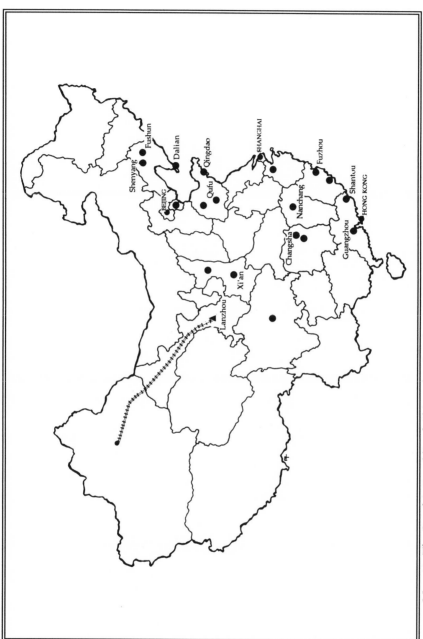

Map 11. The People's Republic of China, showing the cities from which letters in chapter 10 were written.

dao, daoist (dow): the pinyin spelling of *tao* and *taoist,* an ancient Chinese philosophy most famous for articulating the idea that the universe is a constant flux of alternating yin and yang forces: light and dark, mountain and valley, rain and mist, jade and peony, male and female. The Chinese daoist symbol represents the idea that the universe and all life within it is not made up of separate "things," but is a constant shifting balance of forces. The white dot within the black field, and the black within the white, mean that when each force is at its fullest, it contains within it the seed of the other side.

mao (maow): cents; here G argues with a vendor over five cents.

xiangfa (she-ahng-fah): idea or concept.

Yin and Yang

PJ: "Be grateful even for hardship, setbacks, and bad people. Dealing with such obstacles is essential training in the Art of Peace."

A friend translated this for me from the wall of a Buddhist temple. You know, I don't think we teach this every day in the U.S. as they seem to here.

DAL HURTT: The China experience has really changed my life. I have fallen in love with the Chinese *xiangfa*. The idea of seeking a balance or harmony between the dualistic properties of nature and man has a pervasiveness in Chinese society that I had never imagined. This underlying yin/yang duality seems to permeate everything, from balanced character strokes to the *qi gong* of *tai ji* to the *qi* of Chinese medicine and the *dao* of Chinese philosophy and religion.

It is this same duality between our diametrically and geographically opposed regions of the world that we somehow have to balance and harmonize. I believe we have many lessons to learn from Eastern civilizations. Americans must stop dishing out moral absolutes with a fork and spoon, at least until they have tried eating with chopsticks.

At the same time, I am excited about the many possibilities for both Americans and Chinese in the evolving world. I believe the Chinese need Western technology for improved transportation, population management, more efficient resource extraction, toxic emission controls, and for protecting and preserving their culture. There is no doubt that our influence may act as an agent of change or that we ourselves may be changed. There has to be balance for there to be harmony.

Foreigners who live a year or two in China often arrive at Dal's philosophical position—that there is a natural duality in the world that requires constant balancing. But the amount of darkness included in this balanced, daoist perspective can shock many Americans back home, especially if they have lived a relatively sheltered life.

Chapter 5 of the classic book of Chinese philosophy, the *Tao Te Ching*, opens,

> Heaven and Earth are ruthless,
> and treat the myriad creatures as straw dogs.[1]

As PJ notes above, this is not the sort of message taught routinely in the United States, but many of these letter writers seem to understand it. You might recall Stephen in chapter 7, for example, who told of being threatened in the streets and the market, having to talk his way out or face down his attackers. Even in the midst of this and other trials, he seems able to take a philosophical view of his own position as a "straw dog."

STEPHEN: Most of what I've been doing this year is being sick. It seems I've been sick nonstop since I got back. A variety of things, the most serious being bronchitis that has been dangerously close to pneumonia, twice. I cannot seem to get healthy even though I am cooking for myself and am eating a lot better than I did last year. I'm always weak and I've lost so much weight.

I have learned a great deal about Chinese philosophy while I have been here. I tend to think in a daoist way. My first year was peaceful and satisfying. This second year, I have been involved with this sickness and in three attacks.

And Teddy sends back a poignant description of how animals are used in China, balanced by her awareness that similar pain exists on factory farms in America, although it is kept out of sight.

---

[1] This quote is from the English version of the *Tao Te Ching* of Lao Tzu, translated by D. C. Lau (New York: Penguin, 1963). In a note on p. 61, Lau explains that "in the *Chuang tzu* it is said that straw dogs were treated with the greatest deference before they were used as an offering, only to be discarded and trampled upon as soon as they had served their purpose."

TEDDY KELLAM: Life here is so rife with intrigue. Last week, I spent Sunday on a motorcycle tour of Guangzhou with a Chinese friend. The highlight was Qin Pin market. How can I describe walking through a dank gray alley with Cantonese peddling their cages of animals—foxes and rabbits and sullen cats, prowling to and fro in their too-small cages; frogs bound in bunches of five, cinched painfully at the waist; woodchucks and chickens, ducks hanging upside down, panting, panting; and skinned dogs, dangling stiffly from hooks their paws bent hideously, their eyes wild. And the little deer—gentle and exotic, heads bent, front hoofs broken off to prevent them from escaping, speaking in tongues as the pain has taken them already beyond this world. Venomous snakes and exotic fowl, beautiful creatures caged so unnaturally—cruel diversion of nature, displaced, and yet routine to the people who march through searching for dinner's creatures.

I've been told that the Cantonese believe that the more painful a death, the more flavorful the meat. Whether true or not, it gives me an explanation for the deliberate abuse of the animals. Perhaps I am overreacting. I, for one, eat chicken, and I've seen the in-humanity of chicken farms in the U.S., which never deterred me. And yet, as with everything here, life in China is so tangible. There are no layers to peel away: you live, and you see the effects of your living immediately. So every moment counts. Every second is exquisite, intense, and vibrant. No gadgets, no grocery stores, no sterility, no delusions.

It seems that so often in the West we delay, we look forward to the future, we avoid *now* because things will be better *later*, we escape. There are no magic bullets here. Here, that logic is foreign and senseless. Here, I recognize detail, I appreciate *now*, I notice the seconds as they pass by. It's as though my eyes are opening and ripening and suddenly thirsty, they sip and gulp and life gushes into me. I am alive! I am alive!

Life, many American teachers learn vividly in China, is a balancing act. Not a static perfection achieved and held, but constant movement from one extreme to another, from the outer edge to the center—a constant alternation of hunger and fullness, exile and belonging, dark and light.

Shenyang, Liaoning

Dear Alice,

The next pages are for your China book. I hope it doesn't come across as being overly negative, but I for one suffered when I first arrived in China because it was not all the romantic land of quaint dreams that I had read of. Not that it's all a hideous mess, but there are certainly elements of it that are, shall we say, character building?

• • •

Unless you happen to be on a brief VIP tour, China is a country and culture that will test your mettle and force a re-evaluation of the self. I taught English for a short time in the city of Dalian. Dalian itself is actually a very nice town of three to four million people, a port city serving as a gateway primarily to Russia, South Korea, and Japan. Dalian hangs like a precious jewel on the southern edge of Liaoning province, whose capital city is Shenyang.

Shenyang epitomizes the more challenging aspects of adjusting to life in China. At nine million people, it is the fourth-largest city in the country. The transportation and industrial hub of northeastern China, it has been ranked by the United Nations as the second-most-polluted city in the world (Mexico City is number one). The city is home to several outstanding universities, most notably the Foreign Languages and China Medical Universities. Through association with these two institutions, I got to know a rag-tag collection of foreigners teaching and studying in Shenyang.

The teachers were mostly British, American, and Canadian, fresh out of college and off to explore the world, while the students came from a hodge-podge of "revolutionary" nations —Syria, Palestine, Poland, Cuba, Nigeria and Russia—nations thrown together by historical events that are now disappearing or completely evaporated. Every foreigner—teacher and student alike —was confronted by an almost unfathomable Chinese society. Everything is done differently in China, whether you are speaking to a Japanese, a Dane, a Slav, an Indian, a Mexican, or a Korean.

Because of this, members of the foreign community—particularly in Shenyang—cling to one another for advice, information, and support.

I came to realize this one evening after a particularly clear day (you could almost make out the circular orb of the sun through the pollution). We were gathered in a Uighur restaurant enjoying a few rounds of after-dinner beers, and Abraham (he was a Palestinian by heritage who held a Jordanian passport and had been thoroughly Westernized by six years' fraternization with the foreign community in Shenyang, yet was forbidden by the Jordanian government, because of his Palestinian heritage, to go to any Western nation for fear that as a Palestinian he might commit some terrorist act) Abraham was telling the unfortunate tale of Natasha, a Russian student of the Chinese language who had remained in the meat grinder of Shenyang just a bit too long and had slowly lost the last of her marbles. Just as he reached the part of the story regarding Mark's birthday, Pyotr (he was a Polish student of Chinese whose family had once been influential enough to get him to China on full scholarship, but the family had, since 1989, fallen completely out of influence and power to the extent that Pyotr was now stranded in China, financially and politically unable to make his way home) Pyotr jumped in, demanding to tell of the parakeet that Natasha had boiled into a stew.

A good-natured disagreement ensued as to who should be allowed to tell the story of the parakeet, but eventually Jane (she was a Canadian English teacher who had suffered a complete nervous breakdown a month earlier and whose mood since that time had been chemically regulated by excessive amounts of Valium easily obtainable from the local Chinese pharmacy) Jane won the right, and the story was told.

Abraham was beginning to lose interest in his own story by this time, so Mark (he was the American teacher on whose birthday Natasha boiled the parakeet and a student of Chinese who had come to see the culture and had discovered that his skin was violently allergic to one of the many industrial pollutants in the water and therefore had not bathed for three months) Mark picked up where Jane and Abraham left off, detailing how Natasha had gradually withdrawn, had stopped attending classes, had cut off all communication with her friends, and then had simply broken down. They had put her in a Chinese mental institution, but she escaped and was last seen heading north, on foot, back to her mother Russia.

I suppose what I am trying to say with this story is that China is not to be taken lightly. Here is an ancient civilization whose ways are completely independent of Western ideas. The fact that the autocratic leaders of China label themselves Communists should not delude you. China is as far removed from Western patterns of thought as can conceivably be imagined. If you come here and try to cling to the cause-effect system of Western logic in which you have always existed, you will suffer. On the other hand, if you realize that China is a completely different ball game with its own set of rules, and if you are willing to temporarily forget everything that you ever learned in the West about right and wrong, cause and effect, up and down, before and after, you will find an invaluable experience in China.

For example, let me mention that Jane has decided to stay in China for at least another year, Mark is currently enrolled at the University of Chicago in a postgraduate degree for Chinese Studies, Pyotr is finishing his last year of study in China, and Abraham continues to practice medicine in China pending the re-creation of the Palestinian state.

China is not easy, but it is absolutely fascinating. It forces you to answer questions about yourself and your culture that otherwise would never have been raised, and it demonstrates more effectively than anything else I have yet encountered that, by god, there is more than one way to skin a cat.

• • •

Alice, you know what I mean.

Bruce Bender

JEANNE PHILLIPS: Capitalism is hitting harder than ever—or as it is called, "the socialist market economy," which has now claimed

fully half of the students in my freshman class to be Avon
representatives! I try to talk about the evils of pyramid schemes,
point out the profits that the rung above is making from their 60¥
start-up fee, the lessons to be learned from honest hard labor in a
factory as summer help—all to no avail. They think they can get
rich quick and that Avon, that "most popular American superior
product line," will draw buyers despite its exorbitant prices. One
student got her mother to back her with a huge amount of money
and so is several rungs up, with a lot of other students selling for
her. So she may do OK, except the market is way saturated for
such a pricey product.

Meanwhile, Mother's Day is being adopted widely, thanks to
the promotions of dealers in flowers, fashions, cosmetics. One
young woman was quoted in an approving article on the business
page of the *China Daily:* "It was the advertisements that told me
I could take this opportunity to express my love for my mother."

Eagerly adopted Western holidays do still cause some confusion, however. Some of my students, too late for Avon, hope to
sell Christmas cards on the street along with ice cream, to earn
money during summer holidays. There are dozens and dozens of
new magazines in print, and some of them (along with some
newspapers) are becoming more and more outspoken in presenting
news and opinions. Also, more and more people see foreign films
and programs on cable or satellite. All we need to do is wait and
soon all our flaws and problems will be staring back at us from
China.

China, says Bruce Bender in his essay on parakeets and cats, is not to
be taken lightly. And, as experts sometimes warn Americans, this can be
true even of friendship. Those who have the time and spirit to make close
Chinese friends often find an unpredictable dark side to such alliances.

The most common problem is that having American friends can cause
trouble for some Chinese. They can be accused of betraying their country
or their family; they can be hauled in for questioning by school authorities
or village elders. Privileges can be revoked, possessions can be confiscated.
These consequences are usually hidden from the Americans involved, but
it is possible to hear of them. If they find out, most Americans feel

simultaneously surprised, outraged, and guilty, partly responsible for the problems.

Close friends can also simply tell about their lives—lives like those of Todd Lundgren's student Zhang, whose father committed suicide during the Cultural Revolution. China has had a difficult history, and this is reflected in the lives of those who have lived it. Moving into the circle of a Chinese family can bring pain to those who learn to care, as well as warmth and love.

Changsha, Hunan

Dear Alice,

We must live life more intensely.
—D. H. Lawrence

I was weaned partially on Hemingway. It wasn't really my choice; I grew up in his hometown and went to his high school. Ever since, I have felt the need to live a fuller life. To live in a deliberate manner, I thought it best to try to learn under intense conditions. That was partly my reason for coming to China, and now, Alice, things are getting intense.

The rumor is that I have many girlfriends in Changsha and that I'll be going back to the U.S. next month, either deported or with a wife. To the best of my knowledge, neither half of the rumor is true. What is true, on the other hand, is that the FAO knows about my friends, whom I've tried extensively to conceal. They know that I traveled in the deep countryside of southern Hunan, and they questioned the two men as to what we did there, where we stayed. I have found and continue to find beauty in Changsha, in its people, but I worry for them as the clash between New China and the dog of Old China heats up. How can such wonderfully warm and beautiful people be raised by such severity?

It is fascinating—painful but fascinating—to experience China and the lives of our friends whose conflicting values cannot be hidden under a rug during this critical period. There is so much confusion as to the right course to take in China. And, as foreigners fundamentally ignorant and unable effectively to grasp the nature of its conflicts, it is easy to make poor decisions, utterly wrong choices. I am powerless here. That is the source of my pain: I can do nothing but watch my friends get boiled in the cauldron of unemotional, practical principles and politics. There are human rights issues that can never, will never, be placed on the agenda for negotiation. China is big, very big, and I have peeled layers off the Chinese onion only to find disappointment, disillusionment.

Ah, Alice, I'm hurtin'. But I've lived a Chinese life, taken the risks a Chinese takes, and I'll have to suffer the agony with a smile on my face. I do not know, nor do we ever, perhaps, know what we need to learn. We just learn it or not, and give up or go on. I choose to go on. I'm not ready to be air-lifted out by a commando force, nor will I be hanging from the ceiling next month. So don't worry. Regardless of what happens, I'm still glad to be here and living in China.

China is a great place for romantics to get slapped in the face by the practical. Fortunately, I'm a little of both. Learning about China can be uncomfortable at times, but more than ever do I recommend this experience. A fascinating place; it will consume me for the rest of my life.

Until next time,

G

Stereotypes

Facing both the dark and the light in China often leads teachers to face evidence of both light and dark within themselves. After all, psychologists tell us that things we hate in the world outside are often mirrors of what we cannot tolerate in the private world within.

In foreign lands, one hint that the private dark side is beginning to surface is a certain kind of irritation that, early on, most teachers manage to control.

DAVID MOLDAVSKY: Nanchang is not a bad city, although

everybody in Nanchang seems convinced that it is. I've got a bicycle, and I usually cruise downtown once a week with students to go to the park or go shopping. It is a provincial capital and they are not used to seeing foreigners, so I get constant attention. The incessant *lao wai* and "hello" really gets irritating, so one trip downtown per week is enough for me. I'm quite a private person, so living here can sometimes be quite difficult, I must say.

JOE MÁRQUEZ: The students touch every book and ask about every music tape. Sometimes this is great, but sometimes I become a little annoyed—but calm.

TODD LUNDGREN: The foreign affairs folks have moved into the new building and now are insanely busy running their restaurant and hotel. They all have blue uniforms and for the last month have been training cooks, waitresses, and maids. It's their first crack at business, and the group forgotten in the shuffle has been the foreign teachers. It's something that's been hard to adjust to—that we don't matter—especially as we had a close relationship two years ago. In some ways, it is do or die for these folks. Even though their treatment of us is rude, it's really only that we're teachers and not paying guests—we're not high on their list of priorities. But we don't take it personally (too often) and we're trying to enjoy our time here.

But finally, perhaps in the ninth month, the dark side may demand its day.

Xi'an, Shaanxi

Dear Alice,

It was good to hear from you. Everything seems to be going as usual. Teaching has its days. This semester is much tougher than last. The students are harder to "teach." I am teaching writing, though. I really enjoy those classes. Xi'an is a great place, although it can be a bit monotonous. One teacher found a hidden microphone in the apartment.

The FAO is all right but they seem a bit lazy at times. Before my parents came to visit, I was asked to do some recording for language practice tapes. Another teacher and I recorded some eight or ten chapters of stuff, then I left for a week—with permission from the dean. When I returned I was called to the FAO because I had received a package. He talked to me outside later and said that he was grateful to me for doing the recording. I said, "No problem." He then replied, "We should have docked your pay for leaving for a week, but we consider us to now be even because of the recording."

Ever since that, I have lost respect for a lot of people here. I am not the most vocal person and have generally done as I was told—not just to be a good teacher but also to escape some of the boredom. So I've been pretty easygoing. But now I am changing my attitude.

It got worse when my family arrived. I only expected my father and sister to visit me, but my entire family came. My mother, oldest sister, and brother-in-law surprised me at the airport. Well, I had requested the use of a school car for the next day to see the terracotta warriors.[2] My family arrived at night and the school office was closed by the time we got them to their hotel.

So the next morning I go to the office to tell the FAO. He looks at me and says, "You should tell us as soon as you know." I guess they had only arranged for the small car. So I start to explain the change in situation, but it doesn't sink into his thick skull. There is so much (expletive) red tape in this country. Not only do they, the Chinese in positions of "power," not appear to care about us, but they seem to have no respect for foreigners and don't care how we feel. I guess I'm at the boiling point. I've been calm for eight months. No more.

I kept explaining to him that it wasn't my fault, but he just

---

[2] An extraordinary archaeological find near Xi'an, a collection of hundreds of ancient Chinese soldiers modeled in clay, each with a different face and slightly different stance.

would not accept it. I guess his little Communist brain is unable to digest new information and, since I am an Imperialist, my only goal in coming to China is to occupy his time with B.S. excuses and disturb his extremely arduous work schedule of talking on the phone, playing badminton, having a nap and lunch. Am I cynical? I think so.

Anyway, life seems to be all right. I was really happy on the day my next one-and-a-half-year plan came together. It feels good to have goals. I guess. Take care.

Joe Márquez

Changsha, Hunan

Dear Alice,

Let me sleep, sleep; today there is nowhere to go. I should have known to stay in bed this morning, the rain was pounding the roof like machine gun scatter fire. Wet, too wet. But after living in Portland for three years and Changsha for nine months—arguably the wettest places in the universe—I finally spent three dollars and bought an umbrella. Could this new umbrella shield me from the passion that would burst out of me today?

At a fruit stand across from the front gate of the university, I went to buy a bottle of orange soda to bring to R——, the 62-year-old Brit who is in the hospital (with a heavy cold and a fever high enough to warrant a few days rest in the cadres' ward).[3] Usually, I walk among the various stands pricing the fruit, forcing the vendors to compete for my business; not bad business for them, as the lowest prices are usually higher than the Chinese pay. A time-consuming process, but entertaining for both me and the locals when I'm at my best.

---

[3] "Cadre" (often pronounced "cad-ray" by Americans and "cad-er" by the British) is an old term for a member of the Chinese Communist Party. Loyal cadres enjoy certain privileges, including special treatment at hospitals.

But today was a little wet, my head slightly groggy. I went to the stall closest to the hospital entrance and bargained for the bottle of soda. We agreed on 4.50¥. I gave the man a 5¥ note and he then decided to raise the price to 5¥, which means he refused to give me change.

Alice, I'm a relatively patient man; anger doesn't suit me, and it comes to me slowly. The vendor, lanky, with only one eye, grinning at me like Captain Hook, refusing to honor our bargain. My head began to boil, thoughts flashing back to the training hall where I'd learned to fight. Whenever I felt this way I was doomed, for my anger would steal my awareness and cool head, my quick hands and feet would tighten up. I'd lunge in and get my butt kicked. This happened enough times I thought I'd learned to release the tension, let it roll off, stay cool. Some black belt.

I was pissed. I began arguing in Changsha dialect, demanding the five mao change. He was smiling, his gritty teeth disgusting me. I repeated my demand as the inevitable crowd gathered to laugh and watch the "big nose." He continued to refuse, so I grabbed a handful of oranges and threw them into the street. Then another, another. Slowly the grin lifted from his face. Good, I thought, now he is upset. Secretly I hoped he would get aggressive, already I had measured him up. All this for about five cents, a nickel. I was prepared to clear his stand of fruit into the street, determined to get my meager five mao. Finally he gave in, gave me the change. The sight of his wife scurrying in the rain after the stray orbs of fruit was priceless.

An unusual day. I rode across the river with a friend to visit a writer-friend of his and stopped to shop in the clothes market. Twice I was passed by small groups of young idiots in their Sunday best, laughing, shouting, "Hey, big nose! Foreigner!" There is nothing quite so despicable as the way they saunter past, ignorant racists that they are. I know they don't know any better and they usually do not bother me. But today . . . ?

We moved on to the vegetable and meat market to buy some food for lunch. As I was bargaining for eggplant, a few young men walked up behind me and shouted to the vendor to charge me more. Unfortunately, I've been here long enough to pick up some of the rude language of Changsha dialect, and I understood their words. Just as I turned back, I caught one of them saying "Foreign devil" in a sneering tone that is quite unacceptable where I'm from. My rage returned, my eyes grew wide and speared him. I backed him up to a low tank of fish and—I don't know what happened—I just pushed him in. Lightly. Poor guy, his nicely coifed hairdo all wet, mussed. What will his girlfriend think?

Strangely, the crowd loved the scene; demanded an encore. Apparently they knew him, and I learned he was known to be a local rascal and possible thief. I walked away, a little embarrassed and disappointed by my inability to control myself today. Maybe I should get rid of the umbrella.

And so it goes . . .

G

G and Joe fell into their dark and cynical sides in the face of primal human foibles—the dead weight of bureaucracy, the racism of street rascals. Especially for visible foreigners in a society that values blending in, the stereotypes that inspire racism and sexism in us all are almost impossible to ignore, particularly when aimed directly at you.

Shantou, Guangdong

Dear Alice,

I am getting a little fed up with the rampant sexism here. It's no wonder more men than women decide to spend two years here as teachers. The "hello"s you get called your way every time you go down the street are often only out of playfulness but are just as often equivalent to catcalls. I don't think most Chinese men think women are as competent as men. One of my doctors told me she had wanted to be a surgeon, but some director of the surgical department wouldn't accept any women because "they're not strong enough." Perhaps, by the same rationale, they figure that Western women can become surgeons because they're bigger. I could definitely knock down about 90% of the men here in South China, and sometimes the thought is rather appealing.

Actually, I was discussing the topic with my friend in Hong Kong, and in the business world it doesn't seem to be as bad. He says it's often better to hire women since they have fewer problems adapting to authority. So, although this is still evidence of the underlying sexual bias, women do have a chance to move up in the business world. Certainly in the markets and the street stores the women have a nice parity, but it seems the great majority of pain-in-the-ass bureaucratic officials are men. So, in the university and the hospitals the bias is more apparent. There are top women who can have as much power, but it seems that a strong, culturally ingrained idea about women's submissiveness keeps many women from trying. Even my friend admitted that, often, the ones who really get ahead are the ones who are not exactly deemed beautiful and thus have less to lose from breaking that small-waisted, demure feminine mold.

Having been here only a few months, admittedly I have a small range of experience to base this on. As a foreign woman I have my own difficulties within the culture as well. For example, a month ago I had an unpleasant taste of the kind of desperation some people have in China. One of the professors in the English Department invited me over to dinner. I went and it turned out it was only him. I later found out that his divorced wife lives in Shanghai and his son (who just failed his college entrance exams) lives with him, but I didn't see his hide nor hair.

I then suffered through my first horrendously bad Chinese meal. The best dishes were mediocre, and I just had to eat enough of them to justify my "I'm full." There were cold, bland shrimp, crab overcooked to white mush, and half-cooked, greasy spring rolls. The worst was when he—playing that obnoxious Chinese dinner game of "What's this? Just try some and see if you can guess."—induced me to have a spoonful of those eggs preserved in the brown-black jelly stuff. They must be preserved in horse urine, because the ammonia taste that immediately hit my mouth nearly made me retch. I forced myself to swallow it after seriously considering going to the toilet to spit it out.

The dinner was bad enough, but during dinner he also decided to make toasts over our syrupy Chinese laurel wine. "To your good luck!" he first toasted followed by "To China." I countered on the next toast with "To the U.S." At this he looked meaningfully into my eyes and said, "Yes, yes, to the U.S. I hope so, I certainly hope so." The dinner had already turned my stomach and this put it into full rotation. I had earlier made some remark about how, with Chinese meals, they go on so long you have to quit at night and finish in the morning and he had said, "That would be no problem; you could stay here overnight." I had chosen to look upon it as a jest. As I tried to hurry through the formalities of a guest-visit and a cup of coffee, however, he sat too close and made a pretty definite move at a kiss, and I finally said I had to go. He then tried to convince me that he would have to take me home on his bike since it was too late (7:30) for a pedicab. I knew that was nonsense and went out to the street to ride one home, disgustedly turning an unimpressed level gaze upon that evening's street-starers. I know this represents an absurdly exaggerated example of the "I want out of the country and you look like a ticket" mentality, but it made its point.

Inger

STEPHEN: There has been an alarming increase in violence in this society in the last year, and an increase in violence toward foreigners. There doesn't seem to be the strict penalty for those mistreating foreign guests that there used to be. There is widespread inflation, people are moving in from the countryside and being laid off from government jobs. Some people are getting rich but most cannot keep up with inflation. Government has no control on the economy, crime is on the rise, everyone is looking for an easy way to make money. Everyone here thinks all foreigners are rich. Much of the population is uneducated, and racial prejudice runs very deep.

JOE MÁRQUEZ: The Chinese are interesting. They have yet to figure out where I'm from. This week I tell people I'm from India.

Almost every foreigner who stays a year in China will explode at least once in the face of frequently expressed stereotypes. "Yes, I can use chopsticks," G recommends for the back of a China Council T-shirt, and "No, I don't own a gun"—because people ask the same questions over and over, because the stereotype is that Americans come from a violent land where people only know how to use forks. As Todd Hamina says, it "can totally grate on your nerves."

But in the yin and yang vortex, many foreign teachers discover that even stereotyping contains a paradox.

PJ: I really like the people in this department, so I agreed to go on their outing to see Mao's birthplace, a trip that otherwise would be pretty dull. We were supposed to leave at 5 A.M.—*not* a good hour for me and, believe me, I was grouchy.

T—— and I are coming up through the dark, everyone else waiting for us at the fountain, and we could hear them talking in Chinese, "Here come the foreigners now. Foreigners don't like to get up early," and they laugh. Inside, I just explode, I hiss through my teeth at T——, "Foreigner this! Foreigner that! I'm *sick* of this goddamn racism all the time! These Chinese are just so—" and I stop dead.

For the first time I heard myself. All year long, even about my own friends, I had been generalizing exactly the same way. "The Chinese," I'd say, "don't like to be alone; often get up early to do exercise." Even though I'm sure there are plenty for whom these things are not true. We are all doing this to one another. Well, I swan.

As PJ suddenly sees, the human truth is that *everyone* stereotypes. Once this idea blooms into awareness, it takes only a quick review of letters like these to see evidence of it scattered everywhere.

Even writers here who are generally positive about their experience in

China have called the Chinese stupid, greedy, dangerous, cheating, racist, aggressive, inefficient, rude, lazy, apathetic, primitive, and unable to use forks—as well as patient, elegant, exciting, short and slim, generous, flexible, and warm and friendly. They in turn have been seen by the Chinese as rude, pushy, violent, selfish, stupid, helpless, dramatic, greedy, big-nosed, too independent, weak, ugly, emotional, and unable to use chopsticks—as well as rich, funny, exciting, blue-eyed and blond, and hard working.

We all generalize, whether we base our generalizations on experience or the latest movie. And we do this because it helps us know what to do when we meet someone new. Nancy Adler, a scholar who teaches organizations about cultural difference, stresses that stereotyping is basically a useful human tool. People tend to miss this idea, she says, because "we have viewed stereotyping as a primitive form of thinking, as an unnecessary simplification of reality. We have also viewed stereotyping as immoral: Stereotypes *can* be inappropriate judgments of individuals based on inaccurate descriptions of groups. It is true that labeling [all] people from a certain ethnic group as 'bad' [or rude or blue-eyed] is immoral. But grouping individuals into categories is neither good nor bad—it simply reduces a complex reality to manageable dimensions. . . . *Everyone* stereotypes."[4]

When used effectively, Adler says, "stereotyping allows people to . . . act appropriately in new situations." The sign of effectiveness is that we are willing to change our stereotypes as soon as experience gives us more complex and accurate information. And this is only possible, says Adler, when we are *aware* of our own stereotypes. "A subconsciously held stereotype is difficult to modify or discard even after we collect real information about a person, because it is often thought to reflect reality" (p. 72).

Now, it is always easier to see the flaw in stereotypes aimed at us than in those we aim at others. Therefore, several of these letter writers realize a strange advantage in being a visible target of stereotyping for so long in China: Constant exposure to the prejudice of others can force awareness

---

[4] Nancy Adler, *International Dimensions of Organizational Behavior,* 2d ed. (Belmont, Calif.: Wadsworth, 1991), p. 74.

of equal and opposite prejudice within. And, as Adler says, becoming aware of our stereotypes is the first step to transcending them. Experiences with stereotyping in China helped several of these teachers discover how, in the world of yin and yang, there are times when getting closer to the dark side can sometimes be a move toward the light.

Shadow Days

Sometimes, however, the problem is not naïve stereotyping or lack of awareness. Everyone is just having a bad day. For example, in 1993 the International Olympic Committee decided to site the next Olympic Games in the United States instead of China.

> AUGUST 1993: I'm here! Beijing was nice, from what I could see. Everywhere I looked I saw signs for the Olympics. I don't think they've gotten the games yet?

> SEPTEMBER 1993: The decision has been made: the 21st century will not be heralded in by dragons weaving about and *gong fu* exhibitions, and the delicate pride of the Chinese has been wounded. On Tuesday, university presidents and local officials all over China met with students and workers to instruct them, whether in celebration or defeat, not to march into the streets or burn down the U.S. embassies. On the home front, our new president charged the students not to threaten the foreign teachers. Good advice!

> JANUARY 1994: The loss of the Olympics did bring a violent reaction here. At first most people said that China couldn't afford to put on the games anyway. They would try again next time. But the wave of resentment that has followed runs very deep. There is a very different attitude toward foreigners here now, especially Americans. There have been several incidents—whether it is all related to the Olympics or partially the rising inflation rates, who knows. But tourists have been attacked—minor scuffles —several incidents I have heard of foreign teachers here—

disagreements and arguments turn into pushing-punching matches. I personally have been in two situations—one a bike accident, the other an argument about buying vegetables that turned into a small lynch mob. A very scary situation.

And, as always, the wheel of dark and light continues to turn.

MARY BRACKEN: I did want to tell you (to make a long story short) that my mother *and* grandmother in Pennsylvania received two mysterious phone calls from Chinese people, from overseas. There is no possibility of a mix-up. Someone wanted to know who I was calling in the U.S. The only two numbers I've ever called on my apartment phone have been my mom and grand-mother. The person called up my grandmother the day after Mother's Day and asked if she spoke Chinese. What a paranoid country! I've been disconnected several times, also. So, I've been pegged. Gee, maybe I even have an active file. Call me "Little Ms. Counterrevolutionary."

JEANNE PHILLIPS: We'll travel to villages where my companions spent several years of the Cultural Revolution living with very poor farmers who treated them kindly and shared the little they had, without demanding that these soft, late-middle-aged (then) teachers do the heavy work. My friends are excited at the prospects of the reunions as well as of showing me the lovely scenery of the mountains, lakes, and waterfalls. But I can't tell anyone about this trip, for they worry about jealous reactions, accusations of favoritism, and especially resentment that they are cozying up to one of the foreigners. So, mum is the word.

The dark of revolution and the light of kindness; the dark of resentment and the light of reunion. As Bruce Bender suggests in his letter above, Chinese philosophy does not see life as a linear chain of cause and effect but rather as a constant shifting, a moving balance among eternal forces. Many Americans find this easier to understand after a year or two of fluctuating reversals in Looking Glass Land.

SAMANTHA TISDEL: Tell everyone—come to live in China, you will surely at some point feel your human rights are being shat upon. You will feel wrath toward the System. You will call it corrupt, inefficient, inept, sloppy, a dinosaur, and maybe other things as well. Like Gollum,[5] you will stroke and fawn over your little blue passport with the pretty golden eagle imprinted on the cover, hide it in a clever place, check it in the middle of the night, call it "My Precious." This is your ticket out, anytime you want, anywhere you want to go. You will marvel at the serendipity that gave you so much power and freedom in the world. You might even feel embarrassed by the birthright bestowed upon you, which is denied to the people here, who flesh out a full teeming quarter of the earth's collection of human beings.

"So," I hear you mutter in exasperation, "why doesn't she brandish her precious birthright and get the H out of there if it's really so bad?" I do have compelling reasons to return to America; and my reasons for remaining are, I have been forced to acknowledge, equally compelling. Here are some of them:

My job. Always a challenge and often a delight in spite of dingy, cold classrooms, unreliable electricity, an utterly disorganized and unhelpful English Department.

My students. For the most part smart, motivated, well-informed about most aspects of the "outside world," opinionated and indignant about the U.S. policy toward China. (What right, after all, has the U.S. government to impose its values on anyone else, especially for the sake of economic dominion?)

And this strange feeling. I come from a land where the deepest roots (with the notable exception of the Indians) go down only several hundred years, and now I stand on a land where roots are measured in multiples of a thousand. It gives you a remarkable feeling of buoyancy—nothing to hold you in place, no deep taproot to nourish you with the sap of cultural identity. It is freedom, weightlessness, and also emptiness and exclusion.

---

[5] A sneaky, passionate character in J. R. R. Tolkien's trilogy *The Lord of the Rings* who, like the heroes, is searching for a powerful ring. He refers to the ring as "My Precious."

Xi'an, Shaanxi

Dear Alice,

Got your letter; it's great to hear from you. Things are better health-wise for me. Not so many problems now that the weather has changed. In fact, the weather here has taken an incredible turn. It seems that there is a stationary high-pressure system over this area, and we have had almost three solid weeks of clear sunny skies and dry warm weather. Almost like Colorado; it is really pleasant.

It has been a great experience to have been here these two years. I've learned so much about people, life, society, civilization—I have experienced such an overwhelming flow of emotions here.

I've been so angry at injustice, ignorance, and prejudice that I swear I could have killed someone—anyone with such distorted views of reality. My reality, I know, but looking at it from theirs still doesn't make it right. I've laughed deeper and enjoyed the very simple pleasures of life with close friends from countries across the world. And I've cried openly, deeply, at the sorrow, the loss, the heartache of living life with always a questionable future.

Alice, I know you understand all this. I look forward to the time one day when you and I can sit down and have a long talk about this China experience. J—— and I used to spend hours drinking beers and talking. It made the pain of it easier. I wouldn't trade this experience for anything in my life, but it's also been one of the hardest of my life.

Stephen

Lanzhou, Gansu

Dear Alice,

I have my answers, but I do not know how I am to arrive at them.

—F. Gauss

I was on the train eating apricots and melon, but mostly I was thinking about my Chinese friends. Unlike most trains I'd been on in China, the train from Urumuqi to Lanzhou lacked the swarm and crush of sweaty, smoking bodies standing in the aisles, stuffed under seats; no boxes or burlap sacks of raisins and grain obstructed the path to the toilet, and I didn't have to climb in the window to board. There was plenty of room to spit and throw melon rinds. I had a bunk in a sleeper car, but was sitting in a hard seat with a Uighur couple I'd met in Kashgar.

They were Muslim, on their way to visit their son in Xi'an. Ali was a cadre and worked for the Public Health Ministry, and he spoke a little English. Wearing a veil of brown gauze over her head and face, his wife said nothing and peeled apricots for her husband and me.

I had met them trying to convince the driver of the three-day bus from Kashgar to Urumuqi to let me board. No room; the tickets had all been sold. I told him that I was late for work and couldn't wait for the next day's bus. He didn't seem to under-stand my Chinese, probably because it was mostly English. Ali, sitting behind the driver, watched all this, then said a few words to him. The driver waved me aboard. The bus was an old, rusty Russian number; half the windows were blown out. No seats, so I sat on my gear in the aisle in the front of the bus. Ali, a tall, middle-aged man whose flat cap did little to shade his big Central Asian nose and lively green eyes, asked me why I didn't speak the local Turkish dialect instead of Chinese. He thought I was from Xinjiang.[6] In discovering I was a foreigner, Ali laughed heartily, his round belly bouncing and disrupting the front of the bus.

We crossed the desert and twice stopped for the night. Outside of Aksu the bus broke down. The heat was maddening, so we stayed on the bus for three hours while the driver and his mate jury-rigged the fuel line, took a nap, then prayed. Everyone

---

[6] In the northwest provinces of China, people of Turkish and Afghani heritage mix with those from Southeast Asia, and it is common to see people who look Caucasian.

prayed—got off the bus and kneeled on the road. The rest of the trip was smoky, crowded, and uneventful, and in Urumuqi Ali and I parted.

Two days later I ran into them at the train station, waiting for the train to Lanzhou. We talked awhile about Xinjiang province and China. He didn't like the Han Chinese much, complained about their lack of tolerance and disrespect for Allah. I understood little, especially when he got heated up and spoke in a pastiche of three languages about the Cultural Revolution and the toll it took on his family. These days, his people are allowed back into the mosque, but public sermons are prohibited and the learned teachers are all dead or in Beijing. He said that the young know nothing of Islam; the only holy books left are general and vague. His face was getting red, and he puffed when the call to board our train was announced.

Lanzhou was two days away. I had hoped to continue our conversation, but by the time I found them in their seats, he had cooled down, his wife had removed her veil. We ate fruit and talked about the United States. The conversation soon waned, and I could see Ali and his wife muttering prayers to themselves, to Allah. Luxuriating in the vacancy of the car, I settled in my seat and read some Carver stories; I fell asleep thinking of friends left behind.

The sound of grinding metal woke me. The train came to an abrupt stop, jolting the passengers from their seats and the luggage from the overhead storage racks. Outside it was dark, only a few lights making the tiny platform of a tinier train station visible. One o'clock in the morning, and I was tired. I dozed back to my friends' gentle songs.

Stirring passengers brought me back to the train: they were craning their necks and huddling up to the open windows. A conductor entered the car and announced that the windows were to be shut. We were told to stay in our seats. Few people paid attention. We were watching a company of soldiers clustered on the platform; orders were given and two soldiers took positions beside the door of our car. The others dispersed. We waited, everyone talking loudly, speculating on the reasons for the train's delay and the soldiers' presence. Another company approached the train, many of whom were plainclothes in black leather jackets, carrying radios.

In a rush the door swung open, and three soldiers with automatic rifles and a plainclothes with a stun gun—all Han Chinese—boarded our car. The plainclothes, the apparent leader, announced that a search was under way for a camera stolen from a foreigner in a sleeper car. Passengers were ordered to collect their luggage and sit back in their proper seats. Chaos. No one sat down as the search party pointed weapons and emptied bags; everyone watched and shouted and pointed fingers. Amid the flurry, I was noticed by the plainclothes; he came up to me and asked what I was doing in hard seat and whom I was with. He told me foreigners were not allowed in this car. Go up and stay with the other foreigners in the dining car, he said.

I wasn't escorted and I had to pee, so I slipped into the toilet between cars with my daypack and opened the window. I forgot to pee and leaned on the sill, looked out across the vast darkness of the desert. I wanted to jump from the window and run, run into the blackness. No more cigarette smoke or grungy toilets; no more friends I couldn't visit or bureaucrats I couldn't kill. The desert spread out like a pizza and I could smell it.

I peed, and the sounds from the car died down. I left the toilet and looked back into the car—the soldiers had left or moved on. The passengers again huddled by the windows. I went back, took my seat, and no one cared. Then the sounds of shouting voices and stun guns emanated from a crowd of soldiers and plainclothes gathered on the platform.

Ali's wife had replaced the veil over her head and sat with her head dropped, her hands folded on her lap. I tried to get Ali's attention and ask him what was going on, but he ignored me. He was sandwiched between two passengers, the flesh of his belly pressed flat into another man's back. As the train's engine fired up and prepared to leave, Ali pried himself free from the window and took the seat next to his wife. I asked him again, but he turned his head away toward the open desert side of the train and said nothing.

I lifted my daypack and decided to go to my bunk and lie down. I passed the toilet, then turned back. I went in, locked the door. The air from the window was cold on my face for the rest of the night. I leaned on the sill and watched my pizza pass by—in darkness, it passed me by.

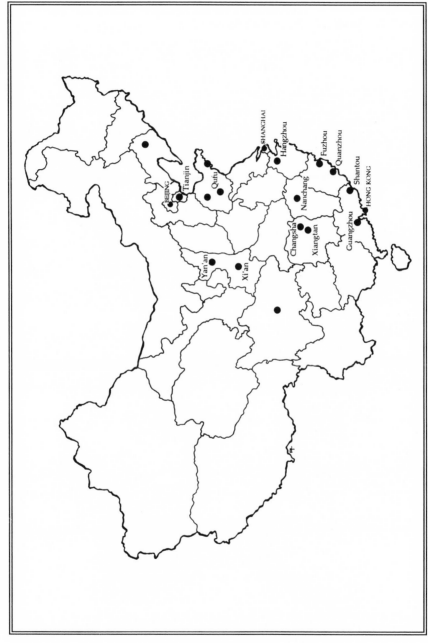

Map 12. The People's Republic of China, showing the cities from which letters in chapter 11 were written.

CHAPTER ELEVEN
VOCABULARY

ma ma hu hu (ma ma who who): so-so.

ni hao (nee how): "Are you well?"—a greeting often used by Chinese speakers to say hello to foreigners.

Making Some Sense of It All

In the spring of each year, Alice usually sends a letter asking her teachers how things went overall at their sites—with teaching, with the FAO, with salaries and facilities. In response, many people are inspired to reflect as well as to report and to send back some advice for anyone tempted to follow them through that Looking Glass.

Looking Back

DALE ASIS: I have decided *not* to continue teaching for another year. It was a very difficult decision to make. Surprisingly, I enjoy teaching and I enjoy the pleasure of seeing all my students speaking English in "happy English" days. The joys of those friendships I have formed with my Chinese friends are deeply rewarding. The sense of accomplishment of fighting through the bureaucratic red tape is overwhelming. But, I made the choice to come home. Maybe I'm scared that if I stay another year I'll lose touch. That if I stay another year, I'll have difficulty finding a job and going back to the corporate world. I hope I will not regret this decision when I look back a few years from now.

What type of teacher will work best here in this small college? Other than the usual survival skills of flexibility, open-mindedness, thoughtfulness, and friendliness, the teacher should be able to handle NO NIGHT LIFE. Unless, of course, ballroom dancing 'til 10:00 P.M. at the student hall or karaoke singing is his or her cup of tea. Then he or she will fit right in. The college is situated outside the city proper, and downtown Xiangtan is not really hopping with excitement. I only go to the city to see movies, to get my fill of Hong Kong ultra-violence or the latest B-movie from the United States. There are no buses to town after 6 P.M., though you can be suicidal and ride your bike in the dark. So life in Xiangtan is slow.

The teacher should also be able to handle the "zoo effect" well. Every move you make is watched by others. Anonymity is non-existent in Xiangtan. And he or she must handle the great red tape of such a small college. If the next foreign teacher cannot handle all this, then he or she is better off in a big city. But on the other hand, you get fresh air, which is quite a premium compared to China's big polluted cities. Vegetables and fish are fresh and plentiful, as farmers bring their produce from the surrounding areas to the college market every morning. And for sure, students would constantly visit any foreign teacher.

INGER: Well, having come through an ass-dragging end of March, I've been cruising steadily through April.

I need to clarify the matter of my opinion of this school. As I said, Shantou is not the most traditional of Chinese cities, and the Shantou people do have a national reputation for being cheaters. On the other hand, it does give one a glimpse of a great deal of new China. It's an excellent place to observe the head-on clash between insular China and the international business world. I do enjoy Shantou once I swallow all those grains of salt. You just have to keep well hydrated to flush it through your system so it doesn't raise your blood pressure.

I had one episode with my boss, but it was only between us, and I can't portray myself as much of a victim. One, I don't actually feel that victimized. Two, when I said stop, he stopped and he's never taken advantage of anything but my state of mind. He's actually been very good about taking care of all my necessities. I think he's a more than fair person to work with and wouldn't cause any headaches like some do. I don't think he's likely to pull moves on just any Westerner. It was all just a foolish episode.

Also, I don't have bad relations with people out here. My

paranoia fueled a lot of suspicion, but now that my schedule and I have relaxed, things are going well. I got stuck in a bad routine last semester. It is difficult being the only foreigner at the college, but now I've gotten the feel of the place.

Altogether, I just want to emphasize that, although I've had my personal difficulties, I do endorse this as a good place to teach. It just depends on what your interests are. I like Shantou, but I like dirty old cities. It's not the place to get the feel for the glory of old China. All you get here is a sad reminder of how the past can lose out to modernity even if it came through the Cultural Revolution.

But it still is China. The Shantou market people (not to be confused with the businesspeople) are delightful. I get to practice my Chinese with them and pick up the odd phrase. I'm an easy mark—they just have to be really nice and I'll buy something. I'm always coming home with loads of vegetables that I don't know how to fix. Everything pretty much gets stir fried. I can't believe at the beginning of the year I thought I'd eat most of the time at the dining hall. I haven't been there for months.

The cat is driving me crazy tonight. He's yowling around the apartment. Even though he was neutered, he still seems to have bouts of kitty-cat testosterone peaks. He is a nice cat and he keeps the pests down. My Chinese friends keep asking if I'll take him back to the States. They really do think we're crazy, don't they?

STEPHEN: Please don't send just anybody over here. China has been great but it does wear on the nerves from time to time—living in a communal situation with someone who just doesn't get it is enough to drive a person over the edge sometimes. I'm really working on developing inner peace and tranquility here, but there truly is the Ugly American, and he or she always complains the loudest. Tell your people it's not too bad a place to be—if they don't mind the *dust*.

Living conditions at this school are probably better than normal. Library is OK. They have a large collection of donated books that they do not use, not catalogued. Classrooms and

equipment are standard, like the rest of China. Tourism department very easy to get along with. FAO is accustomed to foreigners; with patience and small requests life is bearable.

I think the main problems with living here come from the
area itself. Xi'an is a very traditional area, hasn't modernized
much and is taking pains not to, it seems. It is an area of high
crime by Chinese standards, and there are a great many armed
robberies, murders, and rapes here. So far as I know, the only
way foreigners have been affected by this is in pickpocket
incidents and street fights, in arguments over unfair prices or
charges. At this school in the last two years, there have been three
murders, and seven rapes that I know about. In the university
next to us, we heard of two murders this winter. Victims are
mostly students but, increasingly, people who have money.
Robbery is the main motive.

MAX TUEFFERD: Teaching here is equally frustrating and rewarding, but for the most part the students are conscientious. The
library has the usual slew of books in English: Emily Brontë,
Charles Dickens, Shakespeare's complete works (you can brush up
on your classics in China!), as well as *numerous* technical and
science books. They also have a few interesting books on culture,
both American and British.

I brought books on grammar and writing, but I myself didn't
teach them. (Nicky did, though.) Foreign teachers rarely teach
grammar—the Chinese understand it better than we do. The most
useful, I think, is to bring games that will force students to use
their language skills. Books with lots of verbal games are good,
and also certain board games—$20,000 Pyramid is a great example.
Pictures are the best classroom aids. We have only the blackboard.

I recommend teachers bring at least one general U.S. history
and one Chinese history book; it helps keep things in perspective.
Overall, this university is not the greatest place on earth, but it's
pretty relaxed, and we don't really want for anything (except
when they turn off the water).

KEVIN LAW-SMITH: Anyone coming here next year:
- Good pay
- Good space
- Hot water (now)
- Nice club down the street (Health)
- Lovely surroundings—rolling hills, green grass, birds singing, NO people (just kidding)

But honestly, I recommend it.

TODD LUNDGREN: I think China has entered a new stage. Two years ago we were here still in the shadow of Tiananmen: that's history now. And I think that the Chinese will pursue money and glitz with the same fervor that they followed Mao. I often say (to myself) that the Chinese are going to have to go through a period of binge spending and consumption until they see that they have all this shit and no culture or political freedom and then maybe they'll ask "Where are we going?" But now is not the time for questioning. Now is the boom. Get it while you can.

Part of my cynicism is due to one group of students this year, most of whom would be bored with the best teachers or textbooks. Much more interested in their new independence (e.g., dating) and in their clothes, Walkmans, etc. And you can't blame 'em. But to teach 'em is *murder*—partly because they think they know so much. Guess I sound like a seasoned teacher, huh? But that's only one class. The others are still inquisitive.

Before, we thought, "Traveling in China is hell but being a teacher makes it worthwhile." Now our motto is, "Being a teacher in China is hell but traveling makes it all worthwhile." (I'm not really that pessimistic. Maybe it's just the effect of the coffee my friend sent us. Too much coffee in China is a bad thing.)

I think that the last time we returned from China I felt confident to say what China was or wasn't. Now the only thing I'm certain of is my uncertainty. And that's okay. We must look with fresh eyes and know that things are changing and that our time is short and that the beer is (still) good. And now with the heat coming, the last of spring is so refreshing. And the wind through the green wheat outside the campus is truly beautiful.

Ah, China.

MICHAEL MAY: I'm having an interesting time rediscovering who I really am. If there is time to do anything here, it is definitely a time to think. It's very strange, but sometimes I recall long-forgotten memories and I don't know why.

If anyone ever asked me before I came to China my views on China, I think I would have given a completely different answer from what I would now. I re-read my copy of *Living in China*,[1] and now the ideas they discuss seem so much clearer. There really is no way to tell someone what China is like. One can only say, "Just go and discover for yourself."

Simple accomplishments like communicating an idea (because the dialect here is horrible) make me feel on top of the world. At times I say to myself, "I could stay here another year." I don't know though. I love my students, but I don't want to be a teacher. Who knows? I sure as hell don't.

China is one truly screwed up country that I have come to love and hate at the same time, and maybe even in the same day.

Sometimes, of course, people have quite different experiences, even in the same location. On the one hand . . .

DAVID MOLDAVSKY: As far as Nanchang goes—it's been pretty good. I like my students and teaching, although our teaching building is in shambles. They are doing reconstruction on the building, and so we are now basically working in a construction site. There are workers banging on the walls and throwing bricks. Stones and gravel occasionally come smashing through the windows. As you can imagine it makes it difficult to teach, especially conversation class. We've asked our department for

---

[1] This is a useful guide for prospective sojourners by Weiner, Murphy, and Li. For complete information, see the reading list at the end of this book.

help, but they say we should just look for other rooms ourselves and do the best we can. This situation obviously has somewhat marred my experience here.

As far as ranking this school, I'll give it a 7. There's really nothing to see, but it's a good experience in Traditional China. The weather here is supposed to be pretty miserable—real hot in summer and real cold in winter—but I found it pretty sufferable.

I've had no problem at all living on our monthly salary. Unless one plans to eat at Captain Cheng's Grand Seafood Mansions, the money is sufficient. Breakfast is eight mao (0.80¥), lunch about 1.5¥ (at the school's "shiting" establishment). And I cook dinner from food bought at the market—usually adds up to a couple of yuan. For my winter travels (three and a half weeks) I also didn't have to dip into my own resources; I had saved enough from my salary.

The living conditions are quite nice. The apartments are good by Chinese standards (I'm living in the apartment Paige had last year) and most important, we have considerable privacy. The department library is full of useful books and even novels, but some of the equipment we have in the U.S. is not available here (slide projector, overheads, computers, video machines).

Our *waiban* is OK; I've heard of much worse. They are all nice people, but most things take a long time to get done—everything from fixing our heater to getting our promised raise. But this is not America, as I remind myself when dealing with them, and I really haven't had any major problems.

. . . and on the other . . .

PAIGE DAVIES: Our *waiban* is outstandingly wonderful! He helps us buy train tickets, given advance notice, and the office is fairly quick about repairing broken windows and the like. (No, I haven't broken any, but the wind gets so strong at times, it can knock a few windows out!) We play soccer and basketball with our *waiban* also, and visit him at home. He's very relaxed with us, and he tells us how it is—that is, he's not doing the "beat-around-the-bush technique" that so many use here.

Guangzhou, Guangdong

Dear Alice,

I'm on a boat traversing the Pearl River, the ferry hurtling under the bridge we call the "fish bridge" because of its shape.

The fans are flapping madly, as summer has hit. It's 35°C, thickly humid, dusty, mosquito-ridden summer, and the heat burns you right out of bed at 6:00 A.M.

I have my routine down. I wake up at dawn and zip downstairs to buy *baozi* for breakfast. I eat them on the roof above my room or in front of the CBS evening news, which starts here at seven every morning. If I'm feeling restless, I go for a quick walk, or for a swim—the pool is *full* of bobbing students. They come to do a bit of splashing, but mainly to eye the opposite sex. So swimming is almost logistically impossible, but I do my best to weave through the masses.

I teach from 8 until 10 or 12 o'clock, linger to chat with students, then head for the market to buy vegetables. I've been here for so long that I have "my own" vendors—the tofu girl, the noodle man, the water-chestnut couple, and the little old bok choy woman who squats behind her basket and gives me a toothy grin. Back to scrub, slice, spice, stir-fry, and there's lunch. I'll have to buy a wok when I go home—I can't imagine cooking without one now!

When I first came here, I laughed at the Chinese and their *mandatory* one-hour nap after lunch. It was my favorite time of the day, peaceful and deliciously quiet—no phone calls, no visits, a respite to plan lessons or write letters. But now, after lunch, I sleep! China's exhausting. The traffic, the air, the noise, climbing a billion stairs, haggling over eggplant. The more assimilated I become, the more Chinese habits I take on. I ride my ancient Flying Pigeon bicycle everywhere, serve the right tea, and use the greeting "Have you eaten?" as second nature. It's impossible for me to truly become Chinese, but with my eyes open and a lot of care, I do my best to blend into the marvelous tapestry of China around me.

Teddy Kellam

Good Advice

In addition to responding to Alice's questions, many teachers pass on heartfelt practical tips to those who might follow them.

Chengdu, Sichuan

Dear Alice,

I find myself sitting on top of Emai Shan at present. Freezing cold and everything. Actually the sun is shining and I'm leaned back against this monstrosity of a Buddhist temple writing you. The main reason I'm writing is because the most organized people who will be in the program next year shall be inquiring of you soon. If they're going to come here then they'll want to be prepared. I'm not talking mentally but physically, because there is one recurring theme among all foreign teachers, and that is they are cold. I am not. Winter camping has paid off for me. Sure, I look funny, but I'm warm. (Small note—so far I've been swarmed four times by monks who are dazzled by my letter home.)

It's true, I'm warm. I'm also functional. So I'm going to try to give a list of things that will be very practical to have. Some of them will be pricey, but when you compare this to three months of coldness, then it's worth it. First of all, the greatest item is Patagonia expedition-weight capilene long johns. This stuff is just amazing because, unlike most polypropylene products, you don't have to move (i.e., supply friction) for its insulating properties to keep you warm. It also dries very, very fast; less than two hours from washing and you can wear it again. It's also one of the few things so far to take the beating the PRC gives. I'm happy with it in the classroom, trains, anywhere. I also brought my down booties. These are very silly looking but incredibly effective. Also, I didn't bring a single sweater. Instead I brought three types of polar fleece. These are fantastic. Although I didn't bring any polar fleece bottoms, I would recommend them in a second. Warmth is everything and none of the buildings are heated. In our house, three of five heaters are broken. Too bad. Maybe in two months they'll be fixed; until then you freeze.

I also brought a nice Columbia down jacket. Most people who own items similar to the ones I've mentioned didn't bring them because they didn't want them to get trashed. I think this is a silly attitude, but then again I have things to use and abuse. I figure I'll buy even more technologically advanced clothing later and ruin it too. After all, you don't come to China to make or save money. So if you're going to lose money, then do it right and be warm.

The most surprising thing I have that keeps me warm most of the time are my Birkenstocks. "Boston" is the style and they are a clog. And for some reason they're warm. Go figure. Maybe it's my ragg wool socks? I don't know.

Todd Hamina

ANONYMOUS: We're all sitting here on the balcony remembering our first encounters with one another. Two of us arrived early (we were both old hands at traveling), and we just laid out all our supplies on the floor. Public resources, we agreed. Barge cement, duct tape, thumbtacks, and a little hammer. Between us we had about 50 books and 100 music tapes, diarrhea drugs. OK so, "How many condoms did you bring?" We grinned and counted—I think we had about twenty-five between us.

Occupant Number 3 arrives a week later, from a prestigious

Eastern school known for its China program. This man has had ADVICE up the wazoo, though not a lot of experience. Good stuff he brought—Lysol spray, a Hong Kong tape player with tape-to-tape copying capacity. And how many condoms? Seventy. The man had 70. Think of it—the seniors in ivy-covered brick, fantasizing what their compatriot could do with a year in the mysterious East. As far as I know, he did not use a single one.

PAIGE DAVIES: Things I wish I'd brought that I didn't: (1) a pair of sweatpants; (2) more AA batteries; (3) spices (all I can get here is white pepper, salt, soy sauce, sugar, vinegar; I'm craving oregano, cumin, GARLIC powder, onion powder, etc.); (4) shortwave radio (the best bet is to buy one in Hong Kong so you don't have to buy a converter); we ended up buying a portable one here for 100¥, but it totally sucks up the battery power (that's why #2 said more batteries!); (5) tapes of stories in English; (6) *Guinness Book of World Records;* (7) more passport pictures—or any photo you're willing to part with and give as souvenirs; (8) info on applying to U.S. colleges/universities, TOEFL test, GRE exam, etc.; (9) holiday decorations (though these are also fun to make, as I did); (10) potato/vegetable peeler (the ones here are poor quality); (11) if you are going to have a VCR at your school, Disney videotapes are loved.

Also—our frisbee has been a hit and students often gather to watch or play. No butter or milk is available in Nanchang, so maybe calcium tablets are a smart idea? No carpeting, so newcomers should definitely bring wool slippers that have a THICK SOLE.

I recommend bringing world maps along. Students enjoy looking at them on our walls, and I think they would make nice gifts as well. Oh yeah! A compilation tape of Christmas music. Four people requested copies of mine, and I had the words to songs mimeographed so that we could all go caroling. They really enjoyed it (and they thought carolling was very strange!)

TODD HAMINA (again): L. L. Bean Maine hunting boots. My roommate has them and he says his feet love them.

JOE MÁRQUEZ: Advise new teachers to pack plenty of toothpaste. Chinese toothpaste is like putting detergent in your mouth. It feels as if you're brushing with rubber but with bubbles. Also bring plenty of music. And, just enough clothes to wear until you can buy some Chinese stuff. I know people here that have barely a week's worth of clothes. They just do wash a lot. The thing is, I wish I had brought less, but you never know until after the fact.

DAVID MOLDAVSKY: B—— and I wanted to give some suggestions to next year's teachers on what to bring: (1) *Not* books—there are plenty here in the department library, teaching materials as well as novels. I've hardly looked at the ones I dragged with me from the U.S. They don't expect American teachers to give grammar classes since they realize we are all quite poor at it. (2) Clothes—bring polypropylene long underwear, two wool sweaters, and not too many formal clothes. Teachers don't wear real formal clothes; just slacks and a button down. (3) Food—I'll tell you what they don't have: rice (just a joke), peanut butter, butter, mayonnaise, Italian spices, cheese, BBQ sauce. (4) Other—bring two vegetable peelers, can opener, tapes, two teacher's planning books, sticky stuff to hang posters, maps (especially of China *in* English), and deodorant, dental floss, and Q-tips. (5) Others (less essential)—nerf football, *tapes*, an instrument if you play (I would die without my guitar), diarrhea medicine and cold medicine.

TODD HAMINA (again): A long raincoat.

DAVID MOLDAVSKY (again): I'll update the "What-to-take" list I sent you last semester: I have found peanut butter in Nanchang and Miracle Whip, but both taste pretty *ma ma hu hu.*

TODD LUNDGREN AND EILEEN VICKERY: We've just come across a travel book we hadn't seen before: *Southwest China off the Beaten Track.* Its tone and approach are much different from the Lonely Planet's (which tends to be too critical and often outdated). Anyway it's written by Stevens and Wehrfritz and published by

Passport Books. It would be a great asset to anyone thinking about teaching or traveling in China's southwest. It has a section on Kunming where it tells of a cafe that serves "excellent Vietnamese coffee with freshly baked bread." What are we waiting for?

MAX TUEFFERD: You can tell whoever is coming to Quanzhou next year to ignore what the book says about how little China has. You can buy *anything* you want, as far as necessities go. They usually have Western brand names, which are more expensive, but very affordable. There are two exceptions: film of good quality and deodorant. The first is available only in larger cities; the second isn't needed by the Chinese. Unfortunately. But warn them that travel is expensive. (Oh yeah, and tell them we have a Pizza Hut if they want a taste of home.)

PJ: When you think of going abroad, you can't imagine what you'll need. But it helps a little to remember that "those people" are human, too. They wash their hair, brush their teeth. In our house, we were each picky about different things—one didn't like Chinese soap, another didn't like the shampoo. I thought at first they didn't have hand lotion, but then found out it's in little flat tins.

The point is, you can read a lot of lists and bring anything that might make you happier or more comfortable. Health, happiness, and comfort are very important. But everything that human beings *need* exists in China (if you can learn how to ask for it), so you will get by even if it's not ideal.

JIM PAGE: They have banks, barbers, cars, food.

G: My research has made it clear that the real China-haters (not the love-hate majority) hate it so much because they lack solid friendships. Trust a few people along the way—if they use you or screw you, then you've learned a major lesson about Chinese life. If they turn out to be real friends, you will learn a lot from them once they open up.

Yan'an, Shaanxi

Dear Alice,

Howdy and *ni hao*.

The students have finally filed out the door, yet another study session turned into a mentally debaucherous free-for-all: Topics range from comparing Marxist philosophy with Huck Finn, to the inner nature of belly-button lint, to rounding out the evening with a little high-stakes local poker for smokes—a philosophical vice-filled evening for all.

Sorry for my general lack of correspondence. But when every day is a book waiting to be written or a verse screaming for a melody, it's hard to condense generalities into a letter.

How to describe Yan'an? . . . So much beauty and yet so harsh. This sounds simplistic, but I must say that the majority of the people I'm living with are the kindest, most warmhearted people I believe I will ever meet. *Guanxi* and "showing off the *lao wai*" aside, I have found the first seemingly real community I've ever been a part of, where people realize the bluntness of our surroundings and still live for one another.

Whoosh! OK. General information:

- Yan'an—population ranging from 20 thousand to 200 thousand, depending on who and what day you ask.
- Geography: yellow earth, beautiful, terraced over the past thousand years by Huns, Sung dynasty, and the Man himself, Mao!
- Climate: Winter, butt-cold. Summer, Africa-hot. And— except for one day a month—dry, dry, dry.

To a prospective teacher I would advise: Bring a variety of clothes, dark in color and easy to clean. Read Marx's *Communist Manifesto* and Vonnegut's *Slaughterhouse-Five* and Orwell's *1984*, all simultaneously if possible; each one makes sense of the next. Be well acquainted with Salinger's *Catcher in the Rye*, as it describes what is seemingly our chosen profession. If you enjoy the following, you'll love Yan'an:

1. Comical seriousness when discussing the Inner Nature of belly-button lint

2. Caring for humanity and being granted a taste of what humanity is
3. Drinking *baijiu!* (whether you want to or not)
4. Long hours of introspection
5. Long hours of incredible conversation
6. Eating noodles while playing Ping-Pong in a sand storm
7. Being extroverted
8. Never bathing (completely)
9. LIFE!

Yours,

Matthew Rees

Looking Forward

Sometime after the backward look, teachers inevitably turn and look the other way—squinting toward a future that requires them to step back through that Looking Glass. These moments require a sort of double vision and inspire a range of conflicting feelings.

MATTHEW REES: I'm incredibly happy here. However, I am returning to America after this semester. It has nothing to do with Yan'an; in fact it is just the opposite. I feel as if part of me needs to "finish" itself back in the States.

I'm returning—not for a person, a lifestyle, or a cheeseburger —but rather to take a last glimpse of what it is I feel I can leave behind. I plan to return to Yan'an after some more schooling stateside, hopefully with questions answered and self intact.

JEANNE PHILLIPS: Plans for summer are a bit up in the air. I'd thought to stay here 'til September, but the recent hot days have reminded me of what July and August will be like. So either I'll buy an AC and hide to read and write all day, or I'll search out some place cooler but still very cheap (if one exists) to hole up 'til September—or I'll blow the big tax advantage and just come back—though the last is doubtful. It is a *big* difference for only 6–8 weeks.

School won't end until about July 10, officially, though my exams will be given June 25 and I'm free after that. I plan to make some of the Fujian trips I couldn't make with Chinese friends during spring break, then—maybe to the mountains or seashore where it will be cooler! But if you know anyone who needs a house-sitter at the South Pole, let me know.

INGER: *I can't wait* to get back to a place where I feel comfortable with how I dress and can feel feminine even if I'm not in frills or gewgaws or flouncy clothes. When I work at the kindergarten, I always see teachers wincing at my dress, especially my men's shoes and cowboy boots. So last week they gave me a pair of shoes I find atrocious. But I wore them today to make them feel better.

I look forward to theaters, bars, friends' houses where you don't have to eat another bizarre dish. (Yes, I did eat cow penis even after I knew what it was. I'm not chicken.)

It was so nice to call Hong Kong to make travel reservations. It took five minutes, and I had a flight and paid for it with my credit card. No *mei you* or "I don't understand" or *waiguoren* special price. It was so simple. I'm getting intimations of my coming culture shock.

JOE MÁRQUEZ: At present, I am returning to the States in August. I've been asked about staying on and I told them that I cannot. It felt strange saying no because now I must look for more work. I want to teach more (travel more), but I need to pay off a debt. I'll be in the U.S. for a while in order to make some money. I am already looking forward to leaving again. Home or the thought of home seems so distant. It'll be strange to go back. I'm a little nervous.

G (early thoughts): Funny, something strange is going on inside my little noggin. I'm already preparing myself mentally for my return to the USA. I'm working a lot, drinking coffee again, trying to develop a training routine again, thinking about school and cheese.

I keep trying to convince my housemate to stay in China

another year, maybe go teach somewhere else. Learn a little something. One year's for the birds, if you ask me. You spend five months trying to buy food from the market and the next five months trying to make friends. The second year is when you learn about walls and ghosts and the language barriers break down a little; you've stopped looking for Buddhists and begin to see reality.

I know why these teachers return to China. The addiction, the flexibility, the excitement of being in China at a crucial time—it takes a while, maybe a lifetime, to get China out of your system. But hell, I don't want to get China out of my system. And I probably never will.

TEDDY KELLAM (the public plan): As for plans, the contract expires in July, then I'm traveling in China as long as money and patience will permit. I expect to travel for three months or so, visiting a few hometowns of students, maybe Inner Mongolia, Beijing, and back through Sichuan, Yunnan, Guizhou—I have to remember that planning an itinerary is futile. So I'll go where circumstance leads me. I'm very excited, but I'm hoping it won't be lonely. Lonely in China—that's a good one!

Then back to Colorado, to live and work—whatever interesting work I can find, preferably around a lot of people. I'll spend winter and spring working, snow-shoeing, cross-country skiing, hopefully meeting people (maybe even—eeeep—a boy or two! I'm beginning to feel far too celibate for a 24-year-old young lady, Alice!). Then, probably in April or May, to Thailand, unless a graduate program in anthropology or Third World health or development or women's issues bites me on the nose! I want to study Thai language and *vipassana* meditation, and I adore Thailand. And I'm still not ready to settle anywhere, so . . . Ideally, I'd like to avoid teaching English, but I know it's my only real marketable skill around Asia, so I may have to do that at first.

DAVID MOLDAVSKY: I plan to go to Denmark for August and some of the fall and then I'll continue traveling next year—

hopefully to Israel and Africa. I don't expect to be back in the U.S. for quite a while.

G (late thoughts): It will be nice to be back in the U.S. for a time. I'm tired; not burned out, just tired. Lately, I've entangled myself with overcommitments. Besides teaching more than the twelve regular hours, I was asked to teach writing on Saturdays. I also do some lectures, etc.—you know the drill. All by choice, but I have had little time to pursue other interests. I'll know better for next year.

TEDDY KELLAM (the private fear): I'm worried about going back to the States. Somehow I'm hanging over the Pacific Ocean, suspended between two cultures—one an alluring enigma that I don't quite fit into, that I can never quite understand, and one, my history, my country, yet a place that seems more bizarre by the day, unfamiliar, "overcivilized," and damaged. What happens, Alice? How do you unadjust to China, and readjust to the U.S.? I don't feel that I could ever be fully Asian and spend my whole life here, yet the West is repellent for now.

ZUBIN EMSLEY: Any questions? New arrivals will want to prepare to have their hearts melted by these students. I just came from a freshman class where they told me about the Double Dragon Hole ("cave"). Frank and Helen are sweet enough to brighten a year on a hard seat train. This continues to be a wonderful and fulfilling experience. Must it be only a year? I will return to my company as I agreed. I'll see if it feels better there than I suspect it will. I'll stay a while, but if I'm a misfit, I may ask for your help to return to this awful paradise.

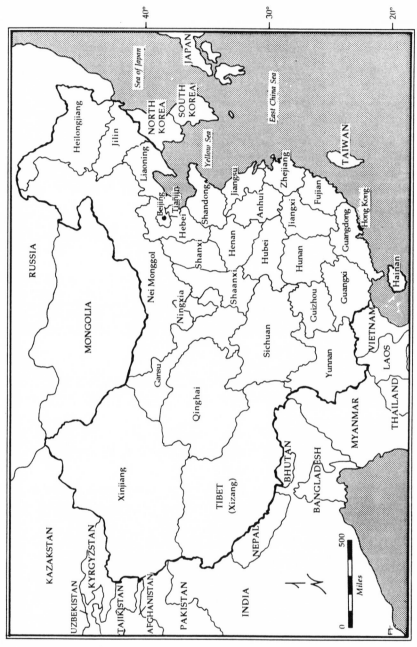

Map 13. The People's Republic of China.

CHAPTER TWELVE

Last Days

Chengdu, Sichuan

Dear Alice,

Things that have semi-happened-by-mistake have turned out to be some of the best "Things" in my life. Thanks for this gift. China has opened a new world to me—in *many* ways.

With Love,

Rachel Coleman

PJ: Betsy was a small nurse in one of my adult writing classes. I have no idea where she got such a perfect name. She was clearly from the country, so short she barely came up to my chest, and she had very long, somewhat frizzy hair—rather unusual in China. She was probably one of the old rural minorities.

Betsy had no English. In the first days, she could only print her name laboriously. I had told her class, since it was a writing course, that they did not need to speak English. I wrote everything on the board and made stencils each week showing models of the forms we studied. Many of these students knew English beautifully anyway, and it was a lively, diligent group. But Betsy never spoke, although she smiled sometimes.

She advanced somehow, and eventually produced at least one correct sentence of English in every writing. On one memo, she wrote three. We all grinned that day—everyone knew that Betsy's village infirmary lay far away from English, that she traveled far to meet us.

On the last day, everyone stood up and reluctantly started to drift out of the classroom. We really had done good work together. But Betsy came to the front and stood before me, with a friend standing a little behind.

"I . . . ," she said, glancing up at me then down. "You . . . ," she said, trying to piece together the words. She looked at me pleadingly and I could see she was going to cry. "It's all right," I said gently and tried to keep very still so the alien sentence could form. "You my!" she burst out and began to weep. I put my arms around her and we just stood there for a long moment. Everyone in the room turned to watch.

"She wants to say, 'You are welcome in my home,'" her friend said. Betsy pulled out of our embrace and looked at me, nodding vigorously. "Every time," she whispered.

"Thank you," I said, knowing she meant "any time," knowing I was already booked with banquets from here until the moment of my flight home. "Thank you," I said again, in honor of this ineffable gift that was being offered across the chasm between our worlds.

Quanzhou, Fujian

Hi Alice!

Things are going very well around here. I can't believe the year is wrapping up so quickly! We've only got about four more weeks of teaching. It's going to be really hard to leave this place!

I'm sure some of my students won't miss me, but my eager little freshmen are preparing songs with which they'll serenade me before I go. I think we'll have a goodbye party and I'll teach them to make apple pie—it's a concept that fascinates them. The hardest part, though, will be leaving all the other foreign teachers. We've really got a great group here.

My mom and my stepfather just ended their visit to China. It was great to see them! My parents finished their tour with a week here, which went really well. My students were thrilled to see some new foreign faces. Mom brought pictures of me from when I was little, and they all thought that was wonderful.

Everyone was healthy the whole time which was a plus—although my mom was a little uncertain about the sanitation. Scary thing is, I've stopped looking at it as dubious. I wonder if everything will seem very sterile back home?

China's still China. The weather is getting super hot and sticky. Our rats are out in full force, along with mosquitos, spiders, and cockroaches. We've mellowed considerably with respect to those creatures too, though.

I do want you to know that I have had a fabulous experience here and would like to encourage anyone else you're sending over.

Good luck with everything, and take care,

Marla Jenks

Changsha, Hunan

Dear Alice,

So, the AC is busted in my room. It's about 90 degrees F and totally humid. Sweating and sitting, you know the story.

I'm on the Countdown and, truthfully, I'll tell you that if I weren't spending most of my time with my girlfriend (American), I'd already have gone mad. I mean it. This place can totally grate on your nerves. We'll talk about this more in person.

Todd Hamina

Guangzhou, Guangdong

Dear Alice,

Every day I try to snap one more thread, to disentangle myself from the glossy web of the past two years, but I cannot. I don't regard China as two years abroad. It has been two years of my *life*, as natural and connected to my life before as it will be to the days after. My best friends are here, my bamboo branches, my wok, my path. Leaving is like a divorce, or a death. I'll have memories, but I'll never get over disconnecting myself from this place.

But contracts end, students go on to new teachers, friends dissolve into their own destinies, and someone new will make this sunny room her own. My phone number scribblings on the wall will be painted over, my dust will be scrubbed away, my old bicycle will lose its spot against the pillar at the foot of my stairs.

My homecoming will be bright, but I'll miss the Chinese roses spangled about my tables, like I'll miss the faces, the people who have blossomed into my life.

Perhaps goodbye will not be for too long. . . . Were you this sappy when you left, Alice? I'm beside myself.

One cannot divine nor forecast the conditions that will make happiness, one only stumbles upon them by chance, in a lucky hour, at the world's end somewhere, and holds fast to the days.
                                          —Willa Cather

Take good care.
Love,

Teddy

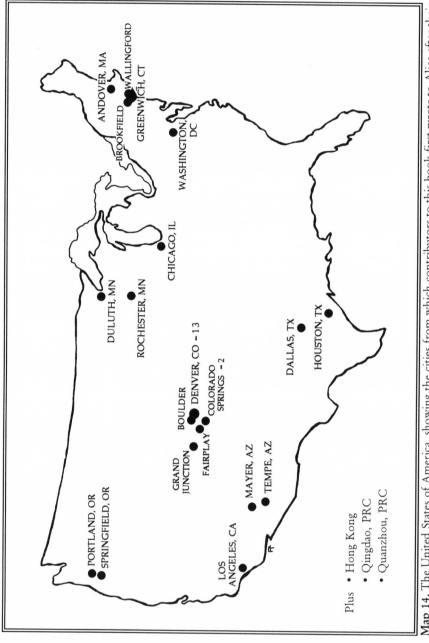

Map 14. The United States of America, showing the cities from which contributors to this book first wrote to Alice after their time in China.

CHAPTER THIRTEEN

Re-Arrivals

In their last days in China, American teachers imagined many ways they might feel upon leaving a year behind the Looking Glass, but they are often surprised by the truth.

Between Two Worlds

KATIE SHOWALTER: I'm sitting in a "cafe" right now, feeling a tad panicky. No reason, except that I'm alone for the first time in ages and I'm in a strange town in the far west of China—key words here being "alone," "strange," and "China." Plus, I have time to think now, something I didn't have my last several weeks in Fuzhou—too busy.

I'm thinking of the students who escorted me to the airport (when one looked at me all teary-eyed, 'twas all over for me). I'm thinking of the crazy, lovable group of fellow foreigners I left behind, having little in common but our very foreignness—we'd never be "one of the guys" in this Middle Kingdom. We will never all be in the same room again—or even in the same country. I'm thinking of goodbyes to Chinese friends—doctors, bartenders, teachers, administrators, tailors. And of P——, who left me yesterday for further adventures on the Trans-Siberian train—Russia, Czechoslovakia, England, Holland, Italy (can you say "envy"?).

I got so used to this Life, to this bubble we were living in, that I forgot it would pop—we'd all move on. And, as psyched as I am to get home, I'm very sad right now.

• • •

Some few American teachers slip smoothly across the Pacific from China into the United States, but most find they have to go through culture shock again. Every culture gets under your skin a little. And the longer you stay, the closer it gets to the bone.

Anyone who lives for a year in China has let go of old rules and assumptions. Or they have learned to look at these old ways from an odd angle. When they come home, they find they have changed a little, and they don't quite fit into once-familiar places. For many returning teachers, the questions "What's going on?" and "What am I doing?" come up again, this time on the very streets and at the dining tables of their birth. "Wait!" they want to cry. "Isn't everything backwards here?" But they cannot cry out. They remember when this was the only way they knew.

Returned teachers who adapted well to China have doubled. They have not lost anything American, but they have gained many things Chinese. In a yin-yang world, this means that the balance of their internal forces has shifted. Who they are has been spun around and turned upside-down twice now. They often step into the sparkling halls of American airports feeling a bit muddled.

> Who can be muddy and yet,
> settling, slowly become limpid?

asks chapter 15 of the *Tao Te Ching*. This becomes a real question for many returned teachers: Who can? Will this muddiness ever settle down? Will I ever come to feel clear again?

Each person must work out an answer to these unsettled questions in the United States—or Hong Kong or Thailand or Denmark—as they did in China. They will balance losses with gains, reason with emotion, there with here. It is not easy, but they know more now about the balancing of light and dark, and they move on.

> TEDDY KELLAM: I miss China. I want to be there, my life per-
> meated with people and caring. The grand "fall from specialness"
> has been a hard one to take. I haven't met many people here, but
> I'm hoping to in grad school. We'll see.
>
> — Working at a bookstore
> Vail, Colorado

KEVIN LAW-SMITH: Such a reality wall returning, going to work in Hong Kong. After teaching all of 12 hours a week, having four days a week off plus all the money you could possibly need, the life of leisure was ingrained. All-day naps, lunch banquets every day, endless supply of beers and ice cream bars. It was a real smack to wake and find myself working 10 hours a day, commuting with six million people, having no free time, not able to afford anything, and no vacation. Almost a year later, I'm slowly adjusting to "Life"—it's brutal.

> — Working as a political analyst for Philip Morris
> Hong Kong

MATT THIBODEAU: I just took Marla Jenks to the airport. We went through all 36 rolls of film I took in China. (I made her help me put them in albums!) We laughed and cried about last year. I got a long gossipy letter from Max Tuefferd, still over there, which was much enjoyed. I guess I'm on a billboard in Quanzhou advertising golf?!

> — Working as a law clerk
> Duluth, Minnesota

ZUBIN EMSLEY: Good-by was sad and difficult. Good-by to students and friends and canals and *tai ji* in the humid morning. A dream ended. I'm amazed to wake up and find the year over. Perhaps I'm not awake. Sometimes it seems that I'm in a half dream, only half awake.

Now what? What not: Slip happily back into that former life; stay in the job permanently; feel content doing my work in a fog of indifference; rekindle the relationships here that are only acquaintances masquerading as friendships; go back to China in a couple of days as I thought I might. With considerable fear of entrapment, I'll move all those boxes and anchors back into that house. The path before me involves figuring out the path before me.

> — Back to aerospace engineering
> Boulder, Colorado

Returning to life and work outside China is a little like walking out of the opera hall after a fine performance. These former teachers find that their eyes take time to adjust to the light. Parts of themselves are still connected to that grand drama for a while, as meanings sort themselves out and feelings reverberate around the heart.

How should I feel when we're to part?	与 君 离 别 意
We're all world-traveling clouds.	同 是 云 游 人
As closest friends in different countries	海 外 存 知 己
No matter how far away,	天 涯 若 比 邻
our hearts always feel very close.	

PAR AVION

ALICE: "Would you tell me, please, which way I ought to go from here?"

CAT: "That depends a good deal on where you want to get to."

For Further Reading

For those interested in scholarly overviews of the differences between the Chinese and U.S. cultures:

Hsu, Francis L. K. *Americans and Chinese: Passage to Differences*, 3d ed. Honolulu: University Press of Hawai'i, 1981.

Hu, Wenzhong, and Cornelius L. Grove. *Encountering the Chinese: A Guide for Americans*. Yarmouth, Me.: Intercultural Press, 1991.

For other stories by American teachers encountering China:

Barlow, Tani E., and Donald M. Lowe. *Chinese Reflections: Americans Teaching in the People's Republic*. New York: Pergamon Press, 1981.

Holm, Bill. *Coming Home Crazy*. Minneapolis, Minn.: Milkweed Editions, 1990.

Kwan, Michael David. *Broken Portraits: Personal Encounters with Chinese Students*. San Francisco: China Books, 1990.

Mahoney, Rosemary. *The Early Arrival of Dreams: A Year in China*. New York: Fawcett Columbine, 1990.

Salzman, Mark. *Iron and Silk*. New York: Random House, 1987.

Woronov, Naomi. *China: Through My Window*. Armonk, N.Y.: M. E. Sharpe, 1988.

For evidence that the culture contrast works both ways:

Liu, Zongren. *Two Years in the Melting Pot*. San Francisco: China Books, 1986.

Useful books for Americans who plan to live and work in China:

Thurston, Anne F., with Karen Turner-Gottschang and Linda A. Reed. *China Bound, Revised*. Washington, D.C.: National Academy Press,

1994. (This is the updated version of Turner-Gottschang and Reed's classic *China Bound: A Guide to Academic Life and Work in the PRC.*)

Weiner, Rebecca; Margaret Murphy; and Albert Li. *Living in China: A Guide to Studying, Teaching, and Working in the PRC and Taiwan.* San Francisco: China Books, 1997.

And of course:

Carroll, Lewis. *Through the Looking-Glass, and What Alice Found There.* Any edition.

Vocabulary

About Pinyin Spellings

If you wanted to learn to speak Chinese, how would you go about it? For anyone who cannot read characters, the language presents a blank wall. Yet it seems possible that you could just listen to the language, write down approximately how it sounds to you, and slowly build up a sense for the oral language. This is exactly what early Western visitors to China did.

Over time, many phonetic renderings of Chinese have been developed by Western scholars (Alice Renouf has learned five!). Until recently, the one most widely used in the United States has been the Wade-Giles system. The pinyin system used in this book is the first alphabetic system developed by the Chinese themselves. Here are some examples of famous Chinese words and places in both Wade-Giles and pinyin:

Wade-Giles	Pinyin
Peking	Beijing
Mao Tse-tung	Mao Zedong
t'ai chi	tai ji
chi kung	qi gong
tofu	doufu
Canton	Guangdong

Why did the Chinese bother to develop an alphabetic system when they can already read characters? There is an official reason that may surprise you, and probably two practical reasons as well. What many Americans find surprising in China is that Chinese people from different regions cannot understand one another. There are so many dialects in China, and they differ so dramatically from one another, that they are almost different languages. It is as though a Welsh shepherd, a Scots factory worker, and an American farmer sat down and tried to speak "English" together.

Everyone *reads* the same language in China, but they speak about things very differently. Therefore, said the government, we will create pinyin so that everyone has a common touchstone for how to pronounce important words. All over the land, children learn in school to pronounce "horse" and "older sister" and "ear" the same way, even if they say them differently at home.

Practically speaking, the Chinese may also have wished to exercise more control over how Westerners represented the language. (Notice, for example, the dramatic difference between the old Western renderings of "Peking" and "Canton" and the Chinese versions.) And the other practical reason may also come as a small surprise: Chinese characters are not alphabetized.

There are approximately 50,000 Chinese characters, and when they are arranged in a dictionary they are organized by stroke count—the number of strokes of the pen required to write each character. Therefore, for example, the Chinese word for "two" (*er*) and the word for "ten" (*shi*) come next to one another in character lists, because each consists of two strokes.

As more and more outsiders who have grown up with alphabets come into China, they find that pinyin satisfies their need for a familiar organizing system. I, for example, was at a loss how to make sense of the "jumbled" lists of student names my department gave me, until a kind graduate student converted them into pinyin. Then I could record grades in "alphabetical order"!

Word List

bagua (bah-gwah): one of several forms of martial art that G practices.
baijiu (by-joe): strong rice wine, which PJ describes as "a white hard liquor in the turpentine family."
baozi (baow-tsuh): rice-flour buns, sometimes stuffed with sugar, meat, or vegetables, then steamed.

baozi cooker (baow-tsuh): a straight-sided round steamer made of woven bamboo that is set over water boiling in a wok.

Beijing (Bay-jing): capital of the PRC.

Changsha, Hunan Province (Chahng-shah, Hoo-nahn)

Chengdu, Sichuan Province (Chung-doo, Sih-chuahn)

Dalian, Liaoning Province (Dah-lee-en, Leeow-ning)

dao, daoist (dow): the pinyin spelling of *tao* and *taoist*, an ancient Chinese philosophy most famous for articulating the idea that the universe is a constant flux of alternating yin and yang forces.

dan, rou, cai, pao cai (dahn, row, tsai, pow tsai): egg, meat, vegetable, pickles—the food words Inger learns first in her stay.

danwei (don-way): the organizational unit for distributing information and necessities in China's Communist system. Usually called the "work unit," it provides a job, pay, housing, rice and cooking-oil coupons, and other basics to its members. Each American teacher's *danwei* is the school in which she or he lives and works.

Deng Xiaoping (Dung Shaow-Ping): the premier of mainland China during the time of these letters.

dim sum (deem-sum): a highly varied selection of bite-sized delicacies, especially popular in southern China.

doufu (dough-foo): the pinyin spelling of *tofu*, a soft soybean cake.

dui bu chi (dway boo chee): "I'm sorry."

Fushun, Liaoning Province (Foo-shun, Leeow-ning)

Fuzhou, Fujian Province (Foo-joe, Foo-gee-en)

gong fu (gong foo): the pinyin spelling of *kung fu*, any of several forms of Chinese martial art—similar in range of meaning to *wushu*. *Gong* by itself is also sometimes used to mean "art" or "well-mastered skill," as when some Chinese say they want to learn the American *gong* of handling money.

Guangzhou, Guangdong Province (Gwahng-joe, Gwahng-dong)

guanxi (gwan-shee): the complex web of obligations and favors that pervades Chinese society, explored at length by Jeanne Phillips in chapter three.

Guilin (Gway-leen)

Guizhou (Gway-joe)

Gulangyu (Goo-lahng-yoo)

Hangzhou, Zhejiang Province (Hahng-joe, Juh-gee-ahng)

hukou (hoo-koh): the Chinese permit system (described in chapter 9 by Rachel

Coleman), which registers most of the urban population.

huoguo (hwoh-gwo): "hot pot," a Chinese type of fondue, where each person dips a wide array of meats and vegetables into spiced boiling water.

jiaozi (jow-tsuh): crescent-shaped wontons (dumplings) that can be boiled or fried.

Jinan, Shandong Province (Jee-nan, Shahn-dong)

Kunming, Yunnan Province (Kun-ming, Yoo-nahn)

lajiao (lah-jiaow): hot pepper.

Lanzhou, Gansu Province (Lahn-joe, Gahn-su)

lao (laow): old; a friendly or informal title in China. Many of the writers here call their housekeepers or immediate bosses *lao*.

laoshi (laow-shuh): teacher.

lao wai (laow wy): foreigner, literally, "old foreigner," another use of the informal title *lao*.

Liu Shaoqi (Le-oh Shaow-chee): one of the early Communist revolutionaries who remained a leader as the Party matured.

ma ma hu hu (ma ma who who): so-so

mao (maow): cents.

Mao Zedong (Maow Tsay-dong): the great revolutionary leader of Chinese communism.

mapo doufu (ma-poh dough-foo): tofu (bean curd) cooked in spicy meat sauce.

mei you (may yoh): "Don't have any," a phrase that is frustratingly common in China!

mei xin (may sheen): "No mail."

Nanchang, Jiangxi Province (Nahn-chahng, Gee-ahng-shee)

Nanjing (Nahn-jing)

ni hao (nee how): "Are you well?"—a greeting often used by Chinese speakers to say hello to foreigners.

pijiu (pee-joe): beer. Since Chinese beer is quite tasty, this is often one of the first words a foreigner learns in China.

pinyin: the alphabetic rendering of Chinese characters.

Puyi (Poo-yee): the name of China's last emperor, member of the Manchu Qing dynasty, who ascended the throne in 1908 at the age of two.

qi (chee): as explained in chapter 7, one of the three vital essences in the body. *Qi* is not only moved and stored but can also be collected from the environment and passed from one living being to another.

qi gong (chee gong): the internal art of collecting, storing, and moving vital energy in the human body.

Qing (Ching) dynasty: the last imperial dynasty, extending from the mid-1600s to 1911.

Qingdao, Shandong Province (Ching-dow, Shahn-dong)

Quanzhou, Fujian Province (Chuan-joe, Foo-gee-en)

Qufu, Shandong Province (Choo-foo, Shan-dong)

renminbi **(ren-min-bee, abbreviated RMB):** the general term for Chinese money, which means literally "people's money."

Sanya, Hainan Province (Sahn-ya, Hi-nahn)

Shantou, Guangdong Province (Shahn-toe, Gwahng-dong)

Shaoxing (Shaow-shing) opera: a style of Chinese opera that emerged from one of the ancient cities of Zhejiang Province.

tae kwon do **(tie kwan dough):** a Korean martial art featuring kicks.

tai ji **(tai gee):** often spelled and pronounced *t'ai chi* in the United States; a flowing exercise and "soft" martial art.

tai ji quan **(tai gee chuahn):** the style of Chinese *tai ji* that is best known in the United States, sometimes written *t'ai chi chuan*.

Tianjin (Tee-en-jeen): Like Beijing and Shanghai, this city has the status of "special municipality" and belongs to no province.

waiban **(wy-bon):** Foreign Affairs Office (or officer); in charge of foreigners.

waiguoren **(wy-gwo-ren):** foreigner.

waishiban **(wy-shuh-bon):** same as *waiban*, the Foreign Affairs Office.

wenzi, zhanglang, tiaozao **(wen-tsuh, jahng-lahng, tiaow-dzao):** the mosquitos, cockroaches, and fleas that plague Inger (and others as well!)

wushu **(woo-shoo):** one of the general terms for Chinese martial arts, similar in range of meaning to *gong fu*.

Xiamen (Shee-ah-mun): one of China's Special Economic Zones.

Xi'an, Shaanxi Province (Shee-ahn, Shahn-shee)

Xiang Jiang River (She-ahng Gee-ahng): also called the Xiang River by G.

xiangfa **(she-ahng-fah):** idea or concept.

Xiangtan, Hunan Province (She-ahng-tahn, Hoo-nahn)

Xiao **(she-aow):** young; a friendly or informal title in China. Many of the writers here develop friends they call *xiao*.

Xinjiang Province (Shin-gee-ahng)

Xishuangbanna (Shee-shuahng-bahn-ah): a district of Yunnan province.

Yan'an, Shaanxi Province (Yahn-ahn, Shahn-she)

Yangshuo (Yahng-shwo)

Yangzi River (Yahng-tsuh)

yin and yang (yin and yahng): light and dark, mountain and valley, rain and mist, jade and peony, male and female. This pair of Chinese daoist concepts represents the idea that the universe and all life within it is not made up of separate "things," but is a constant shifting balance of forces. The yin-yang symbol (see the vocabulary page for chapter 10) shows a white dot within a black field and a black dot within a white, meaning that when each force is at its fullest, it contains within it the seed of the other. In these letters, the concept is most often used in connection with Chinese traditional medicine, where yin and yang represent two essences or types of energy in the body that must be balanced to enjoy health.

yuan **(yu-en, abbreviated ¥):** the primary unit of Chinese currency. At the time of these letters, 5–8¥ = US$1.

Yunnan (Yoo-nahn)

Zhongguo (Jong-gwo): "the Middle Kingdom," the Chinese people's own name for their country.

Zhou Enlai (Joe En-lai): an early revolutionary, now considered the intellectual architect of Chinese communism, who was premier of the PRC from 1949 until his death in 1976.

Names Index

INSTITUTE OF EAST ASIAN STUDIES PUBLICATIONS SERIES

CHINA RESEARCH MONOGRAPHS (CRM)

35. Yitzhak Shichor. *East Wind over Arabia: Origins and Implications of the Sino-Saudi Missile Deal*, 1989

36. Suzanne Pepper. *China's Education Reform in the 1980s: Policies, Issues, and Historical Perspectives*, 1990

sp. Phyllis Wang and Donald A. Gibbs, eds. *Readers' Guide to China's Literary Gazette, 1949–1979*, 1990

38. James C. Shih. *Chinese Rural Society in Transition: A Case Study of the Lake Tai Area, 1368–1800*, 1992

39. Anne Gilks. *The Breakdown of the Sino-Vietnamese Alliance, 1970–1979*, 1992

sp. Theodore Han and John Li. *Tiananmen Square Spring 1989: A Chronology of the Chinese Democracy Movement*, 1992

40. Frederic Wakeman, Jr., and Wen-hsin Yeh, eds. *Shanghai Sojourners*, 1992

41. Michael Schoenhals. *Doing Things with Words in Chinese Politics: Five Studies*, 1992

sp. Kaidi Zhan. *The Strategies of Politeness in the Chinese Language*, 1992

42. Barry C. Keenan. *Imperial China's Last Classical Academies: Social Change in the Lower Yangzi, 1864–1911*, 1994

43. Ole Bruun. *Business and Bureaucracy in a Chinese City: An Ethnography of Private Business Households in Contemporary China*, 1993

44. Wei Li. *The Chinese Staff System: A Mechanism for Bureaucratic Control and Integration*, 1994

45. Ye Wa and Joseph W. Esherick. *Chinese Archives: An Introductory Guide*, 1996

46. Melissa Brown, ed. *Negotiating Ethnicities in China and Taiwan*, 1996

47. David Zweig and Chen Changgui. *China's Brain Drain to the United States: Views of Overseas Chinese Students and Scholars in the 1990s*, 1995

48. Elizabeth J. Perry, ed. *Putting Class in Its Place: Worker Identities in East Asia*, 1996

sp. Phyllis L. Thompson, ed. *Dear Alice: Letters Home from American Teachers Learning to Live in China*, 1998

KOREA RESEARCH MONOGRAPHS (KRM)

13. Vipan Chandra. *Imperialism, Resistance, and Reform in Late Nineteenth-Century Korea: Enlightenment and the Independence Club*, 1988

14. Seok Choong Song. *Explorations in Korean Syntax and Semantics*, 1988

15. Robert A. Scalapino and Dalchoong Kim, eds. *Asian Communism: Continuity and Transition*, 1988

16. Chong-Sik Lee and Se-Hee Yoo, eds. *North Korea in Transition*, 1991

17. Nicholas Eberstadt and Judith Banister. *The Population of North Korea*, 1992

18. Hong Yung Lee and Chung Chongwook, eds. *Korean Options in a Changing International Order*, 1993

19. Tae Hwan Ok and Hong Yung Lee, eds. *Prospects for Change in North Korea*, 1994

20. Chai-sik Chung. *A Korean Confucian Encounter with the Modern World: Yi Hang-no and the West*, 1995

21. Myung Hun Kang. *The Korean Business Conglomerate: Chaebol Then and Now*, 1996

22. Lewis R. Lancaster, Kikun Suh, and Chai-shin Yu, eds. *Buddhism in Koryo: A Royal Religion*, 1996

23. Lewis R. Lancaster and Chai-shin Yu, eds. *Buddhism in the Early Choson: Suppression and Transformation*, 1996

25. Jeong-Hyun Shin. *The Trap of History*, 1998